Life on the Ocean Wave

The second book of a trilogy
"Admiral Jim"

Other books of the trilogy

Book 1   "From Greenland's Icy Shore"

Book 3   "Wider Horizons: Naval Policy
& International Affairs"

I dedicate this trilogy to all my family, and to the fortitude and
faith of those that went before us over several centuries.

Life on the Ocean Wave

by
Admiral Sir James Eberle
GCB LLD

ISBN 978-1-904499-16-9

Further copies of this book may be obtained from
jimeberle@btinternet.com

 First published in United Kingdom of Great Britain in 2006 by
Roundtuit Publishing, 32 Cookes Wood, Broompark, Durham DH7 7RL

Cover image HMS INTREPID
Printed in the United Kingdom of Great Britain by Prontaprint Durham

Preface to the trilogy
"Admiral Jim"

I am not sure when the urge first came to me to write an account of my own personal journey through life. I only know that, as my active life has started to draw to a close, I have became more and more aware of the variety and nature of events in which I have been personally involved – from World War II, the Korean War, the South Atlantic War, the Cold War, and the Cold Peace that followed it, to the 'War on Terror'. All too often when I had been speaking to friends and colleagues about some particular events they had responded 'Oh, you must write all this down'. Indeed, in some cases, these events may not have been previously recorded at all, and may well be of interest to modern political, military and social historians.

However, I had long before been aware that my ancestors had also had very interesting lives about which I knew little and understood less. I believed the Eberle family to be quintessentially English and Bristolian. Indeed, I had at an early age been privileged to become a Freeman of that City. I was vaguely aware that the family had a Moravian connection but I did not really know where Moravia was or how it fitted in to our family history.

Shortly before he died in 1987, my father handed to me a copy of a brief treatise that he had written, entitled "The Eberle Family History". With it, I inherited a considerable mass of ancient books, documents and family papers. Included in those papers was a treatise entitled "The Eberles" written by an American cousin. Engrossed as I was at that time in the very good fortunes of my own life, I gave these papers not more than a cursory glance, and put them aside to be studied in due course. It is only recently that the pace of my life has slowed sufficiently to allow me to look at them more closely.

I soon discovered that my great grandfather was not British at all – he was German, and he had spent very little time in Bristol. The more I delved, the more I became confused. The story that I was trying to unravel seemed to represent a fascinating multi- facetted but incomplete picture of my family's past – of which I had had neither the knowledge nor the understanding to appreciate. I was however inspired by my father's brief foreword to his work in which he wrote: -

> "This is a short record of what we know about the families from whom you and I are directly descended. Some day you may wish to read more about them from the original memoirs and other recorded facts, which have been handed down to us. I hope that you will feel proud in the knowledge that members of our family have lived strenuous and useful lives, in which, by their own unselfish labours, they strove to bring happiness to others. Our story shows, too, in generation after generation, a readiness to accept adventure and responsibility, and to face dangers and difficulties with courage and resolution. There is another reason why I wanted you to know more about those from whom you are descended. It is a proven fact that particular gifts and traits of character are handed on from one generation to another. From this you may learn that you have received a heritage that should encourage in you a similar strength of character and belief in the Christian religion and way of life. May this strengthen you in you determination to be worthy of that heritage in your own life."

These words clearly reflected, not only his own personal experiences in the First World War throughout the four years of which he served in France and Italy in the Royal Engineers which he recorded in his book "My Sapper Venture" published in 1973, but also suggested an earlier and 'deeper' history of the Eberle family.

As I delved through the family papers, I became increasingly aware that there were a number of detailed and fascinating accounts of events involving the family dating back to the seventeenth century and beyond. The more I found out, the more I wanted to know; and the more apparent it became that I must undertake a short pilgrimage to both Germany and Greenland, if I was to be able to answer the many questions that were flooding through my mind.

At that time there was an opportunity. My son was retiring from the Navy, and in October 2005, we were both able to find the inside of a week in which we could visit the places in Germany where our family had lived, to see if we could learn and understand more of our early family history. With the enthusiastic and invaluable support of my son, a fluent German speaker, we enlisted assistance from wherever we could find it. This 'pilgrimage', about which I shall write more, was an unqualified and outstanding success. I learned more and understood more than I could possibly have expected. It was full of fascinating discoveries; and those extraordinary co-incidences that seem regularly to have punctuated my life.

Most fascinating of all was to learn that the Moravian Church called on all its members to write down in their later years a story of their life – their "Lebenslauf". These accounts are carefully preserved, many of them in the archives at the Moravian settlement at Herrnhut. The story that these tell is totally fascinating and absorbing and includes a period of over one hundred years that my forbears spent in Greenland as missionaries of the Moravian Church. I returned to England determined that I must also visit Greenland. This my son and I achieved in the summer of 2006.

As I started to write, I came to realise that the story that I had to tell was not just an autobiography, but was in turn, an episode of social history stretching back for three hundred years; a light hearted account of life in the Royal Navy from the final days of World War II; and the later stages of a career in which I found myself closely involved at a high level in international diplomacy.

JE

April 2007,
Homestead Farm,
North Houghton,
Stockbridge,
Hampshire,
SO20 6LG.

SUMMARY

This, the second book of the Trilogy ("Admiral Jim")

"Life on the Ocean Wave", provides a light-hearted account of life in the Navy after the final days of WWII – from hot war to cold peace. This was the period of Britain's withdrawal from Empire and gradual decline as a global power. It is seen through the eyes of a young Naval Officer who was fortunate in later having a very varied, interesting career and in receiving very early promotion to Flag Rank.

The other books cover:

Book 1, "From Greenlands Icy Shore" tells the story of the Eberle family's origin in Germany in the political and religious turmoil of the seventeenth century; the founding of the Moravian Church and the growing commitment to it of the lives of my ancestors. Their adventures over one hundred years of Moravian missionary work in Greenland; their emigration from Germany and their full integration into British and American society, leading in both countries to prominence in civic affairs.

Book 3, "Wider Horizons: Naval Policy and International Affairs" describes in personal terms the later years of a naval and post-naval career as it moves from national sphere of the men and machinery of war and peace, to a wider experience of international politics and policy. As one of the three most senior NATO operational commanders, he witnessed several defining moments of the cold war'

As Director of the Royal Institute of International Affairs, he was closely involved in events that led to and followed the collapse of Soviet Communism. He was the first senior Britain to visit Buenos Aires after the end of the Falklands War. His worldwide travels enabled him to contribute at a high level to Britain's global interests. This significant historical account ends with a brief look to the future.

The Laws of the Navy

Now these are the laws of the Navy.
    Unwritten and varied they be;
And he that is wise will observe them,
    Going down in his ship to the sea:

As naught may outrun the destroyer,
    Even so with the law in its grip,
For the strength of the ship is the Service,
    And the strength of the Service, the ship.

Take heed of what ye say of your rulers,
    Be your words spoken softly or plain,
Lest a bird of the air tell the matter,
    And so ye shall hear it again.

If you labour from morn until even,
    And meet with reproof for your toil,
It is well that the gun may be humbled,
    The compressor must check the recoil.

On the strength of one link in the cable
    Dependeth the might of the chain;
Who knows when thou mayest be tested?
    So live that thou bearest the strain!

When the ship that is tired returneth,
    With the signs of the sea showing plain,
Men place her in dock for a season,
    And her speed she reneweth again.

So shalt thou perchance grow weary,
    In the uttermost parts of the sea,
Pray for leave for the good of the Service,
    As much and as oft as may be.

Count not on certain promotion,
    But rather to gain it aspire;
Though the sight line shall end on the target,
    There cometh perhaps a misfire.

If you win through an African jungle,
  Unmentioned at home in the press,
Heed it not: no man seeth the piston,
  But it driveth the ship none the less.

Doth the paintwork make war with the funnels?
  Do the decks to the cannon complain?
Nay, they know that some soap or a scraper
  Unites them as brothers again.

See ye, being Heads of Departments,
  Do you growl with a smile on your lip,
Let you strive and in anger be parted,
  And lessen the might of your ship.

So thou, when thou nearest promotion,
  And the peak that is gilded is nigh,
Give heed to thy words and thy actions,
  Least others be wearied thereby.

Uncharted the rocks that surround thee,
  Take heed that the channels thou learn,
Lest thy name serve to buoy for another,
  The shoal, the Courts martial return.

Though Armour the belt that protects her,
  The ship bears the scar on her side,
It is well if the Court shall acquit thee,
  It were best hadst thou never be tried.

Now these are the laws of the Navy,
  Unwritten and varied they be,
And he that is wise shall observe them,
  Going down in his ship to the sea.

As the wave rises clear to the hawse pipe.
  Washes aft, and is lost in the wake,
So shall ye drop astern, all unheeded,
  Such time as the law ye forsake.

                    Ronald A. Hopwood

Table of Contents
LIFE ON THE OCEAN WAVE

Acknowledgments

I'm telling this story without ever having kept a diary. I have been astonished, however, at my ability to recall events of long ago that must have lain dormant in my mind for many years. Where others may find me in error, I apologise.

On more recent events, I am most grateful to many friends who have offered their comments and advice. Where there are still mistakes, the fault is still my own.

I could not have completed this work without the most admirable help of Delia Merrison in its presentation.

The Admiral's Sea Voyages 1944-1976

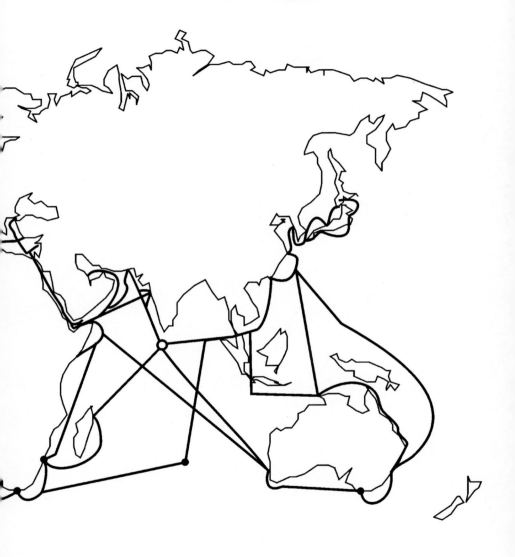

Chapter 1

I Join The Navy

"God, give us men. A time like this demands strong minds, great hearts, true faith and ready hands....men whom the spoils of office cannot buy....men who have honour and will not lie."
Josiah Holland (1819-1881)

My career in the Royal Navy started on a day late in January 1941. I set off somewhat apprehensively from Bristol by train to join the Royal Naval College, Dartmouth[1]. The excitement of joining the College was such that I remember little of saying farewell to my parents, or of the journey itself. However, there was for me some disappointment. The naval uniform for which Messrs Gieves, the naval tailor, had fitted me had not been delivered in time for my joining. This was the result of their premises in Portsmouth having been heavily damaged by an air raid. With several others, also dressed in plain clothes and whom I did not know, I arrived in the dark at the station at Kingswear to be met by a uniformed member of the College staff. We were ushered on to the ferry, the "Mew", to take us across the River Dart to Dartmouth. In the gathering darkness we were just able to make out the outline of the impressive façade of the blacked-out Royal Naval College, overlooking the river and the town, which was to be our home for what we expected to be almost the next four years.

As we wound our way slowly up the hill, our suitcases seemed to get heavier at every step. We eventually arrived at the large, somewhat intimidating front double doors over which is inscribed, *"It is upon the Navy, under the providence of God, that the safety, honour and welfare of this Realm do chiefly attend"*. On entering, we mounted a short flight of stairs to the Quarter Deck, a large,

---

[1] *For the history of the Naval College see (a) "The RN College, Dartmouth" by EA Hughes and (b) "Dartmouth" by Davies and Grove ISBN 0-85997-462-6 (c) BRNC 2005 – ISBN 0-9536361-3-5*

galleried and impressive hall. We were told that on entering in future, we must always salute. We passed on up what seemed like endless broad passages and stairways to the rear of the College in 'D Block', where our 'chest flat' (dormitory) and our 'gunroom' (rest room) were to be for the next two terms.

We were each allocated a bed, at the foot of which was an old fashioned sea chest in which we had to stow all our clothes in neat and standard order. Each chest contained a small lockable drawer, one's private till. This, as it turned out was about the only piece of privacy, other than that of the peaceful dignity of the College chapel, to which anyone was entitled. It was not long before the thirty-one new arrivals, having done our best to get to know those in adjacent bed spaces, were told to "turn in" (get into bed). The lights were turned out, and silence prevailed. I was very quickly fast asleep. In the morning at about six o'clock we were awakened by one of the senior cadets sounding on his bosun's call and shouting in a loud voice "Evo, Evo, Evo, Lash up and Stow – Turn.... OUT." Evo was, of course, the vernacular for Heave Ho, in the days when all sailors slept in hammocks. It was a call that we were going to experience for the next few years of our lives.

Life developed quickly. Our uniforms arrived two days later, as did the cadets of the remaining 'terms' of the College. The College year was divided into the three normal school terms, with a new entry of about thirty cadets, aged between thirteen and fourteen, at the start of each term. One's full spell at the College was eleven terms, with each entry maintaining its own entity and title, although there were usually a few members of each term who did not stay the course. The structure was highly hierarchical; based on an increasing seniority. As a 'first termer', you joined at 'the bottom of the pack', the lowest of the low; as an 'eleventh termer' prior to 'passing out' from the College as a midshipman, your word was law to anyone junior to yourself. Seniority was indicated by the way that the lanyard, which was part of one's uniform at all times, was worn. Woe betides the junior cadet that got it wrong. The first two terms together formed the Drake division. Thereafter, the terms were divided into five other divisions (also called Houses) Blake, Exmouth, Grenville, Hawke and Vincent. Each division had its own section of the College, containing its chest flats and junior and senior gunrooms. This change of status from junior to senior occurred after the sixth term and denoted a step change in the social standing of cadets in the College and their privileges. It also marked a change in the structure of the academic programme, those at the top of results in the important sixth term exams being offered a choice of an advanced 'Alpha' class syllabus based either on science or literary subjects. In a separate part of the College were the special entry cadets, who joined at the age of seventeen and eighteen having completed their academic schooling. They were off to sea after only two terms. We saw little of them.

In the Naval hierarchy of the College, each division was under the charge of a "Divisional Officer", most of whom were senior and experienced Lieutenant Commanders. They were responsible for the conduct and progress of each of their cadets. At the College level, two Chief Cadet Captains, chosen from the senior term, led the cadets. At the Divisional level, a 'House Cadet Captain', was appointed to be responsible to their Divisional Officer for the administration and discipline of members of their division. They had considerable delegated powers, including that of wielding the cane for identifiable offences. Two junior 'Cadet Captains' chosen from the ninth or tenth terms assisted them.

In addition to one's House Officer each cadet was allocated a Tutor from the academic staff. The value of a tutor was very much up to oneself. He represented an academic friend for those who might feel unable to keep up or needed other non-naval advice. They also played a considerable social role by inviting members of their tutor-set to tea in their house on a Sunday afternoon – or perhaps at a local farmhouse where jam and cream were freely available. Such wartime luxuries were only for the very fortunate. Some of the academic staff were elderly, having come from retirement after previous long years of service to many generations of young naval officers, by whom they were remembered with deep regard and respect. However, their continuing ability to remember the names and faces of their current pupils was sometimes limited – a problem that I myself know well in old age! The story, almost undoubtedly true, was of one tutor who, in the process of writing term reports or the academic achievement of his cadets, wrote, "This boy has not made much of an impression in my class this term." To which a subsequent colleague had added, "This does not surprise me because he is in my class not yours."

The structure of any day started at six o'clock with the shrill of the Bosun's call and evo, evo, evo. A cold shower was followed by breakfast and a short divisional period devoted to domestic and naval affairs – and then breakfast. A formal parade, "Divisions", with a Guard composed of senior members of the Duty Division and a Royal Marine Band. This ceremony marked the hoisting of the naval ensign at eight o'clock. On a cold, windy, winter morning this could be something of an ordeal; but against the background of a summer day, the military music and the National Anthem and the view to seaward over the mouth of the River Dart, undoubtedly struck a very emotional chord in the hearts of many young boys. It certainly did in mine and not least when I could hear the drone of an unseen aircraft's engine as it patrolled offshore against enemy air attack.

On some days, Divisions were followed by signal exercises. These required one to read a message in Morse code signalled by a flashing lamp on top of the mast that dominated the parade ground. From time to time the Morse code was replaced by semaphore, which I found much easier. What was even worse, however, were the few signal lessons in a classroom, where one had to read Morse code by a series of 'shorts' and 'longs' on a buzzer. I found this, when conducted at any speed, very difficult. Each 'buzz' seemed to go straight in one ear and out the other. It was only much later in my career, in connection with the escape of HMS AMETHST from the Yangtze River[2] that I regretted this weakness.

---

[2] *See p.92*

Another way of communicating between ships at sea was by flags and pennants hoisted to the ship's yardarm, by which the activities of a squadron of ships at sea could be manoeuvred and controlled. We had to learn the meaning of many of these individual flags and pennants; and to learn how to use the Naval Signal Book. This listed the various flag and pennant groups and defined their meaning in the form of a particular manoeuvre. We were also required to carry out these manoeuvres on the parade ground with each ship being represented by one cadet. The ships (individual cadets) were formed into various formations, each representing a Squadron or Division of the fleet. We were thus manoeuvred around the parade ground using the appropriate flag signals from the Naval Signals Book. The instructor would call out a flag hoist representing a particular manoeuvre. As soon as you understood what your ship (you) was required to do, you raised one arm, and at the order execute, carried out the appropriately ordered manoeuvre - i.e. went slow, or stopped, or turned right or left, either individually or in a group. This almost inevitably ended in a degree of chaos. But it was better happening on the parade ground than in real life at sea.

The academic syllabus was not too different to that which one would have expected in any public school. There were also added periods for seamanship and naval professional training, including engineering, seamanship and boatwork. This professional training increased in frequency and importance at the more senior cadet levels. Training in seamanship was a mixture of classroom time and time spent on the River Dart at Sandquay. This was accessed by long flights of steep stone steps from the College, leading past the old racquets courts and then down to the river. For a fourteen year old, getting down to Sandquay, which also housed the engineering workshops, was no problem. But getting back to the College for the next serial was quite a haul – and excuses for anybody who was late were rarely accepted.

The practical elements of the naval training were, in the early stages, understandably centred on the river where one spent a good deal of time learning how to sail, how to handle a motorboat and generally how to look after yourself on the water. There were a large variety of boats available from small, sturdy skiffs useful for Sunday afternoon relaxation, to Dart–One-Design sailing dinghies which were for the more adventurous, naval whalers and cutters for pulling and sailing, and large twin-engined picket boats, the driving of which was the best fun of all. The achievement of passing a test of competence in the handling of any of these boats was a strong incentive for the use of the river for recreation. Sunday afternoon picnics were much favoured during the summer.

Both the Naval and academic staff also played a strong role in the sporting activities of the College that were happily, at least for me, seen as an important part of our naval education. Within the syllabus there were strictly controlled periods in the gymnasium. "Top of the wall bars - go" was an order from the PT staff that greeted any cadet that might be seen to be slacking – even in the short boxing bouts in which we had to take part. We all had to pass a swimming test of two lengths of the pool, swum in a boiler suit. The fact that we learned that Japanese naval cadets at their academy at Ita Jima were said to have to complete a formation swim of two miles in open water tended to put our achievement somewhat in the shade – but then, we argued to ourselves, our ships would be less likely to be sunk.

Each day during the afternoon in winter, and in the evening during the summer, every member of the college was expected to take part in some physical recreational activity. These activities were measured in 'logs', of which you were expected to complete no less than five and a half logs in every week. A game of rugby or hockey or cricket, or an afternoon on the river was one log. A game of squash or tennis, fencing or the swimming bath was half a log. But what was one to do if heavy rain had made all the sports pitches unplayable and the squash courts were all booked up? What on earth could I do to build up my necessary five and a half logs for the week? The answer came for most of us in the dreaded words "Go for a run". There were two standard runs, one a relatively short mile and a half round the outskirts of Dartmouth, known by the title the Norton Triangle. This involved a bit of uphill struggle for those, such as I, who saw little point in just pounding the road anyway. But this was worth only half a log. The longer run, worth a whole log, took one beyond the outskirts of the town towards Stoke Fleming to round a building at the very top end of Swanaton Road, known as "Black Cottage". Inevitably perhaps, this cottage was actually painted white! This run involved more like three miles along roads, which were at that time mercifully clear of traffic. Nevertheless, this run was for me a form of purgatory that from time to time involved quite difficult decision-making – for unfortunately, all such recreational activities had to be formally recorded each day in a divisional logbook. Repeated failure to achieve your required logs might well be treated as an offence, for which the appropriate penalty could be from two to six 'cuts' of the cane, administered by your House Cadet Captain.

On most afternoons, the very well maintained sports fields, the best of which were sited close to the College, were full of activity - cricket in the summer, rugby in the autumn, soccer and hockey in the spring. Not infrequently, the less convenient overflow sports facilities above the town at Townstal were also in use. The situation today has sadly changed. The Townstal facilities, which later also provided a heliport, have been disposed of. The College sports fields, still carefully tended, are today all too often unused. The pressures of today's professional syllabus, in which young men and women of varying ages have to be turned from the indulgencies of a civilian life, often at university or college, to meet the responsibilities of naval life at sea in a warship in the course of a single year, does not easily permit the inclusion of a large measure of sport and recreation. The path from the College to the sports fields, where, at the age of fourteen, I made my first, and only, century in a cricket match, passed adjacent to some small buildings. These were the kennels that housed the hounds of the Britannia Beagles. The kennels were built in 1889 on a green-field site, the construction of the College buildings not having yet been started. The cadets were then trained in two wooden hulled warships, the BRITANNIA and HINDUSTAN moored in the river Dart at Sandquay. During World War II, many of the hounds were put down, with those remaining being looked after by local farmers. The kennels then housed only pigs - and their smell. However, after the war, the pack was rebuilt and was once again flourishing. At that time, I had no idea of the part that the Britannia Beagles had played in the pre-war life of the College. Nor did I think for one moment that the beagles would come to play such a large part in my own later life.

The dining hall in the Naval College seated all the cadets and provided food, most of which we enjoyed. There was a custom of naming some of the more regular menu items with unusual names. Rissoles were invariably known as 'beagle balls'. The meals were served to us by civilian staff that raced up the long line of tables with trolleys carrying the food and plates. The particular part of the table at which I often sat was served by an elderly steward, short in stature, and nicknamed 'Lightening' for his habit of riding on his trolley - and still being slower than any of the other stewards. All of the stewards wore white shirts with a black tie. Because of Lightening's short legs, when was serving soup, his tie would almost invariably fall into the tureen. If one helpfully remarked, "Lightening, your tie is in the soup," he would invariably say, "Thank you, Sir" - and then remove the offending tie, only to place it in his mouth to suck it clean. Within less than a minute, his tie would once more be back in the soup. In our youth, it never occurred to us that many of these men who looked after us boys would have given service to their country in the field during World War I.

The college had its own naval hospital, with full medical facilities. The first day of our indoctrination to the College brings back only one memory – it was of the Principal Medical Officer (PMO), a naval Surgeon Captain, telling us that if, due to the differing quality of the Dartmouth drinking water to that which we were used to at home, we should become constipated, we should go and see him. This was the last thing that was on my mind at that time.

The hospital had excellent facilities for the convalescence of young cadets from such childhood diseases such as mumps and flu - sympathetic nursing sisters, large airy rest rooms, books and billiard tables. I had taken advantage of all these after an attack of flu in my first term. However, in January 1942, I was taken to the hospital with severe stomach pains that were quickly diagnosed as appendicitis. I was immediately placed in an ambulance to be taken to the naval hospital at Devonport. Having been very sick on the floor, my morale was not aided by the helpful response of the accompanying sick berth attendant, "Don't worry about that, Sir. I've been up to my knees in this stuff before now." On arrival at the hospital, I was put to bed in a spacious cabin, whose windows were protected on the outside by a concrete anti-bomb blast wall. Plymouth and Devonport, like Bristol, had already suffered severely from night-time German bombing. Not before having been acquainted with hospital or surgical procedures, I felt somewhat apprehensive in my unfamiliar environment.

When four masked and green-gowned staff, armed with hot towels, bowls of steaming hot water, soap and a cutthroat razor, came into my room, I thought that they were about to carry out the operation there and then. I was mightily relieved when I realised that they only wanted to shave my lower parts as preparation for the operating theatre. Shortly afterwards I had a jab in my arm and knew no more until I woke up with the noise of a song loud in my ears. It was a song called 'Yours' that was one of my favourites. To this day, I have no idea where this music could have come from. There was no bedside radio, or the like, in the room, and it surely could not have come through the blast protected window. However, it certainly raised my morale. The tune has remained a favourite for me for the rest of my life.

The programme of academic and naval training permitted few moments in any day which one could call one's own. The one privilege of collective relaxation was the canteen. This was of a wooden construction, standing close to the sports pitches and well apart from the College main buildings. Its principal attraction was that you could buy chocolate there. For 'mere civilians', chocolate and sweets of any kind were severely rationed and often unobtainable. We, as 'servicemen', were privileged not to be subject to such rationing. How then could this be used to provide affordable and welcome presents (our 'pay' was just one shilling per week) for family or girl friends, when it was a punishable offence to bring any such food into the College buildings? Considerable ingenuity and the surreptitious use of the private till in one's chest-flat had to provide the answer. The canteen today is much as it was in those days, except that the sale of chocolate is minimal and the sale of beer is great and highly valued.

On the rare occasions that one had time to oneself, it was quite easy to be homesick, as I myself was - for parental visits were only allowed at half term. Today this may seem an unnecessary constraint. But it should be compared with the regime that had existed at the College prior to the war when married naval members of the staff of any rank were forbidden to keep their wives within a radius of fifty miles of the College.

Sundays did provide some form of a break from the rigours of the rest of the week. There were ceremonial divisions (a formal parade) for which one's uniform had to be in perfect order if you were going to have the afternoon to yourself. There was church in the College chapel which I found was an uplifting and emotional experience particularly as the pages of the Book of Remembrance were turned. It was then that one heard the names of those, some quite recently at the College, who had become casualties of the war.

There were outside diversions from what was inclined to be an unchanging weekday routine when VIP visitors, such as our own King and Queen, came to visit the College – with the famous photo being taken in the Captain's Garden of the first meeting of Prince Philip, then a special entry cadet, with Princess Elizabeth. The College also had a visit from the King of Norway. There were also breaks of a very different nature when we were permitted to go aboard one of the operational warships, usually a destroyer, which from time to time came into the river Dart.

After the end of my fifth term, by which time I was firmly established in the junior level of the Blake Division, life at the BRNC Dartmouth changed dramatically. This followed a German air attack. The College leave periods in the spring,, the summer and at Christmas were similar to those of any school – and just as welcome. However, the new entry to the College each autumn term always arrived on a Tuesday, the day before the return of the main body of cadets. To maintain this tradition meant that every eighth year the summer leave period was extended to eight weeks rather than seven. On Wednesday the 18th of September 1942 in the middle of the morning, the Germans conducted a bombing attack on Dartmouth and the local area. Several bombs struck the College, one of which exploded on the quarterdeck without causing casualties. In a normal year at this time, the major body of the cadets would have been mustered there, having just returned from leave, to be allocated and briefed on their defence duties for the coming term. It has been a matter of much conjecture of whether this raid was timed so as to kill a large number of the naval cadets that, in a 'normal' year, it would have done. An interesting novel *"Dartmouth Conspiracy"*[3] has been written on this theme. It is a very good read, which reflects the thrust of another novel written about WWII *"The Eagle Has Landed"*. This contended to be an account of a German attempt to assassinate Winston Churchill. The publication blurb read, "Half this story is true and the rest is fiction". I was forever trying to discern which was which! Other bombs struck the Noss shipyard.

Some fifteen years later when I joined the naval staff of the College as the gunnery officer, I discovered one of the bombs that had not exploded, stowed away in some corner. Having ascertained that the explosive charge had been removed, I had the bomb mounted in a prominent place as a reminder of what had gone before. It is still there.

The result of this bombing was that the College could not open for the autumn term and moves were put in hand to relocate the College to Eaton Hall, the estate and home of the Duke of Westminster, near Chester. The grounds adjacent to the house had previously been home to an army camp and were generously

---

[3] *By James Stevenson ISBN 09536 80207*

provided with Nissen huts and other domestic buildings. It thus provided a reasonable basis for the resumption of naval cadet training. The lack of a suitable stretch of water for training in boats was a particular disadvantage, especially for the new-entry cadets. However, the rather narrow facilities of the nearby River Dee did provide some limited boating facilities. This changeover inevitably took some time, so for the autumn term the junior members of the College were temporarily located in Bristol on the premises of a former orphanage. The facilities there were understandably poor. Nevertheless, under the guidance of Lieutenant Commander Hugh Agnew, we kept up the standards as best we could. Bristol, being my family's home town, I was able to provide an ancient wind-up gramophone to provide the marching music for our daily Divisions. It was not the Royal Marine band, but at least it was better than nothing.

The College reopened in full at Chester in January 1943. The magnificence of the Duke's home was in strong contrast to Muller's orphanage. The Blake Division of which I was now a member was allocated several of the Nissen huts close to the dining hall and not far from the magnificent old building which provided us with lecture rooms. There was no parade ground but Sunday Divisions, held around the long lake of the magnificent rose gardens in front of the house, provided a somewhat special environment in which all the cadets of the College could muster, sing and pray.

Of special interest to me was the fact that the Duke had an indoor tennis court, to which he privately invited several of us cadets to play tennis, usually on a Sunday. What were even more important were his other guests, one of whom was Jill Satheswaite. She was certainly in her seventies and had an international reputation as one of the few lady tennis players to have defeated the famous French champion Suzanne Lenglen. Despite her age, she could still put the ball in the court within a few inches of where she was aiming, on almost every occasion. The other notable feature of the tennis scene was that two of the other guests were often the attractive teenage daughters of the Duke's Factor. My tennis partner, Peter Chambers, and I were not unnaturally delighted every time an invitation came.

The sporting facilities were not quite like Dartmouth but there was a small private cricket ground that provided great enjoyment to those, of whom I was one, that formed the first XI cricket team. It was also the centre of much excitement when an RAF twin-engined Oxford training aircraft crash-landed just outside the leg boundary. There were also open areas in which the army had provided football and hockey pitches.

There was no on-site or nearby hospital at Eaton Hall. However, a fine local residence some fifteen miles away at Hawarden, with most attractive gardens, had been requisitioned to provide the necessary medical facilities. The short period in the summer that I spent there with mumps was one of the few occasions when I enjoyed being ill. The grounds were delightful, the weather was gorgeous, the staff were almost all attractive young girls – and I was growing up!

In my ninth term, I was made a Cadet Captain to assist with the management of the Blake Division cadets. This position provided the privilege of a small room at the end of our sleeping hut, which I and the other Cadet Captains of the division used as a recreation space. It had a large coke stove whose heat was greatly appreciated in the winter and which provided us with the means of cooking our own food to supplement what we regarded as the rather less than satisfying meals provided in the dining hall. The caterer responsible was a formidable Third Officer WRNS, Margaret Buller, a matriarch to many of the younger cadets. She was in due course promoted to Chief Officer and subsequently became widely known and much respected as the caterer for the College on its return to Dartmouth. At one Cadet Captains' meeting with our Divisional Officer (a retired and much liked Lieutenant Commander Harold Greaves, who had rejoined the Navy from retirement), we related the many complaints of our cadets about the standard of food. Our Divisional Officer countered with the words, as I heard them, that we should have no concerns about the food because the First Officer was "a diabetic". This worried me a great deal for some time until I discovered that he had said 'diatetic' - another word, so I eventually learned, for a trained dietician.

As we progressed through the various terms of our naval training, the opportunities to become acquainted with the real Navy, rather than a classroom Navy, expanded. I was much impressed by a visit that we made to an aircraft carrier that was being refitted in Liverpool. I had had no real feel for the size and complexity of a ship of her size. Against the background of a cold dark Liverpool day, with welders and riveters at work seemingly everywhere, it was an emotional occasion that somehow seemed to bring out the realities of war.

On another occasion during my leave, I obtained permission to go to Liverpool to join one of the destroyer escorts for a spell at sea escorting transatlantic convoys through the Mersey approaches. My first experience was not encouraging. Having sailed early, we cleared the Liverpool approaches and headed for the open sea. It was not rough but the ship began to heave against a rising swell. As I sat down at the wardroom table for lunch, I started to feel sick and before long had to beat a rapid retreat towards the heads. I was very disheartened. This, almost my first trip to sea, suggested that I might be forever prone to seasickness. What a start to my Naval career.

A second opportunity to go to sea came not longer after whilst on leave in Bristol. I was able to join a Hunt class destroyer that had been undergoing a short refit at Hill's Shipyard, for a trip round Lands End to return to its operational base at Portsmouth. Fortunately, the sea was calm. I much enjoyed the experience of being on the bridge as we sailed down the river Avon and took our departure from Avonmouth. The Captain having brought the ship to a halt in the middle of the Bristol Channel in order to carry out some magnetic compass checks, asked me to turn the ship round. I had no idea how this might be done when we were stopped. I was soon provided with the answer by making one of the engines go half speed ahead while the other went half speed astern. I was delighted by my newfound skill but somewhat chastened when the Captain said "Now steady her up on a course of 132°." I did get there in the end without running the ship aground.

During the night, I was woken by some heavy explosions. I later discovered that we had carried out a depth charge attack on an underwater sonar contact – which later proved almost certainly not to have been a submarine. We duly arrived off Portsmouth in the very early hours where we became involved in a small action with German E-boats making a nuisance of themselves to the south of the Isle of Wight. Unfortunately the ship did not carry the local Portsmouth area codes, that might have enabled us to take an effective part in any surface action. But it was all rather exciting and I was delighted to have been given the task of manning the bridge radio circuit to our shore headquarters, even though, lacking the local coded grid references, we could contribute little to the action. However, we docked safely the next morning in Portsmouth and I was left with a better understanding of the expression "the confusion of war".

It was in the middle of my eleventh and final term that we all learned of the successful assault of Fortress Europe with the landings on D-Day at Normandy. Attention was now devoted to more war-like studies, aimed at preparing oneself for joining an operational ship. I well recall being instructed in the duties of the midshipman of the 'transmitting station', the TS. This was the central fire control position for the main armament of a large warship. "As midshipman of the TS", pronounced our instructor, "you may well have the duty of operating the Vickers range clock" (this was the clockwork device that kept up to date the range of a target depending on its relative movement to your own ship). It was thus a vital cog in the effectiveness of the ship's main armament. We were told that the worst possible mistake that the midshipman of the TS could make was for his range clock to run down in the middle of a battle. Therefore, on closing up, the first duty of the midshipman of the TS was to wind up the range clock. In the age of the modern radar controlled digital fire-control computer, this brings home the extraordinary pace of technological developments of guided shells and guided missiles.

Such advice must now seem to have been more appropriate to World War 1.

My eleventh term saw me miss out on a promotion to House Cadet Captain but allowed me to add the award of my first team cricket and tennis colours to the first eleven hockey colours that I had gained in the spring term. Then there came our final passing out exams in academic and naval subjects. I was fortunate to gain a first class pass, which governed the length of time that I spent as a midshipman before being promoted to Acting Sub Lieutenant.

As we left Eaton Hall amongst great celebration and partying we were all wondering to which ship we should be appointed. Stories abounded. One of these told of a very youthful looking midshipman joining a large cruiser. He walked rather nervously up the gangway to salute the officer of the watch and announced, as he was required to do, "Come aboard to join, Sir." He was understandably more than a little put out by the unkind response from the officer of the watch, "Are you sure that you have got your mother's permission?" I cannot now but wonder, with our lack of knowledge and experience at seventeen years of age, whether we would be a greater handicap to our Captain, than we were a threat to the enemy.

My short leave was time for me to acquire my first girl friend, Anne Kimber. She lived with her parents in Bristol at Redland; and was about to join the WRNS.

Chapter 2

1944 - MTBs in the Channel and 'big ship' time

"They that go down to the sea in ships see the works of the Lord and the wonders of the deep."

Book of Common Prayer

To my great excitement, my appointment was to a flotilla of fast patrol boats based at Newhaven. These were our Coastal Forces, the "small ships". This was to be an environment totally different to anything that I had been led to expect at Dartmouth. The boats were almost entirely led and staffed by officers and men of the RNVR. Many were experienced peacetime yachtsmen – their knowledge of the sea was appropriately gained in inshore waters. At the Naval College we had been involved almost throughout with the high seas, the open oceans and large ships.

The state of war in France at this time was that the break-out from the Normandy bridgehead was well under way. The Germans, fearing that their forces in the Le Havre area would be cut off and destroyed, were using every avenue to escape, including that of the sea. This involved their ships rounding Cape D'Antifer and hugging the French coast through the narrows of the Dover Strait into their own protected waters of the Belgian and Dutch coasts. This was our battleground. It became the scene of almost nightly contact between our own forces and convoys of German merchant ships escorted by armed trawlers and covered by their fast patrol boats, the E-boats.

Our own forces consisted of three different types of boat. There were two types of 'long boat', some 120ft long; the Camper & Nicholson built boats which carried torpedoes; and the Thorneycroft built 'D' class, 'the Dog Boats', mostly carrying a 6-pounder gun on the forecastle and an Oerlikon behind the bridge. They were powered by two 1500 Paxman petrol engines, giving a top speed, going 'down-hill and with the wind behind', of little more than thirty knots. The third type were the Vosper built 'short boats' of some 75ft in length which mostly carried torpedoes - but

17

were smaller, faster and more manoeuverable than the long boats. The German E-boats were larger and faster than nearly all of our craft. They were also had diesel engines as opposed to our own which used high-octane petrol, thus making our craft more vulnerable to gunfire.

The final phases of action usually took place at very close quarters, since the effective hitting range of the guns that could then be fitted in such small craft, was not more than several hundred yards; and relative speeds could be up to fifty knots. Such close quarters fighting inevitably and quickly became confused. This required very quick thinking by the Commanding Officer in the manoeuvring of his boat. He was on the bridge with the boat's throttles at his hand and stood alongside the coxswain who had the wheel. They acted as a team, instinctively knowing what the other was wanting and doing. They could both see exactly how the situation was developing and If necessary a quick wave of the hand by the CO was enough to tell the coxswain exactly what he required. On the contrary, the Germans had their Commanding Officer on the bridge with the coxswain one deck below in the wheelhouse, with very limited visibility and only able to communicate by voice pipe. Although we were always at a speed disadvantage to the E-boats, our ability to react was far quicker than theirs. This was a decisive factor in success.

Shortly before I joined the 51st 'D' Boat Flotilla, there had been a night action in which they had come off the worst. The nightly actions were also beginning to move up the Dover Strait as the Germans were forced to evacuate their forces from Dunkirk and the other Channel ports. Frustratingly for a very young midshipman 'straight out of the egg', our boats were for some time placed on standby. Much of our days were therefore spent berthed alongside the old railway jetties at Newhaven, carrying out plotting exercises in the chart rooms of our various boats – and longing to get to sea. The chart room formed the boat's 'action information centre' fed by radar, from which had to be deduced which were the enemy radar echoes and which were those of other friendly forces. This enabled the captain to get into a position of advantage before action was joined. Such approach tactics were vital to being able to defeat the German escort, so allowing our torpedo boats to attack the troop and supply carrying ships in the convoy.

It was still summertime and the nights were short. The'boats on both sides were very vulnerable to air attack by day, and so we were keen to be back in our own coastal waters before first light, content that our aircraft would continue to harass the German convoys as they proceeded through the Dover Straits in daylight. For my own part, a couple of night sorties in which we did not make direct contact with the enemy were enough to make me realise that war was not only exciting but also scary.

I was able to have a short diversion when I joined a small landing ship on a cross-channel trip to Dieppe to collect Germen prisones. I thought that this might help to improve my German language skills that I had learned at the naval college. This was not a great success. I was not able to understand a lot of the rather over-excited chatter of the prisoners – and they did not appear to understand much of what I was trying to say.

Somewhat to my disappointment, I was to stay for only a short period at Newhaven with 'the boats'; although a few years later I was to return to return to Coastal Forces at their main base of HMS Hornet at Gosport. My immediate new appointment was to HMS RENOWN , a post WWI built battle cruiser of considerable fame, which was then part of our Fleet in the East Indies based at Trincomalee in Ceylon My instructions were to join a troop ship, the SS Strathnaver in the Clyde for passage to Colombo. My excitement level remained high as I sorted my white tropical uniform, including my solar topee, into 'not wanted on voyage', baggage that was stowed in the ship's hold, and cabin baggage. The latter was rather a hopeful title, since once on board I found that my 'cabin' was a bunk, one of a tier four high, placed in what had been the below deck swimming pool in the ship's happier cruising days. I have no idea how many other bunks there were in this space but I remember that it was very crowded and, with little ventilation, very hot and stuffy. This was bearable as we sailed from the Clyde in winter weather. It was highly uncomfortable, and almost untenable when we later came to the heat of the Suez Canal and beyond.

We sailed in convoy, passing to the west of Ireland and across the Bay of Biscay. As we entered the Mediterranean and steamed along the North African coast leaving the wind and rain behind us, life on deck took on a much more pleasurable hue. There were a number of midshipmen on board taking passage including several who were also due to join RENOWN. We were quickly 'taken in tow' by a Lieutenant RN, designated as midshipman's training officer, to develop our experience of sea time. One of my early exercises was to take a navigational fix of the ship's noon position, using a sextant to measure the angle of the sun above the horizon. I had done the resulting calculation many times in the classroom ashore, where we were given the appropriate sextant readings. Taking accurate such readings at sea was a different matter.

I felt a bit rusty in such matters of ocean navigation, since we didn't do this sort of thing in Coastal Forces. There, after a hectic night off Cape D'Antifer, we merely steamed north at full speed until we sighted the English coast. It was then only a matter of a simple judgement as to whether one needed to turn right or left, to reach Newhaven. However, even this simple drill had its drawbacks. One boat, having been involved in an extensive series of contacts during a long night, headed for home but found some difficulty in identifying any coastline ahead of her. Fortunately, one crewmember spotted land on the port beam. The penny then dropped. They had passed Dover and were heading north into the North Sea. A quick signal to their base confirmed that they had intended to head for Dover anyway!

Returning to my sun sight, I quickly learned that taking angles of the elevation of the sun was not as simple as I had assumed. Having taken what I thought were at least two reliable sextant angles, and double-checked my calculations needed to establish our position, I turned to the chart to plot where the ship was at mid-day. For the first time, this was 'for real'. Unfortunately, the position that I plotted for the "STRATHNAVER" was one that I knew with certainty could not be correct. It was in the middle of a market-place in Tangier. Perhaps I was not born to be a navigator.

We proceeded uneventfully through the length of the Mediterranean to enter the Suez Canal. This provided a welcome change of scenery and activity. The crowd of troops on the west bank exchanged a great deal of banter with our embarked soldiers – which added many new terms to my vocabulary – not all of them complimentary. Traversing the Red Sea was an ordeal. The smell of the oil facilities near Port Tewfik at the southern end of the canal was revolting. The heat was intense and oppressive. Since we had a northerly wind, there was no wind over the ship's deck. Below decks, there was no air conditioning anywhere. Wind scoops placed through the scuttles (port holes) provided some ventilation in a few places well above the water-line. Down below in the converted swimming pool, where we junior officers and others tried to sleep, there was no such luxury; and one spent the night covered in sweat.

In due course we reached Bombay, where we were informed that we would change ship for the final leg of our journey to Colombo. There was a brief opportunity for a quick run ashore and my first taste of the orient. It was hot, dirty, and noisy; and in the notorious Grant Road, there were girls in cages whose services were for sale. However, at a rather different level of interest there were banana sellers at every street corner. I had not seen a banana for more than four years. They were not, in fact bananas, but were plantains, which looked and tasted the same, but were a good deal smaller. I learned that they grew upward and not downward – and if you ate too many you felt sick.

We packed our cabin baggage and transferred to a British India coastal steamer, the SS NEVASSA, hoping that our hold baggage would follow. My own accommodation was almost more uncomfortable than that in STRATHNAVER. I was allocated a small space right in the 'eyes' of the ship, together with others, with seemingly no ventilation. It was infested with the largest cockroaches that any of us had seen before – 'king-cockers' we called them. Fortunately I remember few of the horrors of that trip, only the great relief at arriving in Colombo, on the south west coast of Ceylon. The harbour was full of merchant ships, with little signs of war. For us midshipmen there was to be no break in our journey.

That evening we were put on a train to take us across the island to the east coast where the British East Indies Fleet was based in the large natural harbour of Trincomalee. I had thought that my train journey from the south to Glasgow to join the STRATHNAVER was about as uncomfortable as one could get - but I was quickly proved wrong. The railway carriages had only wooden slatted seats; and there were windows which we thought might provide some fresh air in the very humid heat of the night. Wrong again. The train proceeded too slowly to provide air – and the engine produced copious smoke that seemed to cling to every carriage. Nevertheless it was, as my first journey through the jungle, an interesting experience. The more I saw, however, the less I looked forward to the jungle survival course which we had been warned we might have to undertake. That night itself was indeed a matter of survival.

We arrived at Trincomalee in early November to find a large span of enclosed waters within which the British Far East Feet, comprising battleships, aircraft carriers, cruisers, destroyers, submarines, a large floating dock, supply and hospital ships lay at anchor. In the distance we could just make out the runways of the adjacent Naval Air Station. This was a grand display of naval power - a very impressive sight. A picket boat came to the jetty to pick up our small party of six or so midshipmen joining 'RENOWN'. My dominant thought as we approached the ship was her size. All very different from my last ship – a motor torpedo boat!

Life on board was good. RENOWN was a happy ship. The captain was Captain B.C. Brooke, one of the family of the Rajahs of Sarawak. The commander, Reggie Tosswil was a good leader and a sound administrator. We had an excellent young lieutenant as our 'Snottie's Nurse', Lieutenant Bradbury, who was responsible for our training programme – and our conduct. The midshipmen lived in their own gunroom supervised by a sub-lieutenant, who kept us sensibly under control. We were immediately made to feel at home. We had no bunks but were allocated a hammock billet in the midshipmen's chest flat. There was again no air-conditioning in the ship - and in the tropical conditions, all the internal spaces were very hot. One just had to get used to it. The saving grace, however, was that at night in harbour we were allowed to sleep in the open air on camp beds on the quarterdeck. The hottest space in the ship apart from the engine rooms was the midshipmen's heads. In the chest flat, where we stowed our gear, we each kept a special shirt and shorts, appropriately named, which we donned each time before going to the heads (the loo). However short one's call, one returned soaked in sweat. Sweat rash, particularly in the crotch, was a common highly uncomfortable product of the tropical conditions - and only slightly less painful than the Microsol with which we were required to bathe our more private parts to keep the rash under control.

Our Snottie's Nurse was a good man and we were able quickly to learn a great deal lot about the ship and life in the Navy afloat. Each one of the midshipmen was required to keep a journal, monitored weekly by the snottie's nurse, with comments not only on professional matters in the ship, but also on wider events. Sketches were also required. Being neither able to draw nor to write good essays - I had chosen at Dartmouth to be in the science rather than the literary Alpha Class – I regularly struggled with my journal. One week, I took strong objection to the principle in the ship that midshipmen's attendance at church on Sunday was compulsory. I was indeed happy to go – but not under the threat of punishment for failure to attend. I thought that my view was based on a principle. However, others thought otherwise. I was sent for and told that my journal was not the way to state a complaint. In order to make sure that I remembered this, I was sent to the top of the mainmast, which was along way above the upper deck - it looked even higher from the top - for an hour of contemplation. The midshipman's journals were supposedly kept as a naval archive, rather than as a private document. Sadly, after the war, mine went missing.

One of the particular tasks allotted to the midshipman was as coxswain of the many boats that the ship carried. These varied greatly in size. The largest and most basic was the pinnace, used for taking considerable numbers of liberty men to and from a large Fleet canteen complex that had been set up ashore. Late in the evening, the Canteen Pier was an impressive sight as a mass of sailors, full of beer, tried to sort themselves out to get into the correct one of the many boats that would return them to their own ship. Maintaining order in a boat full of drunken matelots during a return trip from the pier was a task that few junior midshipmen had previously experienced.

The ship to shore trip was itself also not without hazard; for there was a narrow gap through the "Powder Rocks", marked by unlit buoys, through which for a safe passage, particularly on a low tide, one had to navigate. On a dark night, the only marks which allowed the Midshipman of the boat to know his position were the lights of the Dutch hospital ship, the "TITJALENKA", which was moored nearby. I myself nearly came to grief there one dark night. I was on my own driving the Captain's small fast light speedboat, known as a 'skimmer,' on a trip that involved passing though the Powder Rocks. It was very dark, and I had slowed down to look for the unlit 'safe channel' buoys. Not only could I not see them but nor could I make out any lights from the "Titjalenka" Unknown to me, she had gone to sea! I soon realised that I did not know where I was and so stopped. Looking over the side I realised that I was in very shallow and rocky water. I had no option than to jump overboard and push the boat into deeper water so as to prevent damage to the propeller. That was the easy bit. The difficult bit was getting back into the boat again without capsizing it. All good character building stuff.

RENOWN also carried several picket boats with twin engines, a bridge and a crew of three sailors. These were principally used by the wardroom officers, taking them to and from other ships of the Fleet, both on duty and on social calls. Additionally there was a shore-side officers club not far from Renown's berth. Bringing back the officers from the Officers' Club was a much more straightforward task except that it often involved long spells of waiting. When the wardroom officers ordered a boat for 2300, one could be almost certain that no-one would appear at the jetty at anywhere near that time; which made me rather cross. I vowed that I would never in my later life be so discourteous to 'my own' boats' crews. I like to think that I very seldom broke that vow. The officers were not a problem on the return journey; but as you were approaching the ship's officers' ladder, there was no shortage of advice as to how you might better handle your picket boat. One quickly learned to respond, "Aye, Aye, Sir," to such advice - and continue to do exactly as you were doing before.

Sea time for the big ships was limited and confined to exercising. I found myself allotted an action station in a space high up in the forward superstructure above the bridge. It was the ship's Air Defence Position (ADP). Our responsibility was to warn the bridge and the ship's operations room of any approaching aircraft. Thus, in the ADP there was a team of air lookouts, each armed with a pair of binoculars and allocated an arc of the horizon that he was to scan continuously. I well remember listening to the instructions of a senior Petty Officer addressing a group of new lookouts:

"The most important thing about being a naval lookout is not to look further than you can see."

I suspect that this was rather more sage advice than the instructor knew.

The ADP was also required to keep a plot of the area around the ship ,out to perhaps a hundred miles, on which we tried to track the aircraft, some friendly, some hostile and some unidentified, as information came in from our own long-range radar or from other ships. Today, this task is carried out automatically by digital computers. In RENOWN it was a perspex, chinagraph and hand plotting job.

Even in harbour, in addition to daily boat running duties for which each midshipman was allocated a boat and a boat's crew, there were many other activities to keep us at full stretch. Some were specifically training tasks – others were of a less formal nature. At some time before our arrival in RENOWN, midshipmen in a cruiser berthed at Colombo had managed to purloin a red and white striped barber's pole from a shore side barber's establishment. This Barbers Pole soon became a Fleet trophy of considerable importance, the ownership of which carried a great deal of kudos amongst the various gunrooms of the Fleet. The ingenuity involved in planning and executing an operation to remove it from the gunroom of its present possessor, and to return it successfully to one's own, was very considerable. Inevitably it involved such means as the clandestine boarding of another ship at night by clambering up a ship's anchor chain undetected, avoiding the ship's upper deck sentries, and using bolt cutters to release the pole from its fittings in the gunroom – and then to return with the pole to one's own ship without being recaptured or shot at. Deception, diversionary operations and brute force were all used. It was fortunate that no one was seriously hurt in these various operations. I know I spent something like two hours in the water in the middle of the night helping the return of our successful raiding party. Inevitably perhaps, the matter began to get out of hand and the 'game' was outlawed in the Fleet and the trophy confiscated. It is not recorded whether the pole was eventually returned to its original owner in Colombo.

The opportunities for sporting recreation were not good. There were pitches for ship's company football matches but, whilst the bigger ships mainly stayed in harbour, the destroyers and submarines were much more heavily engaged in operations supporting our troops in Burma. The battleships and cruisers performed the task of a 'Fleet in being', a deterrent to any Japanese further attempt to control the Indian Ocean. Fortunately the Japanese were in no position to mount any such threat since their forces were fully occupied trying to stem the growing momentum of the American drive across the Pacific Ocean to liberate the many islands that the Japanese had captured, including the Philippines. The final aim, of course, was an attack on the Japanese homeland itself. Thus, although war operations were in full flood both in Europe and Asia, the big ships in Trincomalee were conducting what was near to a peacetime routine.

One source of serious exercise came from games of deck hockey played on RENOWN's large quarterdeck. This was highly dangerous, particularly to the shins since there were no rules, and the make-do wooden deck hockey sticks made a very effective personal weapon! However, this was less dangerous than the same sport played, as it often was, on the flight deck of aircraft carriers. There was the ever-present danger, not only of the puck being lost overboard, but of it also being followed by one or more of the players.

There was, however, a cricket pitch available ashore, and through some process unknown to me, a match was arranged between the Fleet and a Ceylon XI. For even more mysterious reasons I was selected to play for the Fleet. I'm not sure how this occurred but it may have had something to do with the fact that in the summer of 1944 in Bristol I had played in one or two games at county level, at a time when no formal county composition existed. In my first match I had played for A.E. Gilligan's XI against a team called Essex Services. I don't think I did very well; but this may mistakenly have put me on a level that I did not deserve.

My innings in Trincomalee was a nightmare. Several of the Ceylon XI players were pre-war internationals. Their slow bowler spun the ball to an extent that I had never seen before. He and the wicket keeper, who had the most enormous hands, signalled to each other before each ball was bowled which way the ball would turn. Between trying to watch the bowler's hand and also keeping my eyes open for the wicket keeper's signals to the bowler, I was in total confusion. My innings did not last long.

Curiously, the facilities for swimming were not good other than for water polo played alongside the ship. It is surprising how exhausting this can be when the respite of one's feet on the bottom is only available some thirty fathoms below you. There was however one officers' bathing beach which was not well used. The story goes of a midshipman who went there one evening on his own and was about to dive into the sea when he heard a voice say, "I shouldn't dive in there. There are rocks just below the surface." The midshipman looked round but could see nobody and made ready to dive again. The same voice produced a repeat of the same warning. Looking along the beach the only living thing that he could see was a large frog. Unconvinced, he addressed the frog and asked.

"It wasn't you that was warning me, was it?"

"Yes." said the frog.

"How can a frog speak like a human?" asked the midshipman.

"I am not a frog. I am actually a beautiful young Wren – but I was wronged by a sailor who cursed me and turned me into a frog. He told me that I would remain a frog until a kindly sailor rescued me, took me to his home and laid me on the pillow of his bed – where at the witching hour of midnight I would return to being a beautiful Wren."

Being of a kindly disposition, the midshipman put the frog in his pocket and returned to his ship where he laid it on his pillow as he went to bed. At the subsequent Court Martial the President of the court did not believe his story.

Sleeping in the open air of the quarterdeck under the awning and tropical skies was most refreshing, particularly after the appalling sleeping conditions on our voyage from England. However getting up at half past five to make sure that the quarterdeck was clear for scrubbing at 0600 was not quite so enjoyable. One morning we were astonished to see across the far side of Trincomalee harbour that the floating dock there had changed shape. Closer examination through the binoculars revealed half of a large battleship, HMS VALIANT, hanging out of the front of the dock. This major disaster had occurred when, in docking down the battleship, errors had been made which resulted in the dock breaking its back and VALIANT sliding forward half out of the severely damaged structure.

Despite the peacetime atmosphere, the destroyers and the submarines based with us at Trincomalee were very much at war. During the summer, the advance of the Japanese army from Burma into India had been defeated at Imphal and General Slim's 14th army were driving the Japanese forces south towards Mandalay and eventually Rangoon. Progress in appalling weather and mountainous conditions was slow. Admiral Mountbatten, the south East Asian Commander-in-Chief had requested forces from Europe to be diverted to the south East Asia region but had been refused, since although the war in Europe was going well, earlier predictions that it could be over by Christmas 1945 had been dashed, following our failure to cross the Rhine in the Arnheim operation. Nevertheless some reinforcements arrived for the fleet. The American aircraft carrier USS SARATOGA and the French battleship FS RICHLIEU joined the Far East Fleet in Trincomalee.

At the same time every effort was being made to send naval reinforcements to the Americans in the Pacific. The British Pacific fleet under Admiral Sir Bruce Fraser was formed with a core of British battleships and aircraft carriers being sent east from the Atlantic theatre. In assessing the situation at sea in Europe the British Chiefs of Staff became increasingly concerned that the German fleet might make one final foray into the North Sea and Atlantic with serious consequence for the early ending of the war in Europe. They therefore called for RENOWN to be detached from south East Asia and returned to UK waters.

However, the ship was in serious need of maintenance in a dry dock. The only docks big enough to hold RENOWN in the south East Asia area were at Singapore and Durban. Singapore, however, was still firmly in the hands of the Japanese. Thus, prior to the final decision to call us home, we sailed from Trincomalee in late November 1945 for South Africa. Calling at the island anchorage at Gan in the Maldives, we proceeded at twenty four knots towards Durban. There a very large welcoming crowd greeted us and Perla Mesta, the 'Lady in White', was on the jetty singing popular patriotic English songs, as she was famed to do.

It was an emotional occasion. It was also one in which I learned an important lesson.

As a midshipman I had been put in charge of a small party of sailors to handle one of the berthing hawsers. I was still only seventeen years old and proceeded, as best I knew how, to take charge firmly. Unfortunately, I achieved this by being unnecessarily bossy. The petty officer leading the party was eventually occasioned to remark in a sotto-voce voice, that I was intended to hear, and did, *"If that young man goes on like he is now, by the time he is a Lieutenant Commander he will be a proper bastard."!* That remark made me think deeply about what leadership was all about and how it should be exercised. I have been eternally grateful to that petty officer throughout my naval career.

Before docking the ship we had to unload all the ammunition, and for two days all the midshipmen were turned to helping to place hundreds of 15inch shells and their cordite propellant charges into barges for temporary storage whilst the ship was in dock. It was hot, exhausting work. However, being alongside a jetty meant that when shore leave was given, we had easy access to all the many attractions of a great and peaceful city – and the Durban girls were very friendly! The prize for lack of tact went to a young lieutenant who returned from a run ashore in his dinner jacket at 0600 just as the commander was detailing off the duty watch sailors for the early morning cleaning tasks. It was rumoured that he had returned to the home of his girlfriend rather the worse for wear and had fallen asleep in his dinner jacket on her bed alongside her. In the early morning when they both woke up, they found two cups of hot coffee provided by her mother. Durban was very hospitable. However, the lieutenant did not get another chance for shore leave for another two weeks. We midshipmen took due note.

For us midshipmen there was the opportunity to fly from Durban down to the naval air station at Wingfield in the Cape where British air squadrons were being prepared for air operations in the Pacific area. The aircraft carriers HMS INDOMITABLE and HMS

IMPLACABLE were then heading east from Britain. I flew down to near Capetown in the rear seat of a two-seater aircraft, a lengthy spectacular flight along the coast that, apart from feeling somewhat air sick in the bumpy conditions, I greatly enjoyed. The atmosphere amongst the naval pilots at the Royal Naval Air Station was great, as always – but behind the high spirits there was a clearly operational overlay that contrasted with the almost peacetime activities in which we were involved at Trincomalee. The Commander (Air) of the air station was airborne daily in a 'Japanese' aircraft - and woe betide the young pilot who got 'jumped' by him and was thus a potential victim for the enemy.

It was rapidly approaching Christmas time and South African families had most generously offered hospitality for Christmas to as many officers and sailors as could be spared from the ship. Together with one of my midshipmen colleagues, Peter Chambers, nicknamed 'Jerry' for obvious reasons, and I were invited to go up-country near Johannesburg. An extremely comfortable overnight train journey led to a very warm greeting from our hosts whose home was in the countryside at Nelspruit. Our hosts had two teenage daughters, one of them being particularly attractive – she was immediately 'adopted' by Jerry Chambers, whose social senses were far more developed than mine. Nevertheless we both had a thoroughly enjoyable and relaxing time, including riding, which passed all too quickly. Nelspruit appeared then to us to be a small country town. I am now informed that it is a large flourishing suburban city in the Johannesburg complex. I have often thought of trying to get in touch with our most generous hosts to thank them again for an experience that I have never forgotten.

New Year came far too quickly and very soon afterwards we sailed from Durban heading for home. It was to be at a speed of twenty five knots all the way, and we were the only ship in the navy that could do this without refuelling en route. In every way this trip was the complete opposite of everything that had occurred on my outward troop ship passage. After an uneventful passage, we arrived at Scapa Flow, our wartime fleet base in the Orkneys, to resume our role as part of a deterrent Home Fleet-in-being. A new batch of midshipmen was due and so we were required to move on – but not before we were to take our Midshipman's Board, a series of tests to assess the degree to which we had absorbed our sea-time training. In modern times, I believe that this is done by means of a task book. I was fortunate to gained a first class pass, much of which credit should go to Lieutenant Bradbury, our Snotties Nurse' in RENOWN.

Several of us were detailed to join HMS BELFAST, a large cruiser carrying twelve 6 ins" guns, which had recently completed a major update of its armament following damage incurred from a German mine in the Firth of Forth. We knew she was destined to join the British Pacific Fleet, a prospect that pleased us all. We were now in the last stages of the war in Europe and I was able to take several spells of leave at home in Bristol, one of these covering the VE Day celebrations which I shared with my girl friend, Anne Kimber. By this time she had joined the WRNS. She was a few months older than I but considerably more mature in most other ways. I still remember our first kiss, which from me was no more than a peck on the cheek. I remember thinking there must be more to love than this. There was – much of this occurring in the back seat of my mother's car! I also visited her at a weekend at the WRNS quarters near Bletchley, a top-secret establishment about which I knew nothing. It was a wet rather miserable weekend with not much to do – and overall was not a great success! It was only very much later in my life that I knew that she had been on the staff of the code-breaking establishment at Bletchly.

The VE Day celebrations being over, I rejoined BELFAST in the Firth of Forth on the 6th June 1945. The ship's programme involved some preliminary shakedown exercises in the local areas prior to passage to the Mediterranean where we were to undergo a full operational work-up programme to fit us for Pacific operations. The change from life in an elderly battle cruiser fulfilling a deterrent role in the Indian Ocean to a large, modern, highly capable cruiser fitted with the latest technology and destined for a full operational role in the Pacific was considerable - and once again exciting.

Our workup at Malta concentrated on matters of air defence. In the Pacific War, Japanese air attacks against US ships were causing considerable damage and losses that became increasingly serious in the big ships of the US Navy as the Japanese suicide (Kamikaze) air attacks developed. As in RENOWN, my action station was in the air defence position of the BELFAST. The complexity of this was at least an order higher than that of RENOWN – although in today's computer Navy it would still seem very 'old hat'. We exercised hard all day but had the privilege of returning to anchor overnight in St Paul's Bay at Malta on several days of the week. Our captain, Captain Royer Dick had been an immensely competent and successful Chief of Staff to Admiral A.B. Cunningham in the Mediterranean. He was essentially a very nice man – but I think he found it difficult to relate to sailors and did not therefore win the confidence of the ship's company.

Our forecastle officer, who managed the process of anchoring the ship, was a bearded character, who had made his name as a beach master during the Normandy landings. One morning after a night spent in St Paul's Bay we were due to weigh anchor at 0600 for an important series of exercises that were the climax of our work-up. The anchor was being raised, apparently normally, when the capstan ground to a halt. There was a delay. After an examination, the forecastle officer reported that the flukes of the anchor had caught under the forefoot of the ship. The captain ordered the anchor to be dropped again. Unfortunately it would not move. Nor would the capstan rotate, its driving spindle having been bent. The captain became agitated. It must have taken at least twenty minutes to clear the jam, and the anchor was again dropped to the bottom. On being weighed, the capstan once again came to an unscheduled halt. After a short examination, the forecastle officer, his beard twitching with laughter, reported to the aptain on the bridge, *"You'll never guess, Sir, but it's happened again!"* I had never before seen anyone quite as angry and agitated as our captain. We eventually got underway about an hour later and somehow the rest of the day merely amplified the disastrous start. It takes great leadership to get a ship's company to recover from such a day. Unfortunately our captain, despite his many other great qualities as a senior staff officer, did not have that.

We left Malta for the Suez with a previously planned bombardment of German forces in Crete en route being cancelled following the declaration of VE Day. The banks of the Suez Canal were as usual lined with British soldiers. There was much banter between ship and shore. From the shore we heard a loud, clear, *"What ship?"*

From a mass of sailors on our forecastle came the clearly audible reply, *"The Belsen"*, followed quickly from nearby, *"and we've got The Beast of Belsen on board as well."*

The captain whose hat had been twitching anxiously as he observed the events from the bridge went ballistic. *"Arrest that man"*, he ordered.

Meanwhile "that man" had quickly dispersed himself into the crowd of sailors. This was a very unfortunate and regrettable incident which undoubtedly sapped the morale of many officers and sailors in the ship. For me, this was another lesson in leadership. Good leadership in an administrative context can at times be very much the opposite in another more operational role.

As we sailed on across the Indian Ocean heading for Freemantle in Australia, we began to educate ourselves in the processes of integrating BELFAST into an American Task Group organisation, whose communication and operational procedures were totally new to us. It needed both a change of language and of attitude. It was no small challenge for all those concerned with the fighting of the ship. We arrived in Freemantle early in August. Whilst we were in a peaceful area, the war seemed only a short way away. A few days later all that changed when we heard of the dropping of the atom bomb on Hiroshima and subsequently on Nagasaki. It was clear that the war was now coming quickly to an end. The people of Freemantle celebrated in typical 'Aussie' style and almost overwhelmed us with their hospitality. When we returned to reality and sobriety, there were widely differing reactions within the gunroom officers. Some were disappointed that we had now missed the Pacific war. Others of us, whilst accepting that some element of excitement had now gone out of our lives, were only deeply grateful that the ravages of war for so many people in the Far East were now coming to an end. We sailed on for Sydney.

Chapter 3

The Pacific War ends - HMS BELFAST and HMS TUSCAN

"When you get home, tell them of us – for their tomorrow, we gave our today".

The 14th Army – Burma

Despite the surrender of Japan and the end of the fighting in Burma and the Pacific area, there were very many urgent operational tasks still to be undertaken. BELFAST was ordered to make best speed up to the forward operating area. Passing to the South of Australia, we made a brief call at Sydney in order to collect the appropriate codebooks and operational procedures to allow us to integrate with both the British Pacific Fleet and the American 5th or 7th Fleet Task Organisation. The two American fleets comprised basically the same ships but were operated by different commanding admirals and their staff. Sydney's harbour and bridge provided a splendid backdrop for the ship as she lay moored nearby at Circular Quay against the backdrop of the Opera House.

Now wearing the Flag of Rear Admiral Survais, we sailed north some one thousand miles to the American Forward Fleet logistic base at Manus. The sight of several hundred supply ships of the logistic support force was a powerful reminder of the scale of the American amphibious operations in the region. BELFAST replenished; and then we were off again heading for Formosa (Taiwan). In the very north of the island, there was a Japanese prisoner of war camp in which were detained a considerable number of British civilians. Our task was to give them support whilst they awaited more suitable means for their evacuation. As we steamed into Keelung harbour the ship was at full action stations. However, our arrival was without incident. A few Japanese troops on the jetty handled our berthing lines and then made themselves scarce. We were there for about two days during which time I did not see any of the former prisoners – but I understood that they were not in such bad condition as those from some other camps.

We sailed on north to join an American Seventh Fleet task force, under US Rear Admiral Kincaid, which was due to liberate Shanghai. We reached the mouth of the Yangtze in a couple of days and joined up with the American Flagship the heavy cruiser, USS ST PAUL, and her escorts. The firepower of the St Paul was extremely impressive. In addition to her 8 inch main armament, every square foot of deck space seemed to be taken up by 40mm anti aircraft gun mounts. In contrast, our deck space in Belfast seemed half empty. The Americans had learnt their lesson the hard way, culminating in the vicious kamikaze attacks.

The whole force remained offshore, waiting for American minesweepers to clear any mines in the Yangtze approaches and then the narrower channel of the Whampoa river, which led up to Shanghai. The weather was miserable, damp, and cloudy with little visibility; and with most of us getting increasingly impatient for something to happen. Eventually the word to go was given - and in line-ahead, led by the USS **St Paul**, we steamed slowly up the Whampoa river towards Shanghai, with flat featureless country on either bank. Numerous locally manned sampans, whose occupants made friendly gestures in our direction, followed each ship. The signs of poverty were strong and when any 'gash' (rubbish) from the ship, edible or otherwise, was ditched into the water, the sampans swarmed upon it like a flock of seagulls. After about an hour, we moored in the middle of the river opposite the main waterfront of the City of Shanghai, the Bund. The opposite left bank of the river, the Pudong, was a continuous mudflat. Today, the Pudong is a mass of high-rise buildings, the new business powerhouse of the city.

The Bund was an impressive sight of large run-down western-type business 'houses', a mark of the pre-war international prosperity of this extraordinarily cosmopolitan city. It was divided into 'Concessions', the British quarter, the French quarter, and the German quarter. At one extremity of the Bund lay Soochow Creek, the site of the empty British Consulate. In the middle, stood the façade of the Shanghai Club, a rival to the famous Hong Kong Club of the British Colony, and purporting pre-war to have had the longest bar in the whole of the Far East. From the centre of the Bund ran the Bubbling Well Road, home to a number of hotels and restaurants and one of the main thoroughfares through the city leading to the Shanghai racecourse and the outskirts of the British quarter.

All this provided ample opportunities for exploration and a variety of experiences, some welcome and good. Others not so. Many areas outside the concessions were merely smelly with ramshackle housing that revealed a way of life amongst the ordinary population that seemed to us to be primitive and have little merit. On the first night after the ship was secured, a party of us midshipmen went ashore to land at a passenger pier on the Bund, not far from the ship's berth. An American patrol was already there on duty. We were immediately surrounded by dozens of pedi-cab and rickshaw drivers, all excitedly offering their services to take us anywhere we wanted to go. Our problem was that we didn't know where we wanted to go. We spoke English and they didn't - they spoke a local Shanghai dialect, one of the very many dialects in China. Sign language eventually prevailed and we set off in a small fleet of rickshaws to what we hoped might be a suitable restaurant. After a relatively short journey, we arrived at what we were glad to see looked like a Chinese restaurant, where we paid off our rickshaws. I have no idea what currency we were using, or what the bill should have been. But since they appeared to have been reasonably satisfied we probably paid way over the odds.

Our problems however had only just begun. The very substantial menu was entirely in Chinese characters – and even if we could have read the menu, it was unlikely that we should have recognised anything that we had ever eaten before. It was a matter of picking one or two or three seemingly eatable items – but of course we had no idea what the quantities were. It did not help to try and see what the other customers, who were all Chinese, were having. I can't remember what we ended up with.

However, much of our time was spent trying to use chopsticks to shovel rice with bean shoots and pak choi (a sort of cabbage) into our mouths from a small chow bowl held close to the chin. We drank copious quantities of Chinese rice wine (shaoxing) and beer (pijiu), and by the time we had finished our meal, we found it difficult to distinguish between the two. By midnight, when our midshipman's leave was due to expire, we had managed to make our way back to the jetty where, to our great relief, a BELFAST boat was waiting to return us to the ship. Thereafter, life continued to bring big surprises as we found our way around Shanghai.

After several days, Peter Chambers, a friend since our days together at Dartmouth, and I were detailed off to move ashore to the now-being-occupied British Consulate. Our task was to act in support of a British War Crimes Investigating Unit, headed by an RNVR commander, Gordon Fortin, who were basing themselves there. In more peaceful times, Gordon had been a senior banker. This was great news for us as we would be living ashore and setting up an entirely new outfit in an exciting post-war field of operations. We occupied a well-built annexe to the consulate which was itself a fine building and had been closed since the outbreak of the war. We recruited a few local Chinese as drivers and acquired cars for them. Such acquisition was quite simple - provided you could get there before the Americans. You merely toured the streets looking for likely looking vehicles that had been abandoned by the Japanese and took immediate charge of the best looking. At first, there were plenty to choose from. We did not enquire too closely where the drivers got their petrol from – but that was part of their job. There weren't too many rules in an immediate post-war situation of a defeated enemy.

In the vicinity of Shanghai there were several camps in which pre-war inhabitants of Shanghai had been detained. There had been some atrocities committed by the Japanese; and we found out that the Japanese had frequently used the Shanghai racecourse as an execution ground. Our War Crimes team began by taking statements from British nationals. One of our specific targets was to collect evidence against a certain Indian citizen, Subba

Chandra Bose, who at a high political level, had worked closely with the Japanese and was thus a prime war-crime suspect for charges of collaboration with the enemy.

For us two midshipmen, the main task was setting up in the office some form of filing system of evidence that could be used in future court actions. I am far from sure that what Peter Chambers and I did was of much help in providing evidence of a decisive nature to the War Crime courts, which mostly took place in Hong Kong – but we certainly tried hard and greatly enjoyed ourselves. One evening Peter and I were wining and dining in some not-too downmarket restaurant when we noticed an Indian at another table looking very closely at us. It seemed to us that he looked like a photograph of Subba Chandra Bose that we held on our files. Suddenly, he got to his feet and headed rapidly towards a back door. We followed him, and as we came into the back alley, I put my hand on a pistol, which at that time, I always carried in my back pocket. The next thing we heard were two sharp cracks from the direction of a body running away down the alley. We were being fired at! We were much too surprised, and probably frightened, to do more than take a few more steps in the fleeing body's direction, before discretion became the better part of valour and we abandoned the chase. As we discovered later, it was almost certainly not Subba Chandra Bose.

There were other hazards, some of a minor nature. One of these followed my attempt to have the first drink by anyone since the beginning of the war at the long bar of the Shanghai Club. My plan was to spend a comfortable night in one of the many long-unused bedrooms of the club, rather than on a camp bed in the annexe at the consulate. I had failed to appreciate that there had been no attempt for some years to control mosquitoes in that part of Shanghai. Although it was very hot, I pulled a sheet over me in the mistaken view that it would act as a mosquito guard. It didn't. The final insult was when, having wrapped myself entirely in the sheet with only the end of my nose in the open air; I heard the dive-bombing noise of an approaching mosquito. With unerring accuracy it landed on the exposed tip of my bonce, into which it forced its particularly virulent sting. I gave up and went back to the consulate where at least I had a mosquito net.

Gradually the life of the British inhabitants of the city returned to some normality. We opened up the squash court at the consulate and created a bar from which our chosen local barman, also clearly a competent chef, was able to produce the most delicious fried egg sandwiches. We even found horses to ride at the racecourse and I succeeded in getting one or two of them to jump. The PT staff also created soccer and rugby and hockey pitches there. These were soon put to very good use. We somehow managed to purloin an undamaged and beautiful little theatre, which we found in the French concession of the city. Led by a young lieutenant, Don Willis, who had been a former secretary of the Cambridge University Footlights Society, we put on a pantomime for which I acted as the stage manager. We played to full and very enthusiastic houses for at least three nights. The tap-dancing of hefty sailors complete with wigs, bras and mini-skirts, and wearing black heavy leather boots, always seemed to 'bring the roof down'.

In the middle of October, BELFAST's midshipmen were told that they were all be appointed to Destroyers to do their 'small ship' time. To our delight, Peter Chambers and I were appointed to the Destroyer HMS TUSCAN, which had recently arrived at Shanghai under the command of Lieutenant Commander North Lewis. I packed up my 'billet' at the Shanghai Club and, with the remainder of my gear from BELFAST, moved on board TUSCAN. The idea of moving from the big - ship life of a cruiser, to that of a small ship such as TUSCAN was great news – not least, because I should be living in a cabin rather than in a chest flat. The ship was due shortly to return to England, a prospect that I looked forward to; reminding myself from time to time, but not too often, that I also had there a girlfriend, Ann Kimber. Nevertheless, I knew that I would also be sad to leave Shanghai, as by now I had acquired a local girl friend, Era Kimberly. Her Father was English and her mother a White Russian, of whom many had escaped there from the Soviet Union following the Communist revolution. Era and I had a great deal of fun together, most of which was nightlife as she was working by day. I therefore resolved to keep a return to this part of the world very high in my priorities for the early future.

Life in a small ship soon took on an entirely different tone. The ship was clearly a very happy one with an exceptional small team of RN and RNVR officers. In late October, the back page of the local newspaper, the North China Morning News, carried the back-page headline, *"Tomorrow the turf of the Shanghai racecourse will once more resound to the thunder of ponies hoofs when jockeys of the Royal Navy's 24th Destroyer Squadron will meet in a series of friendly races."* Subsequently we found out that we were in trouble because we had failed to get permission for this event from the local Chinese Authorities – we didn't know that there were any. This was eventually overcome without too much difficulty - for this was a time of neither peace nor war. The first problem in our racing task came from providing the jockeys. If you offer what "Jolly Jack" thinks is a 'good thing', a sailor will volunteer for anything. We had no shortage of volunteers who claimed experience as a jockey. Most of them, as it subsequently turned out, had probably never before even seen a horse at close quarters.

The great day came. The mounts, small North China ponies with very little shoulder, were saddled and taken to the start. During the war, the ponies had been exercised round the racecourse, despite the atrocities that had been committed there. So at least they knew their way back to the stables. However, as the first six ponies were gathered for the start and the jockeys put on board, the jockeys had no idea as to how to get their mounts pointed in the right direction for the race to begin at the right time. The starter got increasingly frustrated as he tried, without success, to get them lined up. Eventually, in exasperation, he dropped his flag and with a great cheer from the crowd, "they're off," the race began. Five of the six ponies immediately dropped their near-side shoulders, wheeled round, and were away. Unfortunately this manoeuvre left four of their five jockeys sprawled upon the ground.

The next race got off to a rather better start and five of the six jockeys came round the last bend into the straight heading for the finish at the far end of the public stands. Unfortunately the leading pony only remembered that its daily exercise always ended at the stable gate that was at the near end of the straight. No effort by the jockey in the saddle was going to make it go in any other direction than back into the stable yard. The other four ponies followed likewise. The crowd was now getting increasingly excited and roaring encouragement. Sensing a possible victory, one enterprising sailor jockey jumped off his pony, put the reins over its head, and ran down the straight to the finishing line towing his horse behind him. With much cheering from the spectators in the stands, he was declared the rather dubious winner.

In the final race, in which I participated having weighed-in at something over fifteen stone, my pony came second. The winner was another young midshipman, Michael Hibbert, who had weighed in at a little over ten stone. We had no saddle weights! As my second prize, I was given a pair of two china vases that, later that evening, I proudly carried back to the ship. On closer examination, I thought they were ugly in the extreme – or more politely perhaps, they were not to my taste. Unfortunately I retained them in my possession for far too long. On three occasions of changing ship, I purposely left them behind only to find that some mistakenly kind person forwarded them on to me. I eventually had to give them the 'float test' (navalese for dropping them over the side of a ship).

There were plenty of other attractions. I managed to play hockey, rugby or squash almost every day until I unfortunately broke my collarbone in a rugby game. A three-day excursion to sea provided a welcome breath of fresh air, literally and figuratively. On return from sea, Era and I also went to see a theatre performance of "The Merry Widow". It was in Russian! Nevertheless it was well staged and we enjoyed the singing. It was at about this time that an extraordinary 'happening' occurred in TUSCAN's wardroom. A Chinese arrived on board one evening and asked if he could perform "magic tricks". After a good deal of humming and haahing and negotiating a fee, he was invited to perform in the wardroom. He was very good, just as good as the 'Gulli Gulli' men of Port Said - and they are very good indeed. For his final trick he produced a medium sized china bowl that was half filled with water from the wardroom pantry and placed it in the middle of the carpeted, steel wardroom deck and covered it with a large embroidered cloth.

After some incantations, he took a heavy looking truncheon and smashed it with some force across the bowl which appeared to shatter. He whipped off the cloth – but there was no sign of a smashed bowl - and no trace of water. He replaced the cloth flat on the deck and again made incantations. To our astonishment, we **saw** the bowl grow as if from the deck. He removed the covering cloth – and there was the bowl, fully intact with the water still in it. He would do no further tricks and left the ship. About six or seven of us had watched this astonishing performance. After he had gone, we all described what we had seen. We all agreed that we had seen the same thing – but not one of us could offer any explanation. The only, but still unlikely explanation that any of us could offer, was that what we thought we had seen happen, had not really happened. But that by some extraordinary feat of collective hypnosis, we all thought and saw that it did happen. There is I believe some evidence that such hypnosis can be achieved. Indeed my uncle when in the Indian Police, believed that he was once the 'victim' of remote hypnosis when he 'saw' a flash flood of water carrying all in front of it flood down the main street of an Indian village. Minutes later, it was clear that no such flood had actually happened. There was only an elderly Indian, seated on the ground on the other side of the street, staring intently at him.

TUSCAN sailed from Shanghai for Hong Kong on the 14th of December 1945. In Hong Kong, I managed to spend a few hours ashore attending one of the war crimes trials of Japanese, which was in progress at Lye Mun. It was interesting, but I regarded my visit as concluding any connection of mine with the war crimes scene within which I had worked in Shanghai.

Our next stop was Australia. As is often the case, timings were critical. The war being over, we were now not permitted to sail at any speed over fourteen knots as a fuel economy measure. This left us with two choices – we could spend Christmas Day in Darwin and then would not be able to arrive in Sydney until after New Year's Day. Or we could sail from Darwin early on Christmas morning and spend New Year in Sydney. The ship's company chose the latter. Darwin was not much of a 'run ashore'; but we found when we got there that there were a number of generous invitations for the ship's company to shore-side Christmas parties.

One of the invitations was for the wardroom officers to join a party at the AWA (Australian Women's Army) mess on the outskirts of the town. There were not many, other than the duty watch, that stayed on board the ship that night. Peter Chambers and I opted for the AWA party – which, from the little that I remember of it, was a most enjoyable affair. However at about midnight, one of the many somewhat intoxicated guests left the mess to spend a penny. He saw what he thought was a suitable bush behind which he could conceal himself. Unfortunately it was not a bush. It was the top of a thirty-foot tree that was growing from the beach below. Inevitably, he ended up on the beach.

The rest of the night passed in some confusion. There was no path down to the beach. A seagoing element in the party, including Peter and myself, all very full of alcohol, was quickly organised to attempt a rescue from seaward. Somehow, with much local assistance, we managed to get safely down to sea level and find a boat. Eventually we succeeded in recovering him and found that he was not too badly hurt - so providing confirmation of the saying that "God looks after fools and drunks". However, by the time we got 'the faller' back to where he could be loaded into an ambulance, dawn had broken. At about 0730 Peter Chambers and I, still in our mess undress and soaked to the skin, managed to get back on board TUSCAN. At 0800 we sailed for Sydney. It was Christmas morning.

Our route inside the Great Barrier Reef required constant and close navigational attention by the Captain, Lieutenant John Hope, our navigator, and the bridge watch-keepers, of whom I was one. It also provided much spectacular scenery for the rest of the ship's company. We duly arrived in Sydney on New Year's Eve, and saw-in the first year of peace with due rejoicing. However, the rest of our week's stay was rather an anti-climax because an electrical power strike had virtually closed down the city – and it was a very hot summer. We also heard that the ship was not to go to New Zealand for a short docking and maintenance period before setting off for home, as had previously been planned. I was particularly looking forward to visiting another country. However, the revised programme took us to Melbourne, and that sounded an attractive alternative.

We arrived at Williamstown, a suburb of Melbourne, in early January for a two week docking. We were immediately showered with offers of hospitality. Nevertheless, there was still work to be done, particularly because on arrival, we lost three of our RNVR sub lieutenants for immediate return to the UK as the post war demobilisation process got underway. This meant that I had to take on a number of additional jobs in the ship, including that of Anti Submarine Warfare Officer. This required some fast learning from me. Nevertheless, I was able to get some tennis and some riding before departing for a week's leave in the mountains some thirty-five miles north east of Melbourne. The family home to which I had been invited was a small wooden bungalow. It had electric light – but no running water. The Reid family was large and immensely hospitable, having had over three hundred British servicemen to stay as guests since the beginning of the war. I spent the time surrounded by magnificent scenery, either walking or riding in the forest amongst lyrebirds, kookaburras, wallabies, wombats and gloriously coloured parrots.

Soon after I returned to the ship, we sailed north from Melbourne to join the three aircraft carriers, HM Ships IMPLACABLE, INDOMITABLE and GLORY at Jarvis Bay, just south of Sydney. They were under the command of Vice Admiral Sir Philip Vian. We were then to escort the carriers back to Melbourne for a week's visit to commemorate the part played by the carriers of the British Pacific Fleet in the Pacific war. A centrepiece for the visit was to be a fly past over Melbourne by seventy-six aircraft from the three carriers. As we neared the approaches to Melbourne, we started flying operations from all three carriers. This was indeed a formidable show of force, the like of which the Royal Navy would seldom be able to mount again. The rehearsals took place over several days in rough weather conditions that made flight operations difficult. TUSCAN was stationed on the Starboard beam of the force as a stand-by plane guard. Sadly, a Firefly aircraft from Glory ditched about a mile on our port beam after its engine caught fire whilst in the landing pattern. I was watching from our gun-deck at the time. We immediately headed for the spot at best speed and lowered our whaler as a rescue boat. The aircraft remained afloat but it took some time to extract the pilot, who was unconscious, from his cockpit and get him on board. Despite the best efforts of a doctor, whom we had to fetch from IMPLACABLE, the pilot did not survive. However, we were able to rescue the observer who was not seriously hurt. This was a saddening start to the visit and I felt very emotional when, on the next day, I represented TUSCAN at the pilot's funeral. Nevertheless, the rest of the visit produced a haze of hospitality of every sort.

Melbourne was in strong contrast to what I had been able to see of Sydney. It was a city of numerous open parks, of broad tree-lined avenues, of big stores and clean streets. There was everything to enjoy. I had learned that two good friends from Dartmouth days were serving as midshipmen in GLORY and we joined up for some great partying. Bill Hart and I also accepted invitations from the Victoria LTA to play tennis on the glorious courts at Kooyong, where the Australians played their Davis Cup matches. This was a privilege that we much enjoyed; particularly when we were invited by two Australians to join them for a 'Davis Cup' doubles - which we won. Even more enjoyable was the opportunity to watch some of the top Australian Davis Cup players practicing, including John Bromwich and Adrian Quist.

The formal visit to Melbourne being complete, we returned in company with the carriers to Jarvis Bay where they were able to operate with a nearby shore 'diversion' airfield at the Australian naval airbase at Nara. Our principal task in TUSCAN was to act as plane guard to the carrier, 'IMPLACABLE'; a duty which required us to keep close station on her port quarter during flight operations. We were then ready immediately to assist if an aircraft should, on take off or landing, go over the side into the sea. It was, however, a somewhat tedious task - provided that there were no accidents. It involved a very early start, and it was 2200 or later by the time we returned to anchor in the bay each night. Sadly, the period was not casualty free. The force lost two aircrew, one flight deck crewman, and two non-aviating sailors who drowned when their launch was swamped in heavy seas in harbour at night. Fortunately TUSCAN was not directly involved in any of these accidents.

The tedium of long days at sea, with no view other than the back end of IMPLACABLE, was relieved by a number of rest days at anchor in Jarvis Bay. These allowed some social contact between our two ships. We were delighted to be able to give her aircrew a change of scenery at lunchtime in our small wardroom. This was followed by an evening party in IMPLACABLE when we sang Fleet Air Arm songs until the early hours of the morning. I can just recall our return boat trip to TUSCAN in a decidedly choppy sea with John Drane, our first lieutenant, practicing head stands on the canopy of our ship's motor boat!

We also managed to fit in some of our own weapon training, including our regular torpedo firing trials. The ship used as the target was anchored in the bay. These trials did not all go well. The torpedoes that were to be fired were set to run deep under the target and were fitted with blowing heads. This meant that at the end of their run the torpedo would surface and could be recovered. Not all went under the target; and nor did all surface at the end of their run! However, the top prize went to the ship that planned to fire two torpedoes on their starboard beam, one from the forward mounted set of torpedo tubes, and one from the after set. The target ship was anchored in the middle of Jarvis Bay. Making a fast approach, the firing ship made a spectacularly sharp turn to fire. One torpedo from the forward set of tubes set off in the direction of the target. Unfortunately, the other set of tubes was pointing the opposite way– and the second torpedo was last seen with its tell-tale trail of bubbles passing between the two headlands that enclosed the bay and heading for the open ocean. It was never seen again. Ah well, we can all make mistakes – and at least the war was over.

After two weeks in the Jarvis Bay area, all the ships returned to Sydney, from where on the 21st of February, with a 300ft paying off pennant flying from the masthead, we set off for home. We were happy to make a brief stop at Melbourne, where the ship embarked a cargo of gold bullion destined for London, the sailors were able to say farewell to their girl friends, and I was able to get a last opportunity for more tennis at Kooyong. On this occasion, I was lucky enough to be playing on an adjacent court to Frank Sedgeman, then Australian Junior Champion and rapidly climbing the ladder of world-class rankings although only aged sixteen. He generously invited me to join in a 'four', in which of course I was thoroughly outclassed. Nevertheless, we all seemed to enjoy it – I certainly did. Sedgeman was very pleasant with no 'side' to his character at all. He became a very great tennis player and a fine sportsman.

After a very rough passage through the Australian Bight, we called very briefly for fuel at Fremantle and set course for Trincomalee in Ceylon. I was sorry to leave Australia without seeing more of the country – but the urge to get home was understandably strong. It was not long, however, before our next destination was changed from Trincomalee to Colombo and thence to Karachi. The post-war political division of India was causing all sorts of racial problems, one of which was a threatened mutiny by ships of the Indian Navy in the Pakistani port of Karachi. So we hastened there so as to act as a calming influence. As we entered Karachi, we passed the Royal Indian Navy sloop HINDUSTAN looking somewhat battered after the attack on her, apparently by the

Indian Air Force, as she was defecting from Bombay. She was also at the centre of political action in Karachi, when rioters broke into the ship's magazines. As far as I was aware, there was no further trouble following our arrival.

One of my two memories of Karachi was that, even in the town, camels provided the principal means of transport – quite unlike India. The other, which was the highlight of our visit, was a wardroom evening fishing trip in a most comfortably fitted and well crewed dhow that we had chartered for the evening. The evening finished with our dhow's Captain, O'Brien by name, cooking a superb meal of freshly caught fish over a charcoal fire, as we lay at anchor in a flat calm sea, with a full moon and a cloudless sky. It seemed as near perfection as could be imagined. It was 0100 before we returned to TUSCAN.

Thereafter, time seemed to drag as we continued alone towards home at a speed of not more than twelve knots, a measure of fuel economy. I don't remember the 'gulli gulli' men as we passed through the Suez Canal – but I do remember a number of happy middle watches as midshipman of the watch with one of two very interesting and amusing RNVR lieutenants. One of these, Alex Bridge, was an expert on the stars. If only I had remembered a small part of all that I learned from him about our universe! Those were, of course, the days of the 'open bridge'. When heading into a heavy sea with rain driven by a strong icy wind and low visibility during the middle watch, an open bridge represented abject misery. But on a calm, warm, clear night in the tropics, with little relative wind, the ship's bow-wave glittering with phosphorescence, the 'open' bridge becomes like a comfortable seat in the dress circle of the theatre of the world. The moon rises, the planets set, the stars shine with a clarity and brightness no longer seen in the industrially polluted air of the northern hemisphere, flying fish and dolphins play in the ship's bow-wave, and with a gentle breeze ruffling your hair, it can seem paradise. Indeed it was a magic paradise, of which the ship and her company were part. Today, the well designed enclosed bridge, which has to hand every comfort and every device needed to sail the ship safely in peace or war, provides a barrier with the real world, of which the ship is no longer a part of its magic. It is only an observer of it.

TUSCAN arrived at Portsmouth early in April to an England that was superficially much changed from the war. There was no blackout, and air raid shelters were no longer the centre of much inner-city life. But the destruction from the air of so many towns and cities was there for all to see. Country signposts, however, were not. Most commodities were still rationed – but without the stigma of undermining the war effort, the black market was flourishing. Arriving from abroad, we were all laden with supplies of fruit and other delicacies that our families had not seen in England since 1939.

My immediate plans were to visit my parents' new home. Whilst I had been away, they had moved to the countryside south of Bristol, where they had bought a somewhat more compact house, with a small cottage attached, a stable yard with garages and horseboxes, a hard tennis court and a much smaller garden than that at Waltham House. The front of the house at Claverham looked out across a ha-ha to a long narrow field of permanent pasture. My sister, Pauline, having just been de-mobbed from the WRAF was now living in the cottage. She began a smallholding enterprise, with pigs and poultry occupying the somewhat aged and small adjacent farm buildings. I greatly approved, especially as my mother promised to get me a horse on which I could hunt in the coming winter.

But it was spring and I wanted to re-connect with my girl friend Ann Kimber, who was about to leave the WRNS. However, I only had a few weeks before I was due to start my nine months of sub lieutenants' technical courses, which were mostly in the Portsmouth area. My head was still spinning with Frank Sedgeman and tennis at Kooyong. Without much idea of what the pre-war British national standard of tennis had been, apart from knowing that my father had played for Gloucester for many years, I entered for the first post-war National Hard Court Tennis Championships at Bournemouth. I had never before played on a hard court and had no idea how slow it was compared with the grass courts of Kooyong. I thought I had a reasonably good service, though I had not expected it to deteriorate as it did when I got onto the court and the umpire called "Play". My opponent was Eric Filby whom I thought was at least twice my age – which he probably was. As I discovered later, he had been a player of some note and skill in pre-war days. As from the first game, and probably from the knock-up, he discovered that I had no backhand – despite having greatly envied that of John Bromwich whom I had watched at Kooyong. From then on, I hardly ever got a shot to my forehand. On the rare occasion that the ball came that way, it was played with slice so that my thundering grass court forehand return either peppered the bottom of the net or ballooned into the stop netting behind the baseline. I think I got one game. It was all over in a very short time and I retired to the dressing room feeling somewhat humiliated and ashamed.

However it did not put me off tennis. It just made me more determined to try to reach the sort of general standard that I was now seeing for the first time. I was not discouraged either, when, as I watched later rounds of the tournament, I saw how often some of the then top players raised their arms and looked up to heaven – presumably for inspiration – when one of their 'should have been' best shots went, like mine, into the bottom of the net or way out of court.

I was now a sub lieutenant – and the weight of the one gold lace stripe on the sleeve of my uniform jacket seemed to weigh heavy! The nine separate specialist courses that all sub-lieutenants had to complete following their service at sea as midshipmen were of differing lengths from two to eight weeks, and were conducted in different naval shore establishments in the Portsmouth area. The most demanding was the Gunnery course at Whale Island – but it also provided the best fun. There were good sporting facilities, one of which was provided within the wardroom mess after dinner on guest nights. This was billiard fives. It was highly dangerous as two officers, who had wined and dined very well, used their hands to propel a billiard ball into the pockets at the other end of the table against the best efforts of their opponent to keep the ball out.

Billiard balls also featured in one of our post guest night projects on the lawn outside the wardroom mess. The object of the exercise was to attempt to fire the billiard balls, from one of the many muzzle-loading cannons captured in yester year, over the roof of a long low building some hundred yards away known as West Battery. The drill was to get as many people as possible holding thunder flashes, to light them simultaneously and put them down the barrel in time for the gun master to load a handful of billiard balls. There was usually then a 'bloody great bang', a check to see that the gun master still possessed all his fingers, followed by a questioning of the observers to determine the range that had been achieved by the furthest billiard ball. As far as I remember, one firing resulted in the loss of one billiard ball which we optimistically claimed must have gone over the roof of the said West Battery. It was rather chancy stuff, but as far as I know, nobody got badly damaged.

The discipline, particularly on the parade ground at Whale Island, was hard and, if one did not get on the wrong side of the parade instructors, could also provide fun. However, clear transgression of the rules resulted in the whole class (we were about fifteen in number) being sent at the double to run as a formed body 'round the island'. The distance round the island was not very great – perhaps a mile. But on several points of the circum navigation a staff instructor would appear out of a neighbouring building and shout loudly, "about turn". Back you went until you met some other 'wizard' coming out from his lair to turn you back in the direction in which you were originally heading. That way, round the Island was quite a long way.

The strict but fun attitude of the establishment was at its peak on the parade ground. Our course instructor was the chief petty officer, Tex Burrell. Even the smallest mistake in drill with a rifle or sword would result in withering criticism. One of our class, perhaps less bright than some of us, had many years before acquired the nickname of 'Batty'. At a point of exasperation from a succession of his mistakes when carrying out cutlass drill, Tex Burrell turned towards this individual to demand, "Do you play cricket or why do they call you Bats?" Stopping in front of him, he made a safe but hefty swipe with his cutlass in his direction. Bringing his cutlass back to his side, Tex continued, "One day I will cut your f***ing head off. And you'll say, yah, you missed - and I'll say "You wag your f***ing head and see."

Despite all this, Tex would come down with us to the pub in the evening and share a few pints. It may have been crude, but this was the way that the gunnery branch played things – and it worked. The gunnery branch was much respected for both its discipline and professionalism.

At the end of each six-week course of sub-lieutenants at Whale Island, they were required to do a ceremonial march past at a special Friday Divisions, which always followed the course's passing-out mess dinner. It was an occasion when each course tried to make its leaving mark on the establishment. One innovative course managed to hoist a broken down car on to the top of the roof of the drill shed where it would be visible to all on the parade. The problem with this sort of stunt was that, following Divisions, the course was ordered to remove the said car before any of them could go on leave. One course, being rather canny, managed to plant a large tree in the middle of the parade ground. They were, of course, told to remove it forthwith. "Aye, aye, Sir", said the course leader, pressing down on the firing mechanism of an explosive charge that had been placed below the roots of the tree. There was a large explosion, the tree rose in the air before toppling to the ground. However, It took a long time for the course to remove the remains of the tree and repair the large hole left in the parade ground.

Amongst the most innovative stunts was that of the passing-out group of sub-lieutenants who managed to borrow an elephant from the local circus, together with its mahout. It was arranged for it to cross the bridge onto Whale Island early in the morning of their passing out parade. The security staff were a little surprised when the elephant appeared at the gate of the establishment.

They quickly rang the duty officer to say that there was an elephant coming on to the Island with a sub lieutenant on its back. Since it just happened to be April 1st, this warning was disregarded. At the parade, this group of sub-lieutenants did a very poor march past and were told to go round again. When they reappeared from behind the far side of the drill shed, they were led by the elephant to do a very smart repeat march past, to the total amazement of all on the parade ground. Returning the elephant was not a problem.

At these ceremonial parades there was a designated 'guard' armed with rifles. The sub-Lieutenants commanding the guard carried swords. If there was a mistake in drill by the guard, the parade training staff would shout, "Steady the guard," whilst suitable remonstrations were made and the mistake corrected. The most intelligent class of sub-lieutenants was that which managed to write these words in large letters on the grassy bank that provided a backdrop to the parade ground, using a strong weed killer. By the time that the weed killer had done its work and the message had become clearly visible to all on the parade ground, the sub lieutenants of this course were all far away.

Such innovation was not confined to the Gunnery School. At our anti-submarine warfare course in HMS VERNON, much of which I found not particularly interesting mainly because one of our instructors was about the most boring lecturer of any that I can remember. He used to deliver his lectures sitting down. After the section of the course in which we had been dealing with demolitions, we managed to take two turns of a piece of cordtex (a type of explosive cord) round the back leg of the chair in which he always sat. He had not long been into his lecture from the seated position when there was a loud bang and the chair, together with a very startled lecturer, collapsed backwards, but unhurt, onto the floor. This seemed very funny at the time, and indeed it was; but it was probably also rather dangerous damage. The penalty was that the leave of our course was stopped for two weeks, so that nobody could 'go ashore' even when the working day was complete. We thought that it was worth it because we did not see this instructor again.

In terms of serious fun, the course that we all remembered was our Air Course at Gosport. This had recently been set up with 727 Squadron providing eighteen Tiger Moths (a two seater biplane) in brilliant yellow colours with ROYAL NAVY on their side, in which we were all taught to fly. Each student was graded on his flying ability. The pilot training was backed up by a series of lectures on the Fleet Air Arm.

On my first airborne sortie in the back seat - the instructor was always in front - and being rather over-confident having once flown before as a passenger during the war in an aircraft of the Air Transport Auxiliary, I failed to do up my safety harness straps sufficiently tightly. Having completed the lesson, in which I learnt how to fly the aircraft straight and level and to make gentle turns, my instructor, Lieutenant Commander Arthur Dennis, took control and said, *"I will show you now what the aircraft can do."* He immediately turned it upside down. I then found myself hanging from my straps, half out of the cockpit. *"Keep hold of the stick,"* he said *"and keep your feet on the rudder pedals."* Both my hands, however, were already in full use gripping the rim of the cockpit, from which I was hanging. My feet were nowhere near the pedals – and I was not letting go my hold on the cockpit rim. After a few terrifying moments for me, he looked in his mirror and where he should have seen my face, he saw my navel. To my very considerable gratitude, he quickly turned the aircraft the right way up and I fell back into the cockpit. On my next flight, I did up my straps so tightly that by the time we landed, I almost had gangrene.

After a minimum of six or seven hours' instruction in the air, one's instructor had the right to send you solo if he thought that you were sufficiently capable. Some of the class never reached this stage. I was sent solo after about seven and a half hours. I don't remember being nervous, but I probably was. I took off safely and after one circuit of the airfield I managed to land back on the airfield in one piece, having crossed the boundary fence in a steady glide at about the required one hundred feet. One of our class, who was nicknamed 'Twitch', was only offered his first solo at the very end of the course. We all watched with interest as he came into land, crossing the boundary fence at about one thousand feet in a steady glide. It was clear that he was heading for the far side of the airfield. He only just managed to get his aeroplane on to the ground before it ran into the boundary fence. There was no room for him to turn the aeroplane round; aeroplanes don't have an 'astern' gear! We cheered loudly as he was eventually towed off backwards so as to taxi back to the squadron's parking area.

I enormously enjoyed my flying and found that in some ways it was rather like riding a horse – that is to say that you needed a good sense of balance. There were of course instruments to tell you what the aeroplane was doing, but for me, as in riding a horse, the 'seat of the pants' was often a valuable addition. I found the least satisfying part of the flying operation was the hours that one spent in the crew room doing nothing but wait for your aircraft to become available from the previous flight - or waiting for the unsuitable weather to clear. Nevertheless, I was able to get in some twenty hours of flying and passed my test to qualify for a civilian pilot's licence. Although I was never able to build upon this very basic experience, nor wished to transfer to the Fleet Air Arm, I never lost the sense of enjoyment that I found when piloting an aircraft. Later in my career when, as a matter of duty, I was spending many hours in the back seats of helicopters, I was able to get more than a few hours flying in the front as a 'second pilot'. I greatly enjoyed every one. Later still, in my retirement, I tried to find time to have fixed wing flying lessons – although my ambition did not stretch to qualifying to fly solo. Sadly, this ambition to take to the air again as a pilot remained unfulfilled.

Other courses were rather less exciting, and some were rather more sedate; such as our course in naval Communications at the signals school at Leydene House near Petersfield. During the course, I came no nearer to mastering reading the Morse code by buzzer than I had done at Dartmouth. However, life was always busy – so busy that I rather lost contact with my girlfriend, Ann Kimber. However, I told my self that I was hoping to return to the Far East to rejoin Era in Shanghai.

When all the exams in all the courses were marked and counted, I was extremely surprised that I had averaged more than a ninety percent mark. This gave me an advantage of some three months seniority for my promotion to lieutenant.

During the weekends of the autumn I had been able to get home to my parents' new house at Claverham, where my mother had very kindly purchased and kept fit a horse for me to hunt. The closest hunt was the Mendip, whose nearest meets were still some distance away. However, Claverham was quite near the railway station at Yatton, where a train ran along the foothills of the Mendips stopping at Priddy and other small stations. I was able to hire a horsebox to be attached to the train for the princely sum of one pound and ten shillings for the day. It took me about twenty minutes to ride to the station from home and another half an hour on the train to the station nearest to the meet. This usually then involved a further ride up the hill to the top of the Mendips. Even if I did not make the meet on time, I was usually able to catch up quite quickly. Often it was a very long hack home, sometimes in the dark - but it was well worth the enjoyment of the day – and the roads were usually quiet. There were some occasions when I would warn the guard that I was planning to catch the train for the journey home. The guard was always extremely helpful and if I was not there on the platform 'on the dot', he would look to see if I was coming and would hold the train for me as my horse and I trotted down the hill. I would apologise to any waiting passengers, some of whom would greet me warmly and ask me for a description of how the day had gone.

Chapter 4

HMS COSSACK and the Far East

"Oh, East is East, and West is West, and never the twain shall meet,
till earth and sky stand presently at God's great judgement seat".

Kipling

My new appointment was to HMS COSSACK, serving in the Far East Fleet. She was one of the 'CO' class of destroyers built in the later stages of World War II. She was a successor to the older and famous 'COSSACK (LO3) which, under the command of Captain Philip Vian, carried out the 1940 rescue of British merchant seamen held prisoner in the German merchant ship "Altmark" in a Norwegian fjord. Later in the war COSSACK (LO3) was sunk.

I wrote my formal letter of acknowledgement to the captain of the ship in the customary form, "I have the honour to acknowledge my appointment to Her Majesty's ship Cossack under your command." I added, using formal civil service language, "I am proceeding East under the directions of the Ministry of War Transport." When subsequently I joined the ship in Hong Kong, I discovered my letter in the office files, across the top of which the first lieutenant had scrawled, "Go west, young man, go west."

Having completed my sub Lleutenant's courses before Christmas, I was now entitled to three months pre-embarkation leave. With a fit horse ready for me in the stables at my family home at Claverham, I was looking forward to doing two days each week hunting with the Mendip Hunt for the next three months. It was not to be. Early in January a prolonged spell of ice and snow set in which stopped almost all hunting, and certainly that on top of the Mendip hills throughout the three months. It was very frustrating.

At the very beginning of April, I travelled North by train to the Clyde to embarked in the troopship SS STRATHNAVER bound for Singapore. It was now peacetime and STRATHNAVER was a 'trooping' experience far more civilised and comfortable than my previous experience two and a half years before. The ship was far less crowded with troops and was much better provided with passenger facilities. There was only a small naval contingent. Some of the passengers were women and children on their way to join their husbands in the Far East. I was not very impressed by the behaviour of either. I was also very unimpressed by the administration of the ship that was now the responsibility of the army. But then, soldiers were never taught how to run ships.

The challenge was how not to become bored. There was no naval training or watch keeping to be done on the ships bridge; and apart from my seamanship manual, I had no books to read – or perhaps I just never found the library! Sun bathing ('bronzy-bronzy') whilst relaxing on deck was very agreeable – and the weather for it was good through the Mediterranean and beyond. But it was all too easy to get badly sunburnt. The alternatives had other drawbacks. To return to the cabin which I shared with some fifteen others was to get insufferably hot or to the lounges that were often cluttered with badly behaved children.

I determined to learn to play bridge. I did this by observing, as best I could, the bridge fours that gathered every day in the card room. One of the players in a four that I frequently watched was an RAF warrant officer. To my unpractised eye, he seemed to be very good. He never sorted the cards in his hand; and when he shuffled the pack, he did it by running it up and down his open arm. This table also played for money – which at sixpence-a-hundred was somewhat too much for my skill level and potentially beyond the depth of my pocket. However, although I was able to learn quite quickly, it all seemed rather too serious for me. Playing for money or gambling was also not my scene. After a couple of weeks, I joined up with a more 'social' group and in due course ventured to do my own bidding and play my own hand. I thoroughly enjoyed the experience. The rest of the voyage seemed then to pass all too quickly.

We reached Singapore on the 25th of April, where I was delighted to be greeted by Peter Chambers who had been a midshipman with me since our first days in RENOWN. He was now the Flag Lieutenant to the Flag Officer Malayan Area, Rear Admiral Faulkner. As the Flag Lieutenant, he had a naval car and driver at his disposal that much facilitated my introduction to Singapore during the two or three days before I could take onward passage to join COSSACK in Hong Kong. During this time, Peter introduced me to a very attractive young girl as his fiancé. Later when I reached Hong Kong, I was sad to hear that they had parted.

The voyage from Singapore to Hong Kong went rather well. The weather was good and I became friendly with one of the lady passengers, Phil Baxter. She was returning to Hong Kong where her husband was in the army. I was young and virginal and she wasn't. The stories she told me about her husband were upsetting. The nights were long, the moon and the stars were romantic, the deckchairs were very comfortable and I found her attractive. We continued some sort of a relationship after arrival in Hong Kong whilst she was preparing the divorce from her husband. There was never ever going to be any future for a relationship for either of us; but I have always been grateful to her because she introduced me to a Hong Kong family, the Thompsons, whose daughter, Ann, became my wife.

As we approached Hong Kong I was still only nineteen years of age. I had worn the Queen's uniform for six years whilst under training. I had seen the destruction by German bombing of some of our great cities, Bristol, Portsmouth and Plymouth. I had seen active service in Europe and the Far East. I had already been through the Suez Canal five times. I had witnessed the end of the war and its immediate aftermath both in Europe and in Asia. Now, I was no longer a 'makee learn', and would take up my first full appointment. I had a clear sense that I was part of an organisation, the Royal Navy, whose duty was the preservation of peace and security throughout the world. I had already seen some of the deep poverty in which parts of the rest of the world lived – but I had no understanding of the world of business and trade.

Not long after my arrival in Hong Kong, I had met at a cocktail party an American who had just come from the States to recommend to his company whether it would be profitable for Coca Cola to set up its own bottling plant there. This depended upon how many bottles of Coke that they could expect to sell weekly. It was his job to assess this. I can well remember thinking, rather pompously, I suspect, how distressingly unimportant was his task in life compared with the career that I was privileged to pursue – that of assisting in keeping the peace of the world. I was still very naïve in many matters!

I was delighted on arrival In Hong Kong to be met by Robert Culverwell, a great friend from school days in Bristol. He was now a young officer in the Royal Marines, his unit being stationed in the New Territories. I was also glad to be able to make contact with an elderly cousin, Don Evans, a distinguished lawyer on the Island, who was sometimes known in family circles as the 'O & A' – the old and archaic. I also found myself, and I am not sure how, stewarding the Alsatian classes at the Hong Kong Kennel Club's first post-war dog show!

Hong Kong was the home port for the smaller ships of the Far East Fleet, the destroyers of the Eighth Destroyer Squadron and the frigates of the Third Frigate Squadron. The naval base and dockyard were very close to the central facilities of Hong Kong, the banks, the clubs, the main hotels, the international restaurants, and the big European stores. But also very near at hand were the dozens of small Chinese shops offering a remarkable range of goods, from the latest cameras, electronic gadgets and gizmos from Japan, to Chinese vases reputedly from the Ming period - all at knock down prices. Hong Kong tailors offered made-to-measure suits and clothing ready to wear within twenty-four hours. Shopping in Hong Kong was an entertainment, an art, a challenge; and an opportunity that was not to be missed.

Across the harbour to the north lay Kowloon and the New Territories, which were attached to the mainland of China. They also provided an element of the 'high life' with the internationally known Peninsular Hotel at its centre and the golf course at Fanling a 'backdrop' for the weekend. But the cross-harbour ferry tended to be a disincentive, both for the local European community on the Island and for sailors in the naval base. In the former case, a well-known comment on the Hong Kong side, to someone who had apparently been absent for a while from the social round, was, "What's happened to you? Have you just got married or do you now live in Kowloon?"

Beyond Kowloon, lay the country of the New Territories[4] that was for the most part strongly rural. Rice paddy fields were widely to be seen, as were large herds of domestic duck, tended by a single Chinese farmer wielding a long bamboo which he used to guide his well disciplined flock. The Chinese walled city at the centre of the New Territories supported a life that had probably not changed substantially for several hundred years.

However, twenty years later when I was again in Hong Kong, the New Territories had changed greatly. Small Chinese villages had become very large European type conurbations. Tunnels rather than ferries linked the Island to the mainland. A large modern racecourse at Fanling had replaced the old home of the Hong Kong Jockey Club at Happy Valley. But Happy Valley, so attractively named, remained a centre of much sporting activity.

A ferry ride to the south west of Hong Kong lay the Portuguese territory of Macau famed for its gambling. It was also a pleasant break from Hong Kong life, and particularly for those who wished to take their girl friend for an away week-end without the danger of running into their own wife or her husband. I later enjoyed a visit there in the company of a strong wardroom team from COSSACK. Macau has a colonial nature very different from that of Hong Kong. Although being of a non-gambling nature, I nevertheless found it fascinating to watch the game of fantan that was played everywhere. In this, the Chinese croupier removes sticks (like fined down chop-sticks) four at a time from a large higgledy-piggledy pile. This he does with remarkable dexterity. The players bet on how many sticks will be left at the end. Later that

---

[4] *This was land leased by China to the Government of HongKong and was not British Crown property*

night, I was not minded to accept the offer of a Chinese girl to share my bed, who had came to my hotel room in the middle of the night as part of the hotel's normal service.

The ship that I was to join, HMS COSSACK, was the leader of the Eighth Destroyer Squadron and as such was commanded by an officer of captain's rank. She carried the various squadron specialist staff officers, mostly of the rank of lieutenant commander, some of who also carried out ship's duties. One of these was Lieutenant Commander Michael Woolcombe who, in addition to being the squadron communicator, was also COSSACK's ships signals officer. Later in my life, I was to meet and know distinguished members of his family in Devon. I discovered all too soon after I had set foot in the ship that I was very much the junior boy. Although the welcome was very friendly, I found out that my duties, in addition to being the ship's gunnery Officer (COSSACK carried four 4.5 Inch Guns controlled by a modern, radar assisted fire-control system) were as victualing officer, sports officer, confidential books officer, press relations officer, film Officer and divisional officer to the Quarterdeck and Top Divisions of the ships company. No wonder perhaps that I found myself struggling a bit at first. As the ship's unqualified gunnery officer I was particularly glad that COSSACK also carried the well experienced squadron gunnery officer, Lieutenant Commander Philip Goode, to guide me.

Some of the pressures came off not long after I had joined, when we left our buoy in the naval anchorage to do some basic exercises in Mirs Bay, a large area of the ocean to the north of the Colony. This was the home of much Chinese piracy; although not in Hong Kong territorial waters. Mirs Bay was well suited to Naval operational exercises, for unlike the near approaches to Hong Kong and the Pearl River approaches to Canton, its waters were not heavily congested with merchant traffic. It also provided a small secluded inlet at the northernmost edge of the New Territories, Plover Cove. Here the ship's company could enjoy a much-relaxed routine, ideal for painting and cleaning ship and completing the more arduous domestic tasks of administration to which one otherwise never got round when directly faced by the temptations and distractions of runs ashore in Wanchai and Kowloon. Nevertheless, I came slowly to realise that, In the wider context of the Navy's task at Hong Kong, it was not going to be easy to preserve a fair balance between the peacetime priority of contributing to the political and social stability of Hong Kong, through smartness, efficiency and 'good order and naval discipline'; the need for relaxation for ship's companies; and the more operational task of maintaining the fighting effectiveness of our ships.

After a few days in Mirs Bay and at Plover Cove, we returned to our buoy in Hong Kong's naval anchorage so as to top up with fuel, victuals and ammunition before setting off for Singapore. Unlike Singapore, the Hong Kong naval base provided a very limited number of alongside berths. The destroyers therefore frequently found themselves at buoys in the harbour. This required a full programme of boat running for the ship's motorboat whose inevitable inflexibility was not fully compensated for by the availability of Chinese sampans, small local craft propelled by an oarsman using a single oar over the stern. They were colloquially known as 'wiggle-stick' boats. Each ship had its own 'side-party' sampan, which not only looked after the cleanliness of the ship's side, an important feature of the ship's general character, and provided a 'hook-rope' party[5] whenever required. The side part' were very much a family unit always with a woman as its head. In COSSACK, she was called Jennie. The following year, a hazardous situation once arose when HMS CONSORT was manoeuvring in harbour and was blown down onto COSSACK. Our side-party sampan was crushed between the two ships, throwing our side-party members into the water. One of our lieutenants, George Cousins, jumped in without regard to his own safety and rescued Jennie. Sadly, two members of her side-party crew were killed.

---

[5] *Navalese for a general clear up party*

Another major facility provided to each ship by the Hong Kong Chinese was a laundry service. Destroyer-sized ships were not provided with appropriate facilities. A bucket and a bar of 'pussers' soap had long been the normal practice for a sailor's 'dhobi'. A Chinese laundry firm, usually part of a larger Hong Kong semi-officially recognised organisation, was a major and essential asset to any ship of the Far East Fleet. Under a 'No. 1 boy', a team of several laundrymen, working and living in whatever spare space that could be found for them, produced a remarkable twenty four hour service, seven days a week. By local standards, they made good money – but the ability to travel, particularly to Japan, provided substantial opportunities for illicit trading. The market for penicillin in Japan was extremely profitable. When, during a planned search whilst at sea between Hong Kong and Japan, I discovered a pillow case full of drugs amongst the laundry bags. I was offered large-sized sums of money to overlook this. However, the drugs having been given the 'float test' (i.e. been thrown overboard), I was never aware of any personal bad feeling against me from any of the firm, even though the money might well have represented a fortune to them.

As we left Hong Kong through the Laimun Pass, I was very much looking forward to the prospects for this, my first deployment in COSSACK. We had, however, not got far to the southeast of Hong Kong, when the first excitement occurred. A large merchant ship that, without engine power, was being driven by strong winds onto the inhospitable Hainan shore, was asking for assistance. After a spell at high speed, we located the ship and took her under tow back to Hong Kong where we submitted claims for salvage money.

We were soon off again for Singapore that was the main base for the Far East Fleet. The island hosted not only the Joint Headquarters of the Commander in Chief, Far East, but also the Far East Fleet Commander; and those of the other two UK services. Situated on the north side of Singapore Island in the Jahore Straits, was HMS TERROR, the naval shore base. This contained extensive dockyard facilities, including a large graving dock, good berthing for large and small ships, and was very well provided with sports grounds and shore-side facilities, including accommodation. There was a thriving Fleet Club and an Officers Club. A naval air station at Changi, also on the Island, provided vital support for the air squadrons of the Far East aircraft carriers.

As a result of our 'tow job', our time at the Singapore naval base was inevitably short. However, I was able to have a brief run ashore with Peter Chambers who confirmed that he and his fiancée, whom I had only met very recently, had parted. I discovered that only shortly before, he had had another 'fiancé' whom he had made pregnant and whom, on the insistence of his Admiral, he had married. They had then parted on the evening of the wedding. Not long after, Peter returned to England to start naval flying training. The next that I heard of him was that he had left the Navy and joined the French Foreign Legion. It was rumoured that his presence in North Africa, where he served for some five years with distinction, had much to do with the wrath of a number of fathers in England whose daughters had unwisely succumbed to his charm. Despite my efforts to regain contact, I saw him only once more for a very short time before he died in sad circumstances quite early in his life. This was the loss of a man, a born leader of many talents not least in the sporting field, and of a most engaging character – unfortunately not all of it was good.

A few days later, we sailed for the east coast of Malaya for visits to the coastal villages of Mersing and Quantan. It was only a few miles off the coast here that the two battle ships, KING GEORGE V AND REPULSE had been sunk on the 10th of December 1941 by a Japanese air attack. It was said by local fisherman that the tops of their masts could still be seen above the surface when the tides were low. We attempted to locate their position accurately with our sonar but failed, as the set was not working properly. Nevertheless, it was a somewhat eerie and emotional occasion to be in close vicinity to where so many lost their lives in one of the Royal Navy's worst disasters. Having anchored off Mersing, a small party from the ship's company were invited to visit a local rubber plantation. This involved a walk along a jungle track. At one point, the guide stopped excitedly and, dropping to his knees, closely examined what he claimed were the footprints of a tiger. By popular consent, the return trip was made before dark.

We returned to Hong Kong in June for a short maintenance period alongside in the naval basin at HMS TAMAR. This was the starting point for my social life. Firstly, my cousin Alan Eberle, a doctor, had arrived to join a thriving well-known local practice, 'Anderson and Partners'. Alan, a well-qualified doctor who had served in the RAF during the war, came to join a thriving practice in Hong Kong. He quickly became a much-respected character on the island. He was a first class rugby referee and quickly made an impact on the Hong Kong rugby scene, centred on Happy Valley. Secondly, I was invited, at the instigation of Phil Baxter, to a small evening party given by Mr and Mrs Edgar Thompson, where I first met their eighteen-year-old daughter, Ann. She had been born in Hong Kong, and was evacuated to Canada, together with her mother, some months prior to the start of the Far East War. Her father, Edgar, was a senior engineer in the Hong Kong Electric Company. When the invasion by the Japanese took place in December 1941, he was a member of the Hong Kong Volunteer Defence Force and was captured by the Japanese at the North Point power station. He was held as a prisoner throughout the war in a camp on the south of the Island. Despite the rigours of the Japanese prisoner of war camp, Edgar fared remarkably well. He was a man of small stature but remarkably resilient. He survived when many others, apparently of a much more robust physique, had died.

For most of the war Ann and her mother had lived in Canada at Banff in the shadow of Lake Louise in the Canadian Rockies. For three years they did not know whether Edgar was alive or dead and were effectively without money, being supported as guests of the Canadian Government. Ann had almost idyllic teenage years, swimming all summer and skiing almost all winter. Calgary, now one of the principal oil cities in the world, was merely the 'not-too-far-away' town to which they went for visits to the dentist. In

1945, Ann and her mother returned to England where Edgar joined them in a small cottage at Bampton, in Devon. Ann, having completed her education in England, returned to Hong Kong with her mother. Her father, now chief engineer of the Hong Kong Electric Company, was engaged in the demanding task of restoring electrical supplies throughout the colony. At one stage, a British submarine in the naval dockyard was used as a temporary power station.

The Thompsons, prior to being able to return to their pre-war Hong Kong Electric Company house at 530, The Peak at the Wong–ni–Cheong gap, lived in a small flat at the head of Dudell Street in the City area and not far from the Hong Kong and Shanghai Bank. This was then the most dominant skyscraper in Hong Kong. Later, it was outdone by a new Bank of China building that was a little bit taller. When the Japanese had invaded in 1941, the Thompson's house had been a temporary headquarters for the Canadian battalion helping to defend the colony. In fierce fighting there, many on both sides were killed and the house destroyed. It was in Dudell Street, that I learnt my first words of Cantonese. Returning with Ann late in the evening, the door of the flat was invariably locked. To get in, we had to resort to throwing stones at the windows of the amah's room and shouting for the key - "Amah, sau-ci ah" - until the key was thrown down to us.

Life for me became rapidly very good. I began to see as much of Ann as I was able. She had several girlfriends, some of whose parents were also senior members of the Hong Kong Electric Company. We saw a great deal of each other, and the more that I saw of Ann, the more I wanted to be with her. On the mainland at Kowloon, the Services had established an Officers' Club that we visited on as many afternoons as possible, to swim, to sunbathe, to eat fried egg or cucumber sandwiches, and act as if there was no tomorrow. There was of course also plenty of nightlife. The Hong Kong Hotel, the many excellent restaurants and nightclubs were a great call - as long as the money lasted.

For those, but not I, who were more inclined to a bachelor-like lifestyle, there was the Hong Kong Club, with its famous bowling alleys. There was also the Cricket Club that was a favourite watering hole for the many young men who had come out from England to join the junior management levels of the great British trading companies, Jardine Matheson, Butterfield and Swire and the Hong Kong and Shanghai Bank. Both clubs, situated close to the gate of the naval dockyard, provided facilities of the highest standard. Also, very close at hand, but in the opposite direction, lay the China Fleet Club and the teaming Chinese community of Wanchai. This was the most popular run ashore area for ship's companies, with life of every sort and very much less decorum, being readily available, at all hours of the day or night.

Also in Dudell Street, was a well-known restaurant called the "Cock and Pullet". It was popular with young naval officers, as it served excellent food from an enormous menu at a price that was a great deal less than at the Hong Kong Hotel or at "Jimmy's Kitchen", both of which were much favoured by the many prosperous local residents. I soon had earned the dubious reputation of being the only member of our wardroom to have eaten my way through the whole of the Cock and Pullet's menu. When I got back to the ship, I lay on my bed groaning. I admit that I was a heavy eater.

At breakfast in the ship's wardroom, for which we were charged by our Chinese messman, I would not infrequently ask for a second helping, colloquially known as "going round the buoy". I later discovered that the messman was recovering the cost of my second breakfast, by adding in the mess account's book, the notation "Lieut Eberle – one guest" My shore side reputation was also not improved by my cousin. On the south side of the island there was a very good and popular hotel at Repulse Bay adjacent to the golf course. They had introduced the principle of the 'Guinea and the Piggy' for their buffet Sunday lunch for which you paid five Hong Kong dollars and ate as much as you liked. My cousin Alan spread the rumour that the hotel paid me twenty dollars a week to keep away. Life was fun, both by day and night.

COSSACK remained in Hong Kong for about a month, during which I saw as much of Ann as I possibly could. There was however strong competition. There were only a small number of attractive young English girls in Hong Kong and there were rather more young naval officers. Having to be duty officer on board, usually for one night in four, could also be inconvenient to one's love life. However, there were frequent calls for junior officers with administrative tasks like mine as victualing officer, sports officer, or film officer which could provide good reason to go ashore on duty during the working day. These allowed useful opportunities for meeting with friends and colleagues at popular places such as the 'Dairy Farm', at the base of the Hong Kong Hotel, where they served coffee, ice cream and delicious fried egg sandwiches.

The more I saw of Ann, the more I wanted to see her. It all seemed so different from my first ever girlfriend in England, Ann Kimber. But I soon learned that our time together was limited. Ann was shortly to sail for Canada where she had enrolled as an undergraduate at the medical faculty of the University of British Columbia in Vancouver. COSSACK was also due soon to sail north for Japan. A few days before our parting, we went for a walk around the Peak, a path about eight hundred feet above sea level that gave breathtaking views across the seas to the south of the Island and a fascinating view 'from the gods' of the teeming centre of the life of Hong Kong below. I decided to 'dip my toe in the water'.

"Darling Ann, if one day I was to ask you to marry me, what do you think you might say?"

"Yes", she said," *I will."*

Delighted, but somewhat nonplussed by the form and vigour of this reply, I rather ungallantly responded,

"But, steady on, I haven't actually asked you yet".

"Well", she said, *"why not try again?"*

I did; and that was the beginning of our very many happy years together.

Before our two ships set sail from Hong Kong, we discovered that both were due to be in Tokyo Bay on the same morning. Our hopes for a farewell wave across a few hundred yards of sea were raised. But it was not to be. I had not realised how big Tokyo Bay was - nor that Yokahama, where Ann's ship was calling, and Yokasuka, which was a naval base for which COSSACK was heading, were many miles apart. Anyway, there was thick fog that morning across all of Tokyo Bay. It was not to be.

That evening, whilst at anchor at Yokasuka, with an American Hospital ship at anchor nearby, we invited a number of the nurses to join us for the evening in our wardroom for a film. The fog had by now cleared as the wind had freshened. Our motorboat was sent to collect the nurses. As Officer of the Day, I was at the head of our shipside ladder ready to greet our guests, with the assistance of our quartermaster, able seaman Hickey, a delightful and colourful Irish man. As the first girl scrambled to the top of the ladder after a rather long and uncomfortable boat trip, she announced in a loud voice "Gee. Is my fanny sore." Hickey's eyes came out like organ stops in an expression that I shall never forget. I think he was reassured about our prospects in the wardroom when I later explained to him some of the differences between the American and British usage of the English language.

It was to be two years and many letters later before Ann and I saw each other again, in England. Despite our separation, these two years were for both of us to be very happy ones. Ann was, of course well familiar with Canadian ways, having spent most of the war years there. She greatly enjoyed university life and made many good and lasting friends. For me, life in the Far East was still full of interest, excitement and adventure. It was all too easy for me to forget that the reason I had been so keen to return to the Far East was to get back to my girlfriend, Era Kimberly in Shanghai.

In COSSACK, we had a very good wardroom and ship's company. Under our two Captain's (D), firstly John Jeffries and secondly Dick White, our whole squadron of six ships worked and played well together. Each year, ships of the Far East Fleet deployed to the north during the summer months to provide a much-welcomed relief from the heat and humidity of Hong Kong and Singapore. Japan had also become a forward base for the US Pacific Fleet. The US Fleet's main base was at Honolulu, with Yokasuka in Tokyo Bay providing major port facilities for forward deployed USN ships. The British fleet maintained our northern base at Kure at the southern end of Japan's inland sea. The approach from the open sea was through many small, uninhabited islands that was navigationally 'interesting' and scenically extremely attractive. On occasions, there was an early morning thick mist covering the water and reducing visibility at sea level almost to zero - whilst at a level just above the bridge of the ship, it was brilliantly clear. To stand on top of the ship's gun director, which stood about twenty feet above the bridge, revealed an almost magical picture of beautifully sculptured tree tops thrusting through the mist and with the top of the masts of accompanying ships being all that could be seen of them.

Kure had been one of the principal naval operational bases for the Japanese Fleet and was where the giant Japanese battleships had been built in total secrecy during the pre-war years. It was from Kure, in the last few days of the war, that the giant battleship YAMATO had set sail before being sunk by American aircraft having just reached the open sea. Her mission was to destroy American ships supporting the US landings on the island of Iwo Jima. It would however have been a 'kamikaze' mission because she did not have enough fuel to allow her to return from this sortie. It was not then widely known that, although the dropping of the atomic bomb at Hiroshima, not far from Kure, brought to an end the war, the war at sea could not have continued for long because there was no fuel left anywhere in Japan.

Kure had been totally flattened by American bombing. It was not even possible to identify where the graving docks or the large factory sheds that had supported them had been. The Royal Navy ships were berthed at piers that had been restored. Contracts, with whom I never discovered, had been arranged for HM ships to have dockyard assistance with repairs and routine maintenance such as boiler cleaning. It was also possible to have all sorts of small, non-essential but welcome 'tiddly' jobs to be done - smart wooden gratings for the bollards, or the capstan. Ashore, there was a policy of total non-fraternisation so there was limited nightlife for the sailors. But somehow they always enjoyed themselves.

The Japanese also provided us with harbour launches, known as hubba-hubba boats. They were popular for banyans on the many adjacent small islands where the sea was calm and warm. These boats were also just fast enough to allow 'ski boarding'. Our attempts at water skiing failed, not least because of the absence of proper water skis – but the boats could also not go fast enough. However, we were able to have made a small flat, shaped wooden board, so that, when towed behind a hubba-hubba boat, It could be mounted and offered limited opportunities for 'tricks'. We later progressed from a 'towed board' to a lighter 'free board', which offered more of a challenge. However, the lack of manoeuvrability and speed of the hubba-hubba boats was a very limiting factor. The very rare opportunity of using a destroyer at twenty-two knots as the towboat offered all sorts of new opportunities, with recovery after a 'fall', providing good 'man overboard' training for the ship's company.

There were other parts of Japan and Korea to be explored during our summer deployment. Whilst at Yokasuka, I had taken the opportunity to spend a day visiting Tokyo. Little did I know that the south shore of the Bay of Tokyo, under the shadow of Mount Fiji through which I was passing, had some one hundred years before, following Commodore Perry's dramatic arrival in Tokyo Bay, seen the permanent deployment of a contingent of the British army to the Yokahama region where the British had built port facilities. Finding foxes in the area, the Regiment imported a pack of hounds from Shanghai, and began the sport of fox hunting[6].

The centre of Tokyo, in the area of the Emperor's Palace where General Macarthur had set up his Headquarters, was not as badly damaged as I had imagined. But vast other areas of this great sprawling city, with narrow streets and houses of mainly wooden construction, had been devastated by fire. It was a scene not to be forgotten. A visit to Kobe on the inland sea, had to be cancelled. Nevertheless, we made use of the fascinating inland route to regain the open sea though the Shimonaseki Strait before heading for the west Coast of Korea for visits to Chemulpo and Pusan. In the middle of the nineteenth century, the freedom of passage through the straits was the cause of several actions by US ships to bombard Shimonaseki[7]. It had also been the scene of a confrontation between a British business man and a local Samurai Chief over a 'right of way'. The British business man was killed. In retribution, British warships bombarded and sacked the town.

The American army were in full force in Korea. On our second day in Pusan, we were to receive a courtesy call by the local American Commanding General. We were to provide an honour guard to greet him. I was the Officer of the Guard. At the rehearsal on the jetty, all went well until I ordered the guard to "present arms". Bringing my sword smartly to the 'recover' position (ie thrust at arms length firmly above my head) I accidentally drove the point of my sword with considerable force into a wooden beam that I had failed to notice above me. As I could not free it quickly, I left my sword there and stepped forward to offer a handshake to the 'General' and to accompany him on his inspection of the guard whilst holding an imaginary sword. I thought this novel procedure

---

[6] *See penguin books (1988) "The Coming of the Barbarians" by Pat Barr. p.169/70. This book provides a fascinating account of Japanese history from 1853 to 1870 under pressures of a growing Western influence.*

[7] *Ibid. p.167/8*

would provide a 'moment of history' if I repeated it for the real General on the next day. Unfortunately, the Captain thought otherwise!

As always on such occasions of a ship visit, sport is an excellent way of expressing mutual respect. Accordingly, a football match had been arranged in Seoul for our ship's team to play a Korean team. The Americans didn't play soccer. A rather large and tall member of the ship's engineering department, who was also a highly competent football player, captained our team. As both teams came on the pitch, we realised that the Koreans, by nature of small stature, had as their Captain by far the smallest man on the field. The two captains met to exchange 'presentos'. The Korean captain, seeming to stand on tip-toe, handed a splendid bouquet of flowers to our Captain, who, looking rather embarrassed, clutched them to his hairy chest. Our 'presento' was a large and heavy, metal ship's crest. The Korean captain, clearly not expecting something of that weight, was seen to buckle slightly at the knees! What we did not know was that the Korean team included several members of their national side who were being groomed for the Olympics. The final score was Korea 11, Cossack 0. Nevertheless, the game was played in good spirit and at least was enjoyed by the several thousand Korean spectators. None of us had any that some five years later this would be in a war zone in which The Royal navy would be closely involved.

We returned to Japanese waters to call at Sasebo, a port that was later also to play a major role in the support of Her Majesty's Ships, and also in my own life, during the Korean War. Some fifty miles to the South West lay the Gotto Islands where we gathered with our sister ships of the 8th DS for a regatta. It was then back to Kure and return to Hong Kong.

This was a difficult time for the Royal Navy. Demobilisation following the wars had left ships with severe shortages of trained men in all branches of the service. Nevertheless we continued at Hong Kong with an active operational practice programme. As the ship's Gunnery Officer, I was primarily concerned with the ship's ability to fire our 4.5-inch guns. As a very young, unqualified and inexperienced gunnery officer, I had a great deal to learn. I was particularly concerned at the very poor performance of the crew of 'A' guns crew, our forward 4.5 inch gun mounted on the forecastle. At harbour drill the crew did well. But not when it came to firing 'live' rounds at sea. 'A' gun's crew were much slower than the crews of our other three 4.5-inch guns. Careful observation by my Petty Officer Gunnery Instructor showed that the young 'number seven' of the gun's crew, whose task it was to take the next shell to be fired, out of the shell-room hoist and place it in the gun's loading tray, was gun-shy. When he should have been making this transfer, he had his fingers in his ears until the gun had fired. This greatly slowed down the rate of fire. I tried my best to cure him of this fault. "Look", I said, "the gun can't hurt you. There is no point in putting your fingers in your ears. I can stand outside the gun shield and when it fires, it won't hurt me". I walked forward on the forecastle, ordered "Load" and then "Fire". I heard a very loud bang – and my right ear-drum has never been quite the same since!! I learned from that! Perhaps he was wiser than I.

Our surface firing practices were usually at a Battle Practice Target towed at low speed on a steady course by a tug at a range of about six to eight miles. This did not represent a very realistic gun-action scenario, but it was the best we could do. When firing by visual aiming, it was not difficult for the aimer to identify which was the tug and which was the target. But when aiming only by radar, as at night, this was not always so easy! It was even less easy when firing against an air target being towed by a manned aircraft.

The shoot itself was only part of the difficulty in any exercise firing – the subsequent analysis of what actually happened was much more complicated. One such surface firing exercise involved the simultaneous engagement of the target by five ships of the squadron. This went off rather well. On our ships' return to harbour, we five gunnery officers agreed to go on what we thought was a well-earned run ashore in Wanchai. One of our numbers, however, did not show up. Next morning when we gathered together to 'parcel out' the recorded direct hits so that we could each complete our individual ship's analyses, we discovered that our 'missing' colleague had stayed on board his ship on the previous evening so as to finish and forward his own ship's analysis; having claimed for himself all but one of the recorded hits! But we got our revenge later.

The Eastern shores of mainland Hong Kong provided excellent facilities for live bombardment practice firings in close collaboration with the army's Forward Observation Teams. The Squadron was also delighted to be given the ex-Japanese destroyer "Sumire" to sink. This was a practice to be greatly enjoyed. It eventually sank but I rather suspected that her final demise may have been assisted by some internally fitted 'scuttling charges'.

This operation reminded me of an incident that occurred with the Far East Fleet near the end of the Burma campaign when, a destroyer which had been conducting a bombardment on the Japanese held island of Ramree, came across a drifting Japanese oil barge. The destroyer's Captain, anxious to get out of Japanese aircraft range as soon as possible, closed the barge to very close range and told his young and inexperienced Gunnery Officer to get on and sink it. Firing over open gun sights at such short range, the initial flat trajectory of the shell meant that a small error in the elevation of the gun resulted in the shell falling several thousand yards on the far side of the target. This did not look good! The gunnery officer, under some pressure asked his Captain to 'back off a bit'. As the range of the target opened, so did more of the rounds hit the target and make holes in the side of the barge, so causing the oil to run out. As the oil ran out the barge got lighter. As the barge got lighter, the barge visibly rose in the water. In eventual exasperation, the Captain, turned to the Gunnery office, said "Guns, I told you to sink this f***ing thing – not make it fly away."

However, gunnery was not the only name of the game. Anti submarine exercises, night encounter exercises, sector torpedo attacks, close quarter manoeuvring, landing and boarding party exercises, damage control exercises, and practicing towing, were all part of the weekly programmes. With good sporting facilities available when the ships were in harbour, life for me was extremely active.

The end of the year was soon upon us. The Christmas and New Year festivities came thick and fast – and with the Chinese New Year coming late in January, seemed to be almost never ending. I was particularly fortunate in being extremely well looked after by my future in-laws and by my Cousin Alan, the doctor, who had been joined by his wife, and now lived in a flat at 'Hillcrest' at the top of The Peak. Maisie and Edgar Thompson had also now been able to return to live in their Hong Kong Electric Company house at the Wong-ne-Cheong Gap overlooking the South side of the Island, which they had occupied before the war. To get the surfeit of Christmas activities out of our systems, Cossack took the ships of the squadron round to Mirs bay, some forty miles North of the Colony, for a thoroughly enjoyable 'shake down' period before the spring deployment to the South in late January. Thailand, Singapore, Malaya, and Borneo were all on the visiting list.

Unfortunately, COSSACK developed engine room problems and we were unable to go. When the squadron returned, COSSACK was still in HK dockyard hands; where she remained until the squadron again deployed, this time to the North. For this deployment, Captain (D) and a number of his staff transferred to CONSORT. It was mid June before the ship was again 'ready for sea', by which time the rest of the squadron had again returned to Hong Kong. This was the time for the Fleet Rifle Competition.

The Fleet Rifle competition was very much a 'high visibility' occasion. It took place on Stonecutters Island, just off the Kowloon peninsular, where the ship's company's land fighting skills were practiced. This was a popular venue with ship's companies as a change from the routine of mess-deck life. The accommodation there was in tents; and there were reputed to be snakes on the island. (As there were indeed on Hong Kong Island itself). Although this was my first experience of competition shooting, I was made captain of the Cossack team. We were all complete newcomers to this game and found ourselves somewhat overawed by the sight of all sorts of 'professional' looking 'sharpshooters' carrying slings, spotting telescopes, and various sorts of other shooting 'aids', things that we had never seen before. Nevertheless, we did very well. Our Cossack team came second, by just a single point, in the in the Small Ships Rifle Cup; with the third placeholder being fifty points behind the winner. Cossack was also the only small ship winner of one of the six team-trophies. This was the Team Tile Competition. The competition called for the team of four to run thirty yards carrying their rifles, to lay down prone, load, and attempt to knock down all of twenty six-inch white square metal tiles set in a row at a distance of one hundred yards. The winner was the team that completed this in the shortest time. Our winning team was myself, Chief Petty Officer Adams, the Chief Ordnance Artificer, Petty Officer Freeman, my Gunnery Instructor and Leading Seaman Salmon, the Gunner's Yeoman. To our astonishment we each fired five rounds and demolished all twenty tiles in a winning time. Petty Officer Freeman was later to figure prominently in the Amethyst incident.

At the end of June, COSSACK left HK in company with the cruiser, HMS Jamaica for a short visit to Sasebo and Kure. We were back in HK again by the middle of July but only for a week. Then, together with the rest of the squadron, it was back to Japan. On the passage North, we ran into some very heavy weather when a typhoon to the north of Taiwan recurved rather more sharply than we were expecting. The sea became very rough and we were reduced to slow speed. However, as the 'eye' of the storm got closer, the wind blew up to over 100 knots. The very speed of the wind 'knocked down' the waves, and the movement of the ship became a little less uncomfortable. Nearer still to the centre of the typhoon, the horizon disappeared. There was no longer a sharp interface between sea and sky – just a grey area of driven spume.

After conducting exercises with the Americans, which went well, our first stop was at Iwakuni, on the Inland sea. Iwakuni had been a Japanese Kamikazi air base from where, during the latter part of the war, attacks had been launched on US warships. An Australian air-force squadron now occupied the base. The facilities at the base were excellent and included an Olympic-size swimming pool. The Australian Air Force had a reputation for being friendly and generous. Offshore, there was also a convenient anchorage for destroyers. A visit to Iwakuni was therefore very welcome to us all.

The visit was a great success. Australian beer was in plentiful supply and, apart from more traditional sports, competitions between the sailors and the airmen as to who could drink the most beer in the shortest time, were not infrequent. One somewhat alcoholic evening party given by our Australian Air Force hosts led to ships of the squadron carrying out an early morning gunnery practice that none of us had expected; and for which none of us were prepared.

Adjacent to our anchorage was a small former Japanese lighthouse, situated on a rocky outcrop. The Australian aircraft used this as a practice target for their rocket attacks. Very early in the morning the Australian Base Commander was commenting that, despite numerous accurate attacks by their aircraft, the lighthouse was still standing. This led our Captain to claim that if the Group Captain's aircraft rockets could not knock the lighthouse down, the 4.5-inch guns of his destroyers would undoubtedly do so. On the Captain (D)'s return to Cossack in the early hours, a signal was sent to the assembled ships to be ready on departure at half past seven to open fire with their main armament using HE shells so as to destroy the lighthouse. As Cossack's gunnery officer, I was awoken from an alcoholic haze at six o'clock and told that I must be ready to have the ship open fire in about a half hour's time. We achieved it, although I don't know how - as did the other four ships. Where the shells from all the ships went was entirely another matter - since several of the aimers could hardly see as far as the target. As the ships

81

departed over the horizon towards Kure, the lighthouse was still standing. Fortunately there were no mishaps among local fishermen. This incident was perhaps an example of the spirit that had helped to win the war, but not one that was appropriate to a post-war climate. Indeed, in retrospect it was irresponsible. Sadly, that is what tends to happen in, and after war.

After four days in Kure, during which we were able to make a very short visit to the nearby Japanese Naval Academy at Eta Jima, our next stop was Ominato. This is a large expanse of enclosed water on the most northern tip of Honshu, the main Japanese island. Ominato provided no shore-side distractions, and thus only organised recreational leave. This was good for all of us. The visit provided ideal opportunities for carrying out equipment overhauls and inspections. It also provided an ideal venue for the Fleet Regatta; and for other competitions like water polo.

The Fleet regatta greatly enlivened inter-ship rivalry. Training was hard and continuous. Whaler racing was a highly disagreeable sport but one in which we all entered with remarkable enthusiasm. At 0600 every morning, bleary-eyed Cossack officers led by our stroke, Michael Woolcombe, could be seen carrying towels as they manned the whaler for their morning training session. The point of the towel was to wrap it round the thwart on which one sat in an effort not further to aggravate the blisters that one invariably got on one's bottom. Naval whalers did not have sliding seats! There was no such 'remedy' for the hands – gloves just did not help. The overall winner of the regatta was awarded a special and traditional trophy of a Cock, which was worn with great pride at the ship's masthead. COSSACK did not win this trophy; but we did win the wardroom whaler race – and indeed came third in the Fleet Open Whaler race, an almost unheard of success for a ship's officer's crew.

Ominato did provide one weekend that was decidedly more alcoholic than bucolic. Some fifty miles to the south at Aomori was a base of an American Airborne Division. They kindly invited a large number of the Fleet's officers and sailors to join them for the weekend. This provided a very popular break from life on board. To get us there, we boarded a Japanese train. On arrival, the Commanding Colonel of the regiment, a Colonel Condon, greeted us. We were told that he weighed two hundred and thirty pounds, was six foot two inches tall and had done more parachute jumps, and practically everything else, than anyone in the regiment.

Our 'leader' was the Captain of HMS SUSSEX, who to us junior officers, appeared rather elderly, indeed almost infirm - and he had hair growing out of his ears. As was expected, the Americans had provided themselves at Aomori with every comfort and facility - bowls, swimming pools, parachute jumping, shooting, riding, and just boozing. On the last evening, there was a farewell party at their Officers Club, with splendid music and dancing until the early hours. Alcohol was in abundance. Our American hosts regaled us with stories of the Colonel's partying ability and assured us that there was no man in the regiment that could drink him under the table. It was thus somewhat of a naval triumph when, at about 0100, the Captain of the Sussex could be seen on his feet, with a glass of whisky balanced on his head, doing the hoki-koki - whilst the Colonel lay 'defeated' and slumped over the table. The reputation of the Royal Navy in the minds of the US Airborne has never been higher.

The return train journey next morning was a nightmare. As the US troops said a very warm and genuine farewell to our sailors, they most hospitably, but rather unwisely, threw case after case of beer into the train. Whilst the journey down to Aomori had been unremarkable, though slow, the journey back was even slower. It was broken by numerous stops. At each one, inebriated sailors would leap from the train and whoop it off into the uninhabited countryside. It inevitably took some time for the regulating staff to encourage them back on board. As far as I remember, we were 'all on' when we eventually arrived back at Ominato - but it was long after our locally expected arrival time.

The Americans also very kindly brought a dozen Japanese horses up to Ominato for our enjoyment. This was great delight for me – although the blisters that I had on my bum as a result of the whaler racing were particularly unwelcome. It was glorious open country and I only wished we could have stayed longer. We had, however, accepted that before moving south, COSSACK would pay a brief visit to Hakodate, the capital of the northern island of Hokkaido, the land of an ancient indigenous tribe 'the hairy Ainu' and now the home to a widely respected university.

As we proceeded south, and after a brief call at Yokasuka, we entered the Inland Sea to visit Kobe, our visit there in the previous year having been cancelled. Kobe was renowned amongst the pre-war maritime community for its sex store. The Japanese geisha was, and is, certainly not a prostitute. But, rightly or wrongly, the Japanese before the war had a strong reputation for being leaders in the exploration and exploitation of sexual enjoyment. Our ship's company was disappointed to hear that the sex store had been totally destroyed by American bombers. Nevertheless, they enjoyed themselves as we were particularly well looked after by a small but flourishing English and European community. A particularly popular visit there was to the Noritake China works where good quality tea-sets or dinner-sets could be bought at very attractive prices. A 58-piece dinner service cost me the equivalent of four Pounds Sterling. However, finding appropriate space on board Cossack for stowing the very well made wooden boxes in which the china was packed was not easy.

Our next call was at Nagoya. From there, we were able to make two outstanding visits. The first was inland to Gifu, where on the Nagara River we watched the age-old practice of cormorant fishing. A number of cormorants were trained to sit on the gunwales of small but long open boats from where they were directed, one by one, into the water in order of 'seniority'. Each cormorant had a ring placed round the bottom of its throats. The birds would immediately dive and very shortly resurface having caught an ayu, a fish like a small trout. They carried it in their gullet because the ring round their throat prevented any further digestions. Having returned to the boat, they regurgitated the fish into the boat in perfect condition for subsequent human consumption. One bird could, we were told, catch up to 180 fish in an hour. This was a traditional form of fishing, practiced on this particular river for many, many years. It was fascinating to watch.

We were also able to visit the nearby Takaratska Girls Opera. Their theatre was large and well appointed, with a revolving stage. The all-girl cast first performed a Japanese traditional opera. This was most colourful and I thought rather more attractive than the few Chinese operas that I had seen. This was followed by a very professionally produced Broadway style American song-and-dance musical, with girls dressed in tuxedo's with black bow ties taking the men's parts. I am not sure how this would have gone down in a European city, but it was a magnificent cultural and enjoyable experience in the topsy-turvy world of post-war Japan.

It was then Kure once more, where I enjoyed meeting a very pleasant young Australian couple who were serving on the UN Hiroshima Atom Bomb Evaluation team. Hiroshima, which was not very far away, was still 'hot' and closed to all outsiders. But I found their description of what they had found there both fascinating and horrifying. More than ten years later, I was privileged to captain the first British and foreign warship, HMS INTREPID, to visit the city.

Back to Hong Kong, and for myself, the prospect of a fresh challenge. I was to be temporarily detached from COSSACK in Singapore to take command of a small armed Naval Motor Launch, ML 1333. This was to be commissioned for coastal patrol duties in the Straits of Malacca. The Malayan Emergency was then at its height, with Communist Guerrillas trying to overthrow the British Colonial regime in the Malayan peninsular. The guerrillas were well armed, and intelligence suggested that their arms were being smuggled across the Malacca Straits from Sumatra. Following the defeat of Japan, the Indonesian Government had had little success in restoring its own authority. Even today, a strong separatist movement holds much sway. The small port on the Sumatran coast from which most of the smuggling was thought to originate was a former pirate stronghold named Bianazi-appi-appi[8]. My task was to patrol a 150-mile stretch of the narrow Malayan Coastal waters from Malacca down to the Jahore Strait to intercept any such arms flows. Since Bianazi-appi-appi had the reputation of having been a pirate stronghold for many centuries, I knew that the would-be arms smugglers would have very much better detailed knowledge of the Malayan coastline than I, and that consequently, my chance of success was not great. But that certainly did not dampen my enthusiasm. At least our presence might act as a deterrent.

I arrived at the Singapore Naval Base at the beginning of November and was able to locate ML 1333. I was relieved to find her in a reasonable condition. However, there was a problem with the two propeller shafts, a defect that I found the dockyard frustratingly slow to resolve. I collected together my crew of a Petty Officer as Cox'n, a leading mechanic engineer, a signalman and a handful of seamen. As something of a very junior 'pirate mob', we set about getting our act together so as to store, victual, fuel and ammunition the boat. ML1333 was armed with a 20mm Oerlikon gun, several rifles and pistols; to which I added my own private 0.32 pistol. It was hard and frustrating work since I was trying to get things done by dockyard staff in a situation which neither they nor I had ever met before! I thought very little of Singapore, as it was very hot and it rained incessantly. After about ten days, having done a check 'swing' on our magnetic compass, we were ready to go. I collected the necessary charts, agreed my patrol plan with the operational staff, hoisted the white ensign, and sailed off into a gathering sunset.

It was dark by the time that we had got to Singapore's Eastern Anchorage. It was already choc-a-bloc with merchant ships at anchor; there were many others trying either to get in or out of the anchorage. We successfully avoided all of them and with some relief rounded Raffles Light and headed to the NW to enter the

---

[8] *I have no idea if this is the correct spelling. I only know that the 'sound' is more or less correct!*

Malacca Strait. This as usual was also full of shipping going in both directions. At about midnight, having established a magnetic compass course taking us outside the main shipping lane – I had never before been at sea without a gyro compass - I decided that I must hand over the boat to the Cox'n for the rest of the night. I wrote my first-ever Captain's 'night orders', which I suspect read something like this. (1) "Steer Course ...N by ....W - This should keep you roughly parallel to the coast. (2) Try to keep clear of the nets of the many fishing boats that you will encounter. (3) If you think you might be about to hit something, try to call me first".

I dropped off to sleep quickly, but was awake again as dawn was breaking. I clambered up to the bridge and took a look round. There in sight on the coast was the prominent hill that I had hoped to see in exactly the place that I had been expecting to see it. I was both surprised and relieved. All those hours that I had spent in classrooms on a chart trying to get from A to B safely taking into account varying wind, tide, compass errors and other hazards, the system did actually work in practice.

We proceeded, so to arrive at Malacca as planned that afternoon. Our signalman, however, was unable to raise the Naval Base on the radio to report our safe arrival. I, therefore, went ashore and telephoned the operational staff from a public phone box. The Singapore Staff were happy to learn of our safe arrival – but I gather that the receipt of this message personally from the Captain by means of the public telephone system caused some amusement. I continued my patrolling for about six weeks, before ML 1333 was ordered back to Singapore so that I could be relieved in command, to allow me to rejoin COSSACK. In that period I had had great fun and learned a lot. The only one of the very many fishing boats that frequented the coast, of which I was suspicious, escaped. I had ordered him to follow me into Malacca – but he soon turned out his lights and disappeared into the mass of other boats. I learned from that.

During this time, I had made a fascinating trip up the narrow river to Muar, a small Malay village with nothing much there except a planters 'club'. Having just scraped over the bar at the river mouth, I was a bit concerned as to whether I would be able to get out again. The many monkeys that screamed at us from the riverbank seemed to be of the view that we might not! After a couple of 'sundowners' at the club, I felt reassured. Nevertheless, I was relieved when we did make a safe departure from the river.

This very short visit to Muar led to yet another of the extraordinary coincidences that have so often lighted my life. Many years later in London, I went to have my hair cut at my Jermain Street barbers. Ivan told me that the girl that usually cut my hair had left, and that he was putting me with a new girl whose name was Marie. I went downstairs and Marie appeared. She was middle aged, plump, and cuddly; and had a lovely face. I thought that she was almost certainly Malay.

I tried *"Where are you from?"*

"Malaysia", she replied.

"Yes, but where in Malaysia?"

She clearly misheard me, and not having had good experience with the geography of the English, responded:

"It's the other side of India – but not as far as Australia".

"Yes, I know Malysia. But where in Malaysia were you born?"

"Muar" she said.

"Yes, I have been to Muar"

*"You know **Muar**?"* she asked getting very excited.

I assured her that I had indeed been to Muar.

"You must be Harry" she replied in even greater excitement.

I told her that my names were James Henry – but never Harry.

"You must be Harry" she asserted and continued to repeat excitedly during the next half hour.

The story gradually emerged. In 1946, her mother, who was an actress, was living in Muar. When the Japanese Army with its brutality had left, the British army arrived as their 'saviours'. Amongst them was a young officer named Harry who became very friendly with her mother, and apparently spent many hours playing with her baby daughter, Marie. It took me a long time to convince her that I was not Harry.

I took passage back to Hong Kong in a Dutch destroyer. I was made to feel much at home and the experience re-enforced my high regard for the Netherlands's Navy. My only problem was that I never established how they all seemed to manage the 'loo' without the use of lavatory paper! Having rejoined COSSACK, we sailed from Hong Kong on passage to Nanking, where we arrived on the 25th of February 1959. This visit was to become the precursor to what became known world wide as the 'Amethyst incident'[9].

Nanking was a major Chinese city lying some 200 miles up the Yangtze River. The reason for our being sent was to protect the interest of the British Embassy and the sizable British community there. A British warship was to be similarly stationed in Shanghai. The threat to the British communities lay in the southward march of Chinese communist forces seeking to overthrow the dynasty of General Chiang Kai Shek. The British government had negotiated with the Chinese Government for a British warship to be stationed at Nanking and Shanghai as a factor in trying to stabilise the situation in this area, and if necessary, to provide protection for British civilian residents. The daylong passage up the Yangtze, one of the longest and widest rivers in the world, was fascinating in its strangeness; and not least for its display of wildlife. There were thousands of wild duck on the water. At one of the river's wider points, we experimented with attempting to add to the variety of our diet by shooting duck in our path from the forecastle with rifles, whilst using nets boomed out from the stern to catch the 'casualties'. This was neither sporting nor, fortunately perhaps, successful.

---

[9] *The Amethyst Papers By RADM David Scott – The Churchill archives centre.*

My memories of Nanking are twofold. The first is of the enormous derelict factory buildings adjacent to our berth, which pre-1939 had been the centre of a flourishing trade with the UK in eggs and poultry. These were bought in their thousands from Chinese farmers in the outlying areas. The egg yolks having been packed into large barrels, the cargo was loaded into refrigerated ships at Nanking for direct passage to England.

The other memory is of the plan for the protection of British citizens. One part in this was to provide gunfire support for an evacuation. Our ship's plan was to provide a creeping barrage of 4.5-inch VT fused shells down the main street as cover for those attempting to reach the safe haven of British ships alongside or anchored in the river. At that time after so many years of war, the collateral damage to the city and its Chinese inhabitants that would inevitably have resulted, raised few qualms of conscience; despite this being somebody else's country with which we were not at war.

Our stay in Nanking was planned to be of four weeks duration. It passed without particular incident – although several others and I beat a hasty retreat back to the ship in our ship's motorboat whilst fishing near the North bank of the river, when the sound of rifle fire seemed to indicate that it was being aimed in our direction. I was principally involved as stage manager of a 'sod's opera' which we produced for the locals in an ancient disused warehouse. The eventual show turned out to be an outstanding success performed before no less than seven different national Ambassadors. The 'can-can' performed by sailors dressed as girls nearly brought the roof down – literally!

Our relief was to be HMS CONSORT, which duly arrived, so allowing us to go down river to Shanghai. There were, however, problems as to what ship should relieve CONSORT and when. The normal endurance in fresh produce for the CO class of destroyers being twenty-one days, we had taken special measures to top up to four weeks so as to last us through the period at Nanking, where we were doubtful about obtaining local supplies. CONSORT had failed to do this, and after three weeks, was running short of fresh provisions. She was thus keen to be relieved as soon as practicable. This was a tricky period because the Communists were now threatening to cross the river. There were also political difficulties over the possible use of an Australian ship as her relief in this region.

HMS AMETHYST was therefore designated to relieve CONSORT, but at a time that might co-incide with a possible Communist Chinese attempt to move south across the river. Regrettably, this was indeed what happened. On the way up river, communist gun batteries from the north shore fired upon AMETHYST. She fought back but was severely damaged with a number of casualties, including Commander Skinner, her Captain. An attempt to rescue AMETHYST by CONSORT coming down the river from Nanking failed. CONSORT, having also received significant damage and casualties from the Chinese guns, had no alternative except to escape down river. A relieving force coming up river from Shanghai, led by the cruiser HMS LONDON, was also forced to turn back having received damage and casualties. AMETHYST was trapped. I was to learn later from Petty Officer Freeman, my former Gunnery Instructor in Cossack who had been drafted to the AMETHYST, that some aspects of the dire straits in which the ship's company of AMETHYST were found some days later when help arrived overland from Shanghai did not reflect all of the finest traditions of the Royal Navy. It was indeed a very sad, difficult and serious affair.

Our short stay in Shanghai brought back many happy memories of the days immediately following the ending of the war with Japan. These memories were re-enforced by the chance arrival from America of my former girl friend, Era Kimberly - another remarkable coincidence. It was great to see her again - and we had fun together. But my mind was far too focussed on my efforts to make an early return to England to be with Ann. The 'apple cart' stayed firmly on its wheels! Whilst at Shanghai, we very successfully put on for the locals a shortened version of our 'Nanking Opera', using the lovely little theatre in the former French concession that we had used in 1945.

By early April COSSACK was back in Hong Kong. The events on the Yangtze and the company in the HK Naval base of the ships damaged in the AMETHYST's attempted rescue, seemed to rest very uneasily with the feeling of peaceful normality there. The funeral and memorial service for the British casualties in the Cathedral at Hong Kong provided us all with an emotional reminder that the world was still not at peace. Meanwhile, despite local and regional negotiations and plans for her release, Amethyst remained trapped.

On the 9th May, COSSACK was once more on her way north, heading for an anchorage at the mouth of the Yangtze, where a force of our ships, including HMS BELFAST, was being gathered in case of further action on the river. However, we developed serious evaporator problems, stemming from our refit, which very severely restricted our ability to make fresh water. Having damaged ourselves in an attempt, during a gale, to replenish our water supply from BELFAST, we had no alternative but to return to Hong Kong. By the end of June, we had completed and tested our repairs and were ready to go again. In the company of the cruiser JAMAICA, we sailed north in order to join up with the rest of the Flotilla for our summer visits in Japan.

By this time, I was getting extremely agitated about the absence of an appointment for my relief, which was considerably overdue, and my return to rejoin Ann in England. She had arrived from Canada and was now staying with her parents, who had already returned from Hong Kong to England to take six months home leave at a small house in Dartmouth.

On the 30th July, COSSACK was in Japan at a buoy in Sasebo harbour. I was the Officer of the Day. At about half past one in the morning, our on-watch telegraphist came running from the radio room to tell me that he had heard Amethyst transmitting her call sign on the radio and saying that she was coming down the river. I asked him if he was sure and he said "Yes Sir. Come and listen". I then much regretted my lack of skill in reading Morse on the radio; but vaguely recognised the letters of her call sign. I accepted fully the accuracy of our telegraphist's report and immediately called the Captain and helped bring the ship to life. We were at four hours notice for steam – but within three hours, we were steaming at twenty knots through the narrow entrance of Sasebo harbour heading for the mouth of the Yangtze and the Woosung forts.

AMETHYST continued to send out reports of her progress down the river and asked for any ships that could help her in the final stages of the escape, when she had to pass the heavily armed forts at Woosung at the mouth of the river. We proceeded at full speed and prepared for gun action through the night and early morning. We were still some way short of the Woosung forts by dawn and were relieved to hear AMETHYST's signal that she had passed them without incident, and had been joined by HMS CONCORD who was already there on patrol. AMETHYST's signal to the Commander-in-Chief "Have rejoined the Fleet south of Woosung. No damage or casualties. God Save the King" was already beginning to echo around the world.

We met AMETHYST and CONCORD at about eleven o'clock. After we had joined to escort AMETHYST back to Hong Kong, we signalled to ask her whether she was damaged or had other urgent needs. Her first response was "No damage, no casualties." It was only later in the day that she reported, "Regret to report damage to the forward naval store." I never discovered whether this was "for real"; or whether this was a simple way of sorting out the naval stores account. I could well imagine that little attention would have been paid to such matters during her very difficult period of captivity. AMETHYST's return to Hong Kong was a very emotional experience for everyone.

We were soon back again in northern waters with the rest of the squadron for some interesting joint operational exercises with the Americans, to be followed by some very warm and generous hospitality by the USN at Yokasuka. Despite a good and interesting visit in the very south of Japan to Kagoshima, where we learnt bits of British Naval History of which none of the Wardroom had been even vaguely aware, the weeks seemed to drag by very slowly. Both our First Lieutenant and Commander (E) had changed and the spirit of the new wardroom was not the same. Other key players in the 'team', and not only in the wardroom, which had got on so well for the last two and a half years were also leaving. I had already missed the sailing of one troopship for home and was desperately keen not to miss the next sailing from Hong Kong at the end of September. I toyed with the possibility of paying my own fare home by air,as I did not want to rush the wedding - for Ann's parents had to return to Hong Kong when their six month leave was complete in the new year.

It was therefore with very great joy that we sailed into HK through Lymun just in time to catch the SS ORBITA on the 30th of September, due to arrive at Liverpool on 6th of November. I do not remember a single thing about that ship or the journey home. Even her name does not ring a bell. I know it only from a letter written to my parents. But perhaps I did at the last minute fly home!

It was against the operational background of the Amethyst incident, with the first British casualties suggesting another possible conflict in the Far East, and the worsening situation in East/West relations in Europe, that I left the COSSACK after nearly two and a half years. Nevertheless, the period of 1947 to 1949 in Hong Kong also reflected a strong feeling of return to 'normality'. The long, hard struggle to rebuild Western Europe after four years of bitter conflict and destruction was at least a 'four week sea journey' away. The legacy of the years of the Japanese occupation of Hong Kong had, however, been remarkably quickly swept away; a triumph of reconstruction in which Admiral Harcourt and the Royal Navy had played a significant part. Japan itself was under the firm hand of General Macarthur. Certainly, there was a civil war going on in China, a strong reminder of which came in the hand-over in Hong Kong of the former British Cruiser, HMS ARAURA to General Chang Kai Shek's Nationalist forces. But the war between the Nationalists and the Communists was still far away in the north. The Communists from Indonesia were making trouble in Malaya – but Singapore, which, with Shanghai, was one of Hong Kong's two chief pre-war rivals, was 'booming'. In Hong Kong, it was a 'new world', a world of expanding opportunities with much money to be made.

Chapter 5

HMS HORNET, The Gunnery School, and the Korean War

"Freedom is the sure possession of those alone who have the courage to defend it".

Pericles – 430 B.C.

On arrival in England, I found a basketful of good news. Firstly, Ann, having arrived from Canada in the late summer, announced that she was not planning to return there. Secondly, I heard that my next appointment was to be to HMS HORNET, the Coastal Force base at Portsmouth. This brought back memories of my first Coastal Forces appointment at Newhaven during the war and so gave me a great deal more to look forward to. Thirdly, that I had been selected to do the Navy's Long Gunnery course at Whale Island. This is what I had asked and hoped for. Officers of the gunnery specialisation were at this time dominant in the higher echelons in the Navy. This, therefore, seemed a sensible avenue to pursue. I had also particularly enjoyed the atmosphere of Whale Island during my sub-lieutenant's course there. However, the Long Course did not start until the following autumn – and I had only a few weeks leave before joining HORNET.

HMS HORNET at Gosport was the base for the Navy's post-war Coastal Forces. It was home to two flotillas and sundry experimental Coastal Force craft. One flotilla was of 'Long Boats' (120ft long) of both Thornycroft and Camper and Nicholson origin. The former were of 'hard chine' design and the latter being 'round chine'. Lieutenant Commander Roland Plugge, a wartime Coastal Force's officer, led the long boats. The second flotilla of smaller, faster Vosper 'Short Boats' (75ft Long) was commanded by another distinguished wartime 'boat driver', Lieutenant Commander David Shaw.

Each of the boats had two officers. During a two year appointment at 'HORNET', a young lieutenant would spend one year as a first lieutenant and his second year in command. I was appointed as first lieutenant to a 'D' boat, MGB 5036, with a delightful but mad Irishman, Paddy Langran, as my CO. Perhaps we all appeared slightly mad – but this was the spirit of initiative and boldness that we inherited from our RNVR wartime predecessors. It has to be said, perhaps sadly, that many of our exploits at sea would in today's Navy be criticised for being unnecessarily risky and perhaps foolhardy. But to pose a risk was to propose a challenge. Our predecessors had met that challenge and had won. We were not going to let them down. Thus HORNET provided a unique training ground for young officers.

We carried out frequent exercises in the local area, mainly at night, for with our vulnerability to visual attack by aircraft, day operations could offer a risk too far. Operating at night at high speed and in very close company, and not infrequently close inshore was very demanding for the Commanding Officer on the bridge with the throttles under his hand. Such manoeuvring required a close and mutual understanding with his Coxswain, who stood beside him at the wheel. There was often no time for verbal orders – rapid hand signals had to do. In the charthouse below, the First Lieutenant, using the boat's radar, together with information by radio from other boats, and from a shore headquarters, was responsible for navigational safety and for keeping his CO on the bridge continually informed of the operational situation and what was going on close around him[10]. This required very close cooperation and mutual confidence.

An annual event was the two week "Coastal Forces War" when boats were deployed at Dartmouth, and in St Peter Port in the Channel Islands, so as to conduct operations against each other. The home side's boats used the Fountain Violet Hotel at Kingswear, with a well-known and well-appointed bar, as its operational headquarters. Espionage was rampant. There was no point in putting to sea during the evening to engage the enemy

---

[10] *Later, the use of a surface-radar equipped aircraft ("Velocipede") to provide longer range information on the movement of 'enemy' forces began to be developed)*

if the crews of his boats were still enjoying themselves in the bar at their hotel in the Channel Islands. But that required spies, ingenuity and deception. Great fun and much value were had by all concerned. After one hectic encounter in which we participated off Looe, a small fishing village to the west of Plymouth, a local cottager going out early the next morning into his garden found some form of 'projectile' sticking up in the middle of his cabbages. Ringing up the Plymouth naval headquarters in some concern, he was not very happy to be told that he should not worry – it was only an illuminating device that had failed to 'illuminate' – and his best course of action was to put it in a bucket of water. He did not take this advice too kindly! Subsequently, the matter escalated as the result of a parliamentary question. At our base, we had claimed that it was not one of our illuminating rockets. It must have been a flare dropped by a co-operating RAF aircraft. Unfortunately our story did not stand up, as the offending object was found to be clearly marked HMS Hornet! But no damage had been done, we were practicing the 'defence of our country' and our apologies were abject. We heard no more.

Another activity in which we were then engaged involved matters of espionage at a high security level. The East–West confrontation in Europe was growing in intensity. The iron curtain had come down and it became increasingly difficult to find out what the Soviet Union was up to. Inserting covert agents became very difficult. One 'door' that remained seemingly open was through the shores of the eastern end of the Baltic – through Latvia and Lithuania. This was exploited by the use of German manned E-boats to land western-trained agents.

From time to time, we were visited by one or other of these E-boats that were known locally as 'pssst' boats. We had no direct contact with them. We did however have the task of providing training for such locally trained agents in the procedures and practices of landing clandestinely from a small boat over the beach at the correct time and in the right place. They never spoke when they came on board and our only liaison with them was through a naval officer who worked for the Secret Intelligence Service (MI6). These were very brave men, many of whom, I believe, were subsequently captured and executed by the Russians.

In addition to the first lieutenant's operational responsibilities at sea, he also undertook all harbour movements of his boat. The boats were moored in 'trots' of four between fixed sets of catamarans that lay at right angles to the tidal stream in Haslar Creek. With three boats in place, getting in to the 'fourth hole' particularly at the time of a strongly running tide, took considerable skill and judgement both from the first lieutenant, who had the throttles of the four engines at his hand, and the coxswain at his side who was doing the steering. If the boat was going too slowly, the tide would catch the stern and the boat would get stuck sideways across the entrance. If the boat was going too fast, then it was not easy to stop before you hit something that you were not meant to hit. For a new first lieutenant doing his fourth hole for the first time, the crowd of watchers would not have looked out of place on the touchline of a local football match. The major and frequent requirement for harbour moves was for refuelling with 100 octane petrol. This had to be done under very strict safety precautions with the boat totally shut down and was only possible at a special refuelling berth in the north of Portsmouth harbour.

As well as his operational responsibilities at sea, the first lieutenant was also responsible for the upkeep and administration of the boat and its crew in harbour. This included the feeding of the ship's company. We were not entitled to a professional caterer or cook – so the duty fell on the shoulders of a volunteer from the small band of able seamen. In '5036' we had a splendid chef, one able seaman Hassle. The galley in which the chef had to operate was extremely small. Another disadvantage was that the movement of the boat at sea, in almost anything but a flat calm, was such that it was impossible to cook or heat anything safely on the galley range. The best that one could hope for on a long cold night at sea was a cup of hot soup from a thermos flask that had been prepared before sailing. Some wizard in the Admiralty, when made aware of this problem, hit on the solution of issuing each boat with a pressure cooker, shaped like a large hand grenade that could be lashed down onto the range, thus enabling food to be cooked at sea. It wasn't a bad idea. But it was not popular with the chefs, principally because they were required also to use it regularly in harbour; and more so because they were required, on each occasion, to render a formal report of what ingredients had been used and how the ship's company had reacted to the resulting meal.

Hassle, steadfastly backed by the rest of the boat's crew, straightforwardly refused to use the device in harbour. Thus from time to time, he and I had to get together to make up appropriate reports. In the section of the report, which called for "suggestions for improvement", I had to veto the idea from the crew that the relief valve, which whistled loudly all through the boat when cooking, should be replaced by a flashing red light.

One day as I passed the galley at midday, I heard a loud whistling from the pressure cooker. "Hassle, congratulations – what have we got on for lunch today?" He looked embarrassed. I pressed him. "Come on, Hassle, tell me what have you got in there?" He looked more embarrassed. It's my smalls, sir" he said, "It does the dhobi a treat" He opened the cooker and drew out two T-shirts and his underpants!

The camaraderie formed by life at sea amongst the officers of the flotilla also extended to our social life. We worked hard and we played hard. The boats were all seagoing ships and as such were entitled to duty free liquor. This was normally stowed in considerable quantities below the deck-boards in the wardroom – and included popular brands that were still difficult to obtain ashore. Sunday lunchtime was a favourite time for congregating with as many of your brother officers and their girl friends as you could get in to the small space of the wardroom and the CO's cabin. As young officers, I suspect that, from time to, we probably drank more than was good for us – and certainly more than we could possibly have afforded at duty paid prices.

Christmas came all too quickly. Ann, had been staying with my parents, and we had by now agreed a date for our wedding. Our two families now became increasingly involved in the planning. The wedding would take place from my parents' home at Claverham during the Easter leave period. For our honeymoon, Ann and I decided to go to Ischia in Italy.

During the Christmas leave, we managed to do some hunting together. The first occasion was not a great success. We went to the meet of the Clifton Foot Harriers on the moors to the south of Yatton not far from my home. I persuaded Ann that we should follow the hunt. The moors were very wet and the rhines (ditches) were full of water. Hounds were soon in full cry. We tried to jump a rhine together that was wider and deeper than I had thought. We both fell in. Ann asked to go home, as she was not enjoying being wet through. I was not best pleased, since for me this was something of a normal hazard. However, I did not know at that time that Ann had once had rheumatoid arthritis; and very sensibly wanted to get dried out as soon as possible. This incident added to her doubts about the joys of hunting.

Not long after however, Ann went with my mother in her car to a meet of the Mendip foxhounds. On this occasion, I was mounted. Ann was somewhat apprehensive as she had little idea of what to expect. After the meet, hounds got away to a good start in full view of the car followers. As the field approached the road where the cars were parked, there was one of the Mendip's well-known stonewalls to be jumped. At my turn, my horse refused and I fell off. Ann was much alarmed *"Oh,"* she cried, *"Jim's fallen off. Will he be seriously injured? Oh my poor Jim. What can I do?"* My mother was less than sympathetic. *"Stupid boy",* she said loudly, *"What the hell does he think he's doing. That horse never refuses. Get back up quickly or you'll be all behind."*

I manage to remount without delay, clear the wall without a second refusal, and to catch up without too much difficulty. Ann, however, was not much reassured. Nevertheless, she was thereafter always very supportive of my hunting - but not otherwise enthusiastic. Much later, she did once suggest that she might come foxhunting with me if she could ride a donkey. But it never transpired.

Despite Ann's rude introduction to the hunting field, we were deliciously happy to be together again and we both were genuinely very much looking forward to being married at the earliest opportunity. In retrospect, however, this was probably not a very easy time for either of us. Our childhood upbringing had been so very different. I was a very homespun Bristolian. Bristol at that time was a very closed and merchant orientated society. Members of the prominent Bristol families often married into other prominent Bristol families at an early age, I had taken before the Lord Mayor the oath of an apprentice (this was to my father which was strictly against the rules) as a prelude to later taking the oath of a Burgess and becoming a Freeman of the City of Bristol. However, having joined the Royal Navy, I had perhaps breached the narrow bounds of the Bristolian mercantile convention and might be forgiven for marrying into a non-Bristol family. In contrast, Ann had had a very travel spun and international childhood, living and being at school in England, Hong Kong and Canada. Her family were of an engineering bent and from Birmingham.

Our life together was not made easier at this stage, because as soon as I had returned to HORNET from Christmas leave, I found out that my boat, '5036', was to be involved in a trip with some of the rest of the flotilla to the Baltic. The timing of this deployment was beset with various problems. The first of these was whether or not we could reach our first port of call, planned as Wilhelmshaven, without refuelling. This involved detailed discussion and trials with the base staff on the exact capacity of our fuel tanks and the petrol consumption rates of our four engines at various speeds. These calculations were not an exact science. Our practical experience in the boats varied with the theoretical figures produced by the base staff. There was little clear agreement between us, other than it was going to be a close run thing. The staff solution was to call at Den Helder in the Netherlands to top up on the way. We had, as we have always had, very good relations with the Dutch Navy – and we knew from experience that Den Helder was very hospitable. However, our time was short and our base engineering staff was convinced that we could make Wilhelmshaven in one hop. So off we set.

We turned out to be more right then they. The experience of having to transfer 100 octane fuel by hand pump to MGB 5008 who had run dry and was lashed alongside us, with both boats totally closed down for safety reasons (no lights, no nothing) for several hours with a rising northerly gale and the German Coast not very far to the south, is one that I would never wish to repeat. However we all eventually reached Wilhelmshaven safely – just. One of the other boat's engines 'died' when they were put astern as the boat was berthing. We continued our Northern deployment with a passage through the Kiel canal to Kiel. Non-fraternisation was still the order of the day in Germany. We were thus soon sailing north to exercise with the Danish Navy – and then through the Kattegat, down to Den Helder and home to Portsmouth.

Our wedding day was soon upon us. My best man was Robert Culverwell, a very old school friend of mine who had done his National Service in the Royal Marines. After a good bachelor's run ashore in Bristol the previous night, we arrived at the church in nearby Yatton in very good time. On the approaches to the church was a pub. With time to spare, a quick brandy to steady the nerves seemed a good idea. As we came out, whom should we meet but my elderly Uncle Ellison whom I did not think of as being of a 'pub' culture. To our relief he gave us a very cheerful wave.

The wedding and the reception all went very well. The first leg of our honeymoon, which was to be on Ischia, a small island just off the Italian coast at Naples, was by train from Bristol to London. Ann went upstairs to change into her going away outfit. Time passed and she did not reappear. More time passed and she still had not appeared. Our parents and our guests were beginning to line up for our departure. I was ready, but began to get concerned about getting into Bristol in time for the train. Still no sign of the bride. A little agitated, I went up to my room where I knew Ann was changing to find her sitting on the floor, with not very much on, with a large glass of champagne in her hand, clothes strewn around the room, and being thoroughly egged on by my best man. It was a great party! How Robert managed to get us both, plus our baggage and great handfuls of confetti, onto the train in time, I shall never know.

In London we were staying at the Grosvenor Hotel – that at Victoria Station, not in Park Lane. There, we entered a lift, whose vintage seemed likely to have been that of the First World War, with a bellboy of an age which seemed to match. As we went in to our room, he pointed to the wall and announced, "That is an electric fire. To turn it on, you go...." as he made a downward movement of his hand on the switch. "To turn it off, you go ......" Perhaps we really were in heaven! We reached Naples twenty-four hours later for a much more romantic breakfast and the ferry trip to the island. It was an idyllic place for us both despite my occasional complaint that there was really not much to do. Ahead of us, we had our lives to share – and we were very happy.

On return home we rented a small flat in a delightful Georgian arcade in Alverstoke near to HMS HORNET. It was a very new life for both of us. To allow ourselves to eat-in on the first evening, we had to buy a cookbook for both of us to find out how to boil an egg. However, as often in the Navy, separation was again not far away – but life at the present was great. It was not too long before Ann found she was pregnant. We were both delighted. It helped that the young wife of our senior officer in the flotilla was also pregnant; and the two Anns got on very well together.

The summer was soon upon us, and at the base four boats, including '5036', were being prepared for another northern deployment, this time in the Baltic. Our first call was at Sandifjord in Norway, at the entrance to Oslo Fiord. We could not have been more hospitably received. A very rich Norwegian ship owner generously found business to be done in Oslo so as to leave his large and delightful house, together with his very attractive young wife, to look after us and to entertain the officers for all of our stay. We were only able to return this magnificent hospitality in our boats in a very meagre way. But the wardroom seemed to be full of visitors for most of the day and night – and we left open bottles of Scotch whisky, which the Norwegians had not seen during the war, on the table throughout the twenty-four hours. Our ships' companies were equally warmly and generously entertained.

After several very hectic days and nights in the most glorious summer weather, we sailed for Falkenberg in Sweden. Swedish hospitality was similarly very warm and enthusiastic, as was their appreciation of our ample supply of that rare commodity for them, scotch whisky. The young girls we met were most attractive and delightfully uninhibited. We were also offered sporting facilities. A shooting match with the Falkenberg Pistol Club resulted in a resounding victory for the home side and a lot of misses on ours.

We were also offered tennis. As the only British tennis player present, I was more than happy to accept. The game was arranged for three o'clock, following a magnificent smorgasbord in our honour. The quantity of schnapps, which we consumed in repeated skols was only matched by the quality and variety of the food. I staggered away wondering if I should be able to see the ball at all. When I got on the court my concern did not seem unjustified. My host, and the owner of the court, was a dentist who, I very quickly realised, had 'played before'. As we changed-over after the first few games, during which I had collected very few points, I well remember him saying to me, "How do you like my backhand?" This confused me, as I could not remember seeing him play a backhand. After further observation, I realised that he played his shots on both wings with alternate hands. He did not therefore have a backhand. Despite my winning only a handful of points, I thoroughly enjoyed myself and found him a most pleasant companion.

When we sat down on completion, I began to hear the full story. He had twice won the Swedish National Championship, having beaten both Bergelin and Johansen, two Swedish players whose names were for some years to be seen in the latter stages of the Wimbledon Championships. I found out that he had refused to leave Sweden and thus, despite his undoubted skills on the court, his name was completely unknown on the international tennis circuit. I felt better about that 0-6, 0-6 score line of our game.

Our next visit was to Karlskrona, where we were once again most hospitably received – and I learned that very attractive young Swedish girls were much quicker off the mark than those either in Hong Kong or England! I managed however, to honour my marriage vows. We returned to HORNET exhausted and all too ready for summer leave.

Sadly, in early August, it was time for me to leave HORNET, before my time for a year in command of my own boat had arrived. But Paddy had given me many opportunities at 'driving' so I did not feel hard done by! I had greatly enjoyed and valued every moment of my time 'in the boats'.

At the beginning of September, my new appointment to the Long Gunnery Course started. The first three months of the course were held at the Royal Naval College at Greenwich in London. It was an academic term so as to bring all our course members up to a common standard in maths and science. Ann and I fixed ourselves up with a reasonably comfortable bedsit overlooking Blackheath– and bought our first very second hand car. For me it was back to school', and for Ann it was off to the doctor. To our delight, the baby was due shortly before Christmas. We therefore based ourselves at my home for the Christmas leave period. Having fixed up a nursing home for the birth, we set about finding somewhere for the three of us to live near Portsmouth for the next year of the course that would take place at the Navy's Gunnery School at Whale Island. This was an establishment steeped in naval history and tradition. There was not a great deal of choice. However, we found a small, fairly modern but modest bungalow in a relatively quiet part of Porchester, which would also accommodate a qualified child-nurse for six weeks, which we needed so as to get Ann, the baby and I off to a good start. After all, it was only a year ago when we had first learned how to boil an egg! The nurse that came was called Greggy – and within days she was part of the family. How fortunate we were to have her take the weight at such a time when I had to devote a great deal of my attention to the beginning of my course, one that was widely regarded throughout the Navy as being very challenging.

The twenty members of our course, which included two Royal Marine officers, three Canadians, two Australians and a New Zealander, were from a wide range of backgrounds, both academically and in terms of naval experience. Our instruction was in the hands of two excellent course officers, lieutenant commanders Colin Ross, a kindly and perceptive man, and Bernard MacIntyre, a splendid, rumbustuous, and highly intelligent officer who lived life to the full. We were thus extremely well led. 1951 was the Festival of Britain year – so we called ourselves the Festival Long Course. This brought to us all a great sense of cohesion that was to last throughout our subsequent naval careers and beyond – although, being only a short way into the next century, our numbers are now sadly depleted.

The course consisted of the theoretical study and practical hands-on experience of all forms of naval gunnery, including weapons launched from naval aircraft; and from small arms to a battleship's 16inch gun turret – and their means of control. Naval gunnery had made enormous advances since the Battle of Jutland - and it needs to be remembered that shortly before the turn of the century, there were still Royal Navy ships at sea carrying 9inch muzzle loading guns. Nevertheless, Britain lagged some way behind the technological advances that had been made in America. Electronic computing in Britain was still in its infancy – and our design of hydraulic control systems, and some other equipment, was still somewhat agricultural, 'inch to the acre' stuff.

The Germans during World War II had made great progress in the design of rockets and were developing the concept of orbital weapon systems. Understandably, British resources were primarily devoted to the reconstruction of our national infrastructure that had been severely ravaged during four years of war. Britain's armed services were also operating on the basis of a government policy that there would be a ten-year warning time of any future major conflict. It was nevertheless clear that we were living at the beginning of an era of great technological advance with rocket-propelled guided missiles taking on an increasing role, particularly in anti-aircraft defence. The course was therefore challenging, involving a mixture of the old and ageing with the new technologies that were being developed. This required radical thinking.

The naval gunnery branch was also responsible for all aspects of naval ceremonial. Thus the Whale Island parade Ground, familiar to many of us from the days of our sub lieutenants gunnery course, played a large part in our activities, drilling with swords, cutlasses and rifles of World War I vintage. The Long Course was expected to set the standard for others. A feature of the national 'Festival Year' was a grand parade in London, in which the Navy as the senior service would take the lead. On this occasion, the heads of the three services, the Navy, the Army and the Airforce were to ride on horses behind the carriage of the monarch.

The First Sea Lord was a Scotsman, Admiral Macgregor. He was small in stature and had never before in his life ridden a horse. The riding master of the Household Cavalry therefore offered the three Chiefs instruction. The 'Wee Mac', as he was affectionately called, was not a very apt pupil. It was said that, on a horse, he looked more like a 'pea-on-a-plate' than a jockey. Nevertheless on the great day, he did not fall off. He was not told, however, that his horse had been given a tranquillising shot shortly before the start. When congratulated on completion of the ceremony by the riding master on a splendid performance, he is said to have replied, *"Thank you. It was easy. It is just like steering a boat, except that the rudder is at the other end."* The Army thereafter has never taken naval equitation very seriously.

To drill to a very high standard the sizeable Naval contingent that would line the streets along which the grand parade would pass, was not an inconsiderable task. To assist with this, two Long Course Officers were required to be temporarily withdrawn for two weeks. Much to my surprise, I was one. The other was my good friend, and bachelor, Ian Wright. I had then, and still have now, no clear idea of why we were chosen.

Anyway, it was good fun and a useful experience. The position of my platoon of sailors was at the Trafalgar Square side of Admiralty Arch through which the Queen's coach would pass, on the south side of the road. On the opposite side of the road, was another platoon with which I had not been in direct contact. On the great day, we took up our position with due ceremony at a somewhat early hour. We thus had to 'stand-easy', but with no movement permitted, for more than an hour before anything was going to happen. Twiddling your toes in your shoes, and changing your weight from your heels to your toes, was all that we were permitted to do, and no movement of the head. As time went on, the sailors' rifles, and my sword, became increasingly divorced from one's easy control. At last, the first escort of the Royal coach came up The Mall towards us. We ordered our platoons to 'attention', and then to the 'Present Arms' for the Monarch. As my counterpart on the opposite side of the road brought his sword smartly down from the 'recover' position with the sword handle in front of his face, to the 'salute' alongside his right leg,, it slipped from his grasp and clattered into the middle of the road. Not one member of the great crowd of the British public there would have noticed. Their eyes were glued to the Arch through which the Royal coach was about to appear – until a well meaning policeman on my side of the road dashed across the road, close in front of the first Cavalry Escort, to pick up the sword and hand it back to the Officer who was standing motionless, *"Quick – grab hold of this, Sir, before the Queen comes,"* said the policeman handing him the offending weapon. A thousand and more eyes from the crowd were momentarily diverted from the royal procession as witnesses to this unexpected event. Inevitably, a press camera was there to record the incident for posterity.

One of the two most interesting and enjoyable 'outside' visits was to the Army School of Gunnery at Larkhill on Salisbury Plain to learn about field artillery. There was a traditional rivalry between Larkhill and Whale Island which took the form of sporting engagements, sometimes after guest nights at billiard fives, and sometimes on the hockey pitch or cricket field. The rules of cricket for this purpose were those of Saint Barbara, the Patron

Saint of all artillerymen. All eleven members of each side had to bat and bowl. There were no boundaries. Each batsman had two overs and if he was bowled or caught this merely resulted in a minus score. On our visit to Larkhill, the game was played on a delightful little cricket ground with a pavilion well stocked with beer. The opposition batted first. It was not long before one of their batsman carted an excellent shot over mid-wicket's head (mine) and down a grassy bank. It took me and three of my colleagues some ten minutes to find the ball during which time the opposition had walked about a hundred runs.

When it came to our turn to bat I was reasonably confident that I could do at least the same. On about my third ball I caught one beautifully on the meat of the bat and the ball sailed way over the bank. "No need to run," said I to my partner, "It'll take them ages to find that." Within moments, to my great surprise, a ball was returned from the bank. I thought that they were very lucky to find it so quickly – and that they certainly would not do so a second time. A few balls later, I carted another one. And to my even greater surprise, back it came in no time flat. It was only then that I realised that their leg side fielders all had a spare ball in their pockets.

The other very popular visit was to the Government's missile range in West Wales at Aberporth. We travelled the day before and were accommodated at the remote Cliff Hotel at nearby Gwbert. A few of the Abberporth staff joined us for dinner and the evening developed into quite a party. In the early hours the challenge lay in a competition to see who could get from one room to another in the shortest time via a square hatch in the wall, which was a) narrow and b) at almost head height off the ground. Transit was almost impossible without help, which of course was willingly given to any volunteer who tried to perform this feat. One tall member from the Abberporth staff was a willing volunteer and we spent much time, and consumed much alcohol, in championing him for the fastest time – which he eventually achieved.

The next morning we arrived at the establishment through the security gate and assembled for the first serial of the day which was a greeting by the Superintendent of the establishment. It was more than mildly to our surprise when we realised that we had seen him only a few hours before at our hotel as we stuffed him through the hole for the winning time. He was, however, also a good scientist; but much to our sadness, we heard that in due course he was moved to another job.

Our next serial was about rocket fuels. One of these was liquid oxygen. A young naval officer on the staff produced a bucketful of O_2 and a steel bar that he plunged into the bucket. He pulled it out using gloves and with a sharp knock on the ground the bar broke in two. We got the message.

When the course came to its end in mid December, Ian and I found ourselves at or very near the top of the order of merit and selected to continue our gunnery studies in 1953 with a year's advanced course at the Naval College at Greenwich[11] *was denoted by* '**G.†.**').

My next appointment was as the Second Gunnery Officer in HMS BELFAST. Having served in BELFAST as a midshipman in 1945, I was pleased to be going back to a ship that I knew. However, BELFAST was at this time involved in the Korean War. The prospect of being parted from Ann and Peter, my newborn son, was a serious blow to us both. We therefore agreed that Ann and Peter would come out to Hong Kong to live there with her parents as soon as it was sensible for them to travel. Hong Kong was still a long way from Korea – but at least it was a lot closer than England.

When I joined the ship in spring 1952, having travelled by sea, the war situation on the Korean peninsular had stabilised along a line that was later to mark the divide between North and South

---

[11] *This was very widely known as the 'Dagger' Course, because completion of the Long Gunnery Course was noted against one's name in the Navy List by the symbol* '***G***' *– whilst the completion of the Advanced course earned a* ***G†***

Korea. The American fleet was deployed off the east coast of the peninsular, where a coastal railway line, passing through a number of short tunnels, provided US surface ships with challenging targets for their guns. The trains usually ran at night and were not easy targets. However the end game was to bombard the line at one end of a tunnel so that a train could not proceed; and then switch fire to the other end of the tunnel to prevent the train escaping backwards.

The British ships were deployed on the west coast where there were a number of offshore islands held by the North Koreans. The main effort here came from the British aircraft carriers. Nevertheless the surface ships operating relatively close inshore carried out frequent bombardments on targets of opportunity. I was never convinced that much of this firing did more than chase a few North Korean farmers round their paddy fields. However, a curious American organisation called CCRAK, which stood for Combined and Covert Related Activities Korea, operated ashore on the North Korean west coast. The 'troops' were mostly South Koreans led by American Special Force officers. The CCRAK officers operated mainly from appropriated local fishing craft. I admired them immensely since most of them spoke little Korean and yet they put their lives on the line on numerous occasions.

In BELFAST, we were briefed to provide gunfire support for one particular CCRAK operation, in which they were to land a force of several hundred men. Very early on the morning scheduled for this operation, which was being mounted from one of the smaller offshore islands, the troops came down to the beach to embark in the many sampans that had been acquired to carry the force under darkness over the short sea distance to the coast. These had been readied the previous evening. Unfortunately, they had been readied at the time of high tide. When the troops came to embark at about midnight, it was low tide; and their wiggle-stick boats were high and dry by several hundred yards. The operation was postponed.

At the second attempt a week later, they got the embarkation time right, but had underestimated the strength of the tide that they had to stem to get ashore. As dawn broke, we, in BELFAST, were horrified to see that this fleet of wiggle-stick boats were still half a mile off shore. I was all too glad not to be in one of them. Nevertheless they landed without serious casualties and began their operation, whose aim was to take North Korean prisoners and 'liberate' as many bags of rice as they were able.

We supported the operation with 6inch gunfire throughout the day. The radio reports that occasionally came through to us during that time seemed to suggest that the situation ashore was rather 'hairy'. However, the force was successfully withdrawn before dark. We subsequently learned that they had captured a small number of prisoners, several hundred bags of rice and three cows. It seemed to me a very small reward for what was clearly a very risky operation. I calculated that, in terms of monetary cost, it would have been cheaper for the British Government to have bought three top level cows at Smithfield Market and, together with several hundred bags of rice, shipped them out to the islands by P&O (first class). But war isn't like that.

Our Commonwealth navies and the Dutch also provided a few ships to support the United Nations operation. On the west coast we had several Australian ships including HMAS BATAAN, commanded by a well-known Australian gunnery officer, Captain Bracegirdle, 'Bracers' for short. At a sheltered anchorage at one of the larger islands, we kept a Royal Fleet Auxiliary tanker for refuelling our ships. One afternoon, whilst we in BELFAST were returning towards the anchorage, we received a personal call on the radio, captain to captain, in which 'Bracers' announced that he had a problem. Unlike British ships, the BATAAN was still fitted with depth charges. In going alongside the tanker, a misjudgement caused her stern to strike the side of the tanker rather heavily. A depth charge fell out of its rack and sank. Despite clear advice from his staff officer that the depth charge, having been neither primed nor set, represented no risk to the tanker, the gallant Captain Bracegirdle nevertheless ordered the tanker to slip its cable and towed it to re-anchor some safe distance away.

He then announced he would counter-mine the errant depth charge on the bottom by dropping five primed and ready depth charges in its vicinity. Accordingly he ran the ship over the spot and released his five charges. There were three large explosions. He was then left with one safe depth charge and two unsafe depth charges on the bottom. Not to be discouraged, he ordered a pattern of ten depth charges. He ran over the spot again; and this time there were only six further explosions. His question to our captain was, "I am now not sure what to do. Do you think I should go on dropping depth charges until the top of the pile shows at low water?" The response of our captain is not recorded. However, that part of the anchorage was unusable for the rest of the war.

The Flag Officer Commanding the British ships was Rear Admiral Scott Moncrieff, a most able and well-liked boss who flew his flag in BELFAST. He was joined on one occasion on the coast by the Commander-in-Chief of the Far East Fleet from Singapore, Admiral Sir Charles Lamb. He was a former gunnery officer and was keen to observe one of our shore bombardments. On most occasions of such shoots, we were assisted by an aircraft from one of our carriers to spot the fall of shot so that it could be adjusted directly on to the target. On this occasion no aircraft was available and so correction to the fall of shot had to be made by our own observations from the bridge of BELFAST. Our gunnery officer, Lieutenant Commander Joe Milne, was somewhat concerned that the admirals might wish to take control of the shore spotting procedures. He therefore instituted an internal drill between the bridge and the fire control station (TS) below decks, in which the TS crew did not obey any spotting instruction from the Admirals, or anyone else, unless it was preceded by the words, "no skylark."

Observing this situation from my own action station in charge of the eight 4inch guns that we carried, the situation developed as follows: with a large crash the six forward 6inch guns fired the first ranging salvo. All out binoculars were trained on the shore to spot the fall of shot. Some 40 seconds later a great kerfuffle ashore in the vicinity of the target was readily observable.

"Not bad, Scottie," commented the Commander-in-Chief.

"Thank you, Sir." responded Scottie. *"I think we need to go left four hundred yards and up one thousand."*

The Commander-in-Chief, *"I think that's too much, Scottie, I think it should be up five hundred and left two hundred."*

Scottie, turning to the gunnery officer, *"Gunnery officer, up five hundred, left two hundred."*

Joe Milne, speaking down the voice pipe to the TS shouted loudly *"Up five hundred, left two hundred."*

Pausing slightly whilst the two admirals readjusted their binoculars, he ordered, *"No skylark, up two hundred, no change."* This order being preceded by the words "no skylark" was accepted by the TS below. A few moments later there was another large crash as six more 6-inch shells winged on their way. The next comment from the admirals was music to our ears, *"Well done, Sir"* said Scottie to the Commander-in-Chief. *"Right on the button that time."* 'Switch to Admiral's spotting' soon became a phrase well familiar to the TS operators down below.

Early in the autumn, BELFAST was ordered to return to the United Kingdom, her place being taken by two newly refitted cruisers, the NEWCASTLE and the BIRMINGHAM. At the same time, I was reappointed to remain in the Korean area as assistant to the Fleet gunnery officer in HMS LADYBIRD, our local flagship based at Sasebo on the south west Coast of Japan. Sasebo was also the base port for our ships and those of the US fleet operating in the Korean area. Sasebo, was not for north of Nagasaki, the target for the second atom bomb.

Our headquarters ship, the LADYBIRD, was an aging former Yangtze River steamer. From her, the Fleet staff administered and operated the ships in the forward area on the coast. The ship was berthed alongside and, though bearing absolutely no resemblance to a ship-of-war, she wore the White Ensign. She became much loved by all the staff. Although having no air conditioning, which was a rarity even in many of our operational warships, she had been built for operating in the heat of a China summer and was comfortable, provided you did not mind sleeping in your upper deck cabin with the door open.

My new job was mainly concerned with working with the Americans to arrange practice facilities for our ships and to provide supplies of ammunition. Although at this time the expenditure of six-inch shells was not matching earlier days of the Korean War, when, over several three month periods, our ships fired more rounds than were fired over the three month period of the Normandy Landings. The expenditure of bombs by our carrier aircraft operating off the west coast was also very considerable.

In addition, I acquired the title of "Staff Officer, Fish". My duties in this regard were to assist in a system of fishing licences in the island area on the coast to prevent increased activity by North Korean vessels intent on intelligence activities. Implementing it was a nightmare. I well remember an incident in BELFAST when a curious vessel was seen unexpectedly approaching. It came alongside and fortunately revealed itself in time to be friendly, and commanded by a CCRAK officer. It had engine problems and was seeking our help. As one of our senior engineer ratings went on board and passed through a remarkably well-appointed cabin, he noticed a very attractive young Korean girl stretched out on the bunk .He commented to his assistant, *"Cor, she's a bit of alright."* To his surprise and embarrassment, from the bunk in very good English came the response, *"Yes, I am a bit of alright aren't I?"* Life in CCRAK was not all work and no play.

Life in LADYBIRD was relatively relaxed and my boss, the Fleet gunnery officer, Dick Round-Turner, was a good friend who later became godfather to one of my daughters. There was a tennis court in the American shore base to provide some exercise; but a much more popular activity was a walk of up to two hours or so through the local hills which provided a most magnificent display of wild azaleas. One favourite walk encompassed two adjoining well-rounded and prominent hills known locally as Jane Mansfield, a well known and endowed American film star. There was also plenty of sport and the ship provided both rugby and hockey teams, with both of which I was closely associated. Our hockey matches were against teams from our own ships on their regular breaks from duties off the Korean coast. For rugby, we were able to arrange a number of games against Japanese teams from the region, as far a field as Fukuoka – a three-hour coach trip. On the initiative of our excellent Gunner, Lieutenant Wilfie Smith, who had been a prisoner in Japan near Nagasaki when the second A-bomb was dropped, we 'acquired', as a short-weekend retreat, a small Japanese 'hotel' deep in the countryside where one could relax and live totally à les Japonais'.

There were no arrangements for any of our officers to be accompanied by their wives. I was particularly lucky in that Ann, with Peter our young son, was staying in the region with her parents in Hong Kong. I was even more fortunate to be able to get down to Hong Kong on business and pleasure to join them for three weeks over Christmas. One of our LADYBIRD based staff officers did, however, take the private initiative of bringing his wife to Sasebo, where he was able to find a small Japanese house – nearly all the houses there were small and made of wood – where they lived very happily for many months.

In April 1953, HMS LADYBIRD was replaced as our Headquarters ship in Sasebo by the large and, in comparison, seemingly sumptuous, submarine depot ship HMS TYNE. She had all the facilities that Ladybird lacked – but none of her character. She was also far too large to be berthed alongside. The operational staff had, therefore, to get used to a boat routine whenever we had business or recreation ashore. LADYBIRD was now required by the Admiralty to be returned to Hong Kong. Our Naval Constructors attempted to strengthen the hull for this long voyage – but at her first sea going attempt, she struck a gale and the concrete in her bilge threatened to fall through the bottom. She returned to Sasebo. For the second attempt, she was commanded by my boss, Dick Round-Turner, an experienced destroyer driver as well as a gunnery officer. This passage provided better weather; but to my and everyone else's great surprise, Dick Round-Turner suffered a breakdown during the voyage and had to be replaced. I was only glad to be able to offer the hospitality of my parents-in-law when he arrived in Hong Kong, to assist in his recuperation.

It is clear that at this time, I did not think much of the American operational efficiency. In April 1953, I wrote in a letter to my parents.

"The top-heaviness of American Command structure, the almost incredible lack of knowledge, ideas and ability of so many of their officers, combined with a very general and understandable distaste for the whole war, are not a foundation upon which one can rely. It is difficult to call the American services 'efficient'."

With my boss, Dick Round Turner, the Fleet gunnery officer now being returned to UK on the sick list, I temporarily took on his duties in addition to my own as the "assistant". Apart from thus becoming the youngest 'Fleet gunnery officer' in naval history, with responsibilities both to the Commander-in-Chief in Singapore as well as to the Flag Officer in command in the Korean area, my working practices did not change very much. However, this development certainly complicated the question of my successor, or successors, a problem that was further aggravated by the need for me to get back to the UK and to have some leave prior to starting my Advanced Gunnery Course in September.

The plans seemed to change every week. Eventually, under what I remember was 'Plan E', I took passage down to Hong Kong in Tyne to be reunited with Ann in mid July. At the beginning of August, Ann, Peter and I were able to take a British Airways flight to Heathrow. Even this was slightly complicated by the fact that Peter was still recovering from a broken leg. However, we all arrived safely.

The Greenwich course was the equivalent of a low-level technology degree, compacted into one year by direct teaching for two people. However, we were joined in certain subjects, such as mathematics, by member of an advanced communications course being undertaken by a naval signals officer, Lieutenant Peter Prince. Fortunately for him, he did not join us for lectures and laboratory work in explosive chemistry. One of the tasks set for Ian and I in the laboratory was to make the high explosive TNT – tri-nitro-toluene. The laboratory notes seemed clear. As instructed, we did three nitrations of a small amount of toluene to produce a few crystals of TNT. We placed these in a small hollow in one of two heavy iron blocks that were provided. With one block on top of the other, we hit the upper block sharply with a hammer. Nothing happened. After some thought and discussion, we decided that we had not achieved sufficient quantity of crystals to provide the necessary 'pinch' between the blocks; and thus achieve detonation.

We repeated the experiment. But even with the increased number of TNT crystals, Ian's hammer blow did not achieve the required minor explosion. We repeated the experiment a third time. This time I said to Ian, "let me have the hammer." and gave the top block an almighty blow. There was a very loud bang. The head of the hammer broke from the handle and hit the ceiling. The lower block went through the lab bench and bounced on the floor. The lab filled with smoke. Lots of people came running. Fortunately nobody was hurt. But we understood that there were some amendments made to the lab instructions for such future experiments in explosive chemistry.

The course was very comprehensive and involved concepts in science and mathematics that I had not met before – non-linear integral equations had me rather lost, and the theory of pouring radio waves down a tube (wave guide technology) was something that I never got to grips with in detail. During the course I kept copious notes that I wrote up every night – but I was never sure that I would later understand what I had written. Nevertheless, life was good. The sporting opportunities were good with regular hockey games, good grass tennis courts within the college and two squash courts.

In the previous year, squash at the Royal Naval College had flourished. Two naval officers and one Royal Marine were at the very top of the national level. The College was in the top division of the Bath Cup, a competition open to all squash clubs in London. All these three had left at the end of the previous year. The College was thus faced with a team of very much reduced skill for this year. Indeed, so reduced that I was selected to play at number five for the team – and I did not consider myself a squash player. I was very much involved in naval tennis – but not squash. Very sensibly before each match for the Bath Cup, we informed our opponents that our team was now greatly weakened. There were a number of occasions when I went on to the court to play someone, whom I considered to be somewhat aged, thinking, "If I can't beat this old man, I'll shoot myself". And regularly I came off the court looking for a gun.

A drawback to our family comfort during the year was our accommodation. It had not been easy to find somewhere handy that we could afford. We eventually settled on a small ground floor flat on the other side of Blackheath Common, at 4 Dacre Gardens, Lewisham. It was not self contained and had an outside loo. Our landlady, a Mrs Tapsell, lived on the middle floor. She was a highly religious person, a member of a not-very-well-known Christian community. On the top floor, lived two very elderly former post-mistresses. Aunt Lillie was very large and Aunt Ethel was very small. At one time, Ethel was ill. That evening we could hear her sister talking to a friend in a very loud voice on the only phone in the house which was on the open first floor landing. We could all hear her booming tones, "Doctor has just been to see her. He says she's dying. He said she won't last till the morning."

Ethel did last 'till the morning'; and was still alive when we left several months later. We were convinced that she recovered only because she could hear Lillie recounting to all and sundry the doctor's verdict.

During my earlier Long Gunnery Course, I had been intrigued with the potential of missilery to take over the role of gunnery in future wars. As my 'dagger' course progressed it had led me towards two ambitions. One was to become involved in the naval missile programme; the other was to go to America, which was clearly leading the technological race. Not long before the end, I was delighted to hear that both my ambitions would be fulfilled. The Navy's future guided missile was codenamed 'Seaslug' and it was first to be deployed for trials in a converted merchant ship, HMS GIRDLENESS. I was to be the ship's first trials and gunnery officer. In preparation, I was to spend six months in the United States to gain experience in the field in general and the conduct of seaborne trials in particular. Ian was to go to undertake a course on air-to-air missiles at the US missile school at Fort Worth in Texas. I was to join the USS MISSISSIPPI for a period of six months.

The MISSISSIPPI, based at Norfolk, Virginia, was involved in the operational sea trials of the USN's first generation surface-to-air missile, codenamed 'Terrier'. My task was to gain experience in the practical conduct of such trials. For the previous six months, Commander Terrence Ridley, a weapons engineer, had been there concerned with the technical aspects of putting missile systems into ships. This was for me another very exciting prospect, made the more exciting by Ann's description of her own experiences in the USA and Canada. I would find everything there double life-size - the trains, the cars, the roads, the town houses, the open spaces. I am not sure that I really believed it all. But I certainly got the message that it would be different. It was.

Early in 1954, domestic life for Ann had taken an unexpected turn. A very generous gift of money from my uncle, Ellison Eberle, enabled us to consider buying a home of our own. After much house hunting, principally in the Portsmouth area, and several visits to the London Ideal Homes Exhibition, we were able to buy and furnish a small, but modern and comfortable three bed-roomed house just outside Portsmouth on Portsdown Hill at 94 The Brow, Widley. We planned to move in early the next year. This would, of course, have been most exciting in any circumstances. But after ten months, including a very wet, cold winter in a somewhat insalubrious part of a nineteenth century London suburban house; with three of us in a non-self- contained flat, three elderly ladies as other occupants of the house, an outside 'loo', no garden worth its name, and no garage, our new home at 94 The Brow seemed to offer the prospect of a new 'seventh heaven'.

Chapter 6

Missilery, USS MISSISSIPPI and HMS GIRDLENESS

"For evil to prevail, it is only necessary that good men do nothing."
Edmund Burke

We took possession of the keys of our new house at Portsmouth at the end of July, 1954. The house and garden had been left in very good condition so fortunately we were able to move in and be comfortable several days later. This was particularly fortunate since Ann was due to give birth within the next few weeks. In the event, daughter Sue was born on the 24th of August in a ward of Lewisham hospital, a situation which Ann found so much more convivial than the circumstances of the nursing home in Bristol where Peter had been born. There was one delightfully large London lady in the ward who was having her ninth child. When the nursing staff was trying to convince her that on going home she must continue her programme of exercises, she replied, "Certainly not. I get all the exercise I need clipping the other kids over the ear 'ole." Ann and Susan were soon able to rejoin us at Portsmouth with Nanny Pat, a young, competent and very nice girl, already in residence.

We all settled down quickly. But for me, time was all too short. My departure for America was scheduled for the 26th November in the RMS QUEEN MARY from Southampton. Meanwhile, I was attached to the Experimental Department at Whale Island to start my introduction into the guided missile world. I was fortunate in having control over my own time, so was able to play a full part in helping to set up our new home as we wanted it. Nevertheless, it seemed all too short and it was hard for us both that I should be away for Christmas and have to leave Ann so soon with two very young children. At the last moment, my time for boarding the QUEEN MARY was put back twenty four hours. At the time, this was for me an irritation and disappointment. For Ann it was a further day together to be treasured and blessed. When I left on the next day, I felt guilty and have remained so.

After a further short delay at Cherbourg, and a fairly rough passage, we arrived in New York in the early hours of the 3rd December. Life on board had been luxurious compared with my previous experiences in troop ships, and indeed in HM's Ships – and luxury is surely to be enjoyed. I did. It was also different. In a letter to my parents I wrote of my fellow passengers,

> "The nautical experts in their yachting rig - the 'too British' British – the obscenely flamboyant Americans – the charming and most interesting Americans – the little fat Italian whose coat reaches to well below his knees and whose white open necked shirt cannot have been changed in four weeks or more – the French who turn the lounges into a veritable tower of Babel. They are all here!"

Amongst the Americans was a lawyer, who as an officer in the US Navy had served as flag lieutenant to a British admiral during World War II. He was returning to America with his young British bride. He was a delightful person and had more than a touch of a West of England ancestry. I was later to discover that his forbears owned a paper mill at Ivybridge in Devon, not far from where I was subsequently to spend much of my life. We seemed to share many interests, him in tennis and her in horses. As we arrived in New York, Mark and Jill Willcox very kindly invited me to come and see them at Ivy Mill, Wawa, their home in Pennsylvania. It was an address, which fascinated me. "Wawa, PA, USA" was just nine letters, yet it was enough to find one family in the whole world.

In New York, I was met by a representative of the British consulate, armed with a supply of American dollars that were still strictly limited to British visitors. He most helpfully and effectively guided me through the complexities of entry to the USA – for the procedures required both knowledge and very considerable patience. For the rest of the morning, I was taken for a brief tour of New York. Others were not so fortunate with the US immigration officials. Until recently, members of the ship's company of the QUEEN MARY, which had to meet a very short turn round time in New York, were allowed to go ashore without restriction, the ship being berthed alongside a public pier. However, the New York authorities had recently rescinded this privelege. One British Stoker had been made to stand in a long queue before reaching the immigration official, who then proceeded with a lengthy rigmarole of questions:

"Why do you want to come to America?"

"Are you planning to kill the President of the United States?"

"Are you a homosexual?"

When it came to the question, *"Are there any signs of insanity in your family?"* the stoker had had enough.

"Yes," he said, *"My sister married a goddamn Yank."*

He did not get ashore.

By early afternoon, I was on the train for the four-hour journey to Washington, where I was met there by Commander Bunny Holford, the Gunnery Officer on the staff of the British Joint Services Mission. The short car journey from Grand Central Station to his home in Maclean presented an entirely different picture to that which I had gained from my very brief tour of New York. New York was impressive and dirty. Washington was clean and beautiful. Bunny Holford and his charming wife, Priscilla were to be most generous hosts to me in Washington throughout my tour in the USA. I soon learned that life in America was indeed very different to that in Britain – but very enjoyable. After a couple of days getting my programme and other arrangements sorted out, Bunny Holford took me on a rapid tour of the Offices of the Bureau of Ordnance in the fine old buildings of the US Navy Department that then ran down the side of Constitution Avenue. Several of the offices seemed to be working at a noticeably high level of activity and excitement. I later learned that immediate decisions were being made about the extent of the participation of the US Navy in a number of nuclear warhead programmes. This brought home to me the enormous size and scope of America's military effort.

I was soon on an aeroplane from National Airport bound for Norfolk, Virginia to join the USS MISSISSIPPI. She was berthed alongside one of the many big-ship piers in the huge Norfolk naval base. After distinguished service as a battleship in World War II, she had been converted into a trials ship to carry out the operational evaluation trials of the beam-riding Terrier' anti-aircraft missile, as part of the US Operational Development Force's (OPDEVFOR) programme. My two immediate impressions were of the large size of the ship compared with the planned RN equivalent, HMS GIRDLENESS; and the small size of the Terrier missile compared with the monster size of our Seaslug.

I was greeted most warmly when I arrived on board and was faced with my first decision. Would I like dinner at the normal time of 1700 hours or would I prefer a late meal at 1800? Yes, things were different. There was no tea-break in America. However, I was also soon aware that despite what were many, largely superficial, differences between our two navies, there were also some curious similarities in shipboard life. Captain's defaulters was Captain's Mast rather than Captain's Table. Soft drinks were Gedunks rather than the RN's Gophers – and not a few others. My strongest impression however, was of the different relationship between junior and senior officers on board and ashore. On board the ship in the working environment, I perceived this relationship as relaxed and often informal. Ashore, the social relationship often seemed strict and formal. It was, for instance, the widely accepted custom that an officer joining the ship would, on each Sunday in harbour, make a formal social home call (in uniform with white gloves, leaving three cards) on every officer in the ship who was senior to you, starting with the Captain. If invited in, you stayed for not more than fifteen minutes. I complied with this practice (but no white gloves) for the Captain, the 'Exec' and the 'Gunboss' – but I then called it a day.

I was determined to see as much of the Norfolk area as was possible in the short time that was available. I needed a car. Fortunately, I had been provided with one by my predecessor, Terrence Ridley. It was a 1946 Chevrolet, for which he had paid a hundred dollars. Unfortunately the car was in New York, from where he had sailed for home.

Christmas was soon upon us, and I found myself invited to spend it in Philadelphia with the parents of my cousin in law. My cousin, John Eberle, had been serving on board the British Battleship, HMS NELSON, when, having been damaged by the Germans in the war, she had been sent to the US naval dockyard in Phliadelphia for refit and repair. There he had met, and subsequently married, Elizabeth Hersey. Sadly, the marriage failed in England after the war.

A young lieutenant in the MISSISSIPI, Don Weiss, who was part of the onboard missile group, was driving up to spend Christmas with his parents in New York. He kindly agreed to drop me off in Philadlphia. We had a very good journey in which I much enjoyed both his company and the opportunity to see the 'lie of the land'. The Herseys were extremely kind and hospitable and I was able to have a quiet and most enjoyable Christmas. In American terms, they were 'main line'. To me, their friends, their fine house and the neighbourhood seemed to carry a faintly Victorian aura. Mr Hersey was a Professor of some distinction, and a most interesting man. In the period between the two world wars, he had carried out some of the first formal academic work studies in Germany on the German railways.

Christmas being over, I went on to New York to collect 'my car'. I located the garage where it had been left without trouble. The car, an old 1946 'Chevy', was brought onto the forecourt for me to drive away. I set off trying desperately to remember on which side of the road I must drive. My planned route out of New York took me through one of the East River tunnels. Don Weiss had warned me that they were not infrequently blocked by heavy traffic - and that could bring almost the whole of New York to a halt within minutes. The car had automatic transmission that I had seldom met before. A few weeks earlier in Norfolk I had had some practise when, after a late night party, Don had asked me to drive his very smart car, with automatic transmission, back to the ship, whilst he departed with his girlfriend. Fortunately, though not without some difficulty, I got it, and me, there safely.

I set off rather hesitantly, for not only was I unfamiliar with my 'new' car and its two pedal drive, I was also not entirely sure about the validity of my driving licence. It was endorsed for Europe – but I had failed to check that this was valid in the US. Traffic was indeed heavy through the tunnel, and unfortunately as I emerged, I stalled the engine. The cars behind me immediately started sounding their horns. But, even when I remembered to put the drive lever to neutral, I still could not restart the engine. I did not know how – for when I had collected it from the garage, the engine was already running. I turned the ignition key, pressed every button and pulled every knob that I could find – but to no avail. Out of the corner of my eye, I spied a New York 'cop' looking intently in my direction. He stepped off as if heading my way. I began to panic and my left leg stiffened onto the floorboard where there was what I had thought was the dip switch for the headlights. The engine roared into life. I was away.

My instructions from Jill Willcox were to follow Route One southwards until a certain point in the Philadelphia area, where I was to 'make a right' and follow appropriately listed signs. I estimated a time of arrival as from about seven to eight o'clock in the evening. As I turned right off the highway, I noticed that it was getting dark and I became concerned with my ability to be able to read the appropriate signs. As I was pondering this problem and wondering whether or not I was still on track, a policeman jumped out into the road to stop me, opened the passenger door and said loudly:

"Say bud, drive me to Penn Road - and fast." I replied that I had no idea where Penn Road was.

"No problem," he said – and there followed a long string of instructions – *"make a left"* - *"faster"* – *"take a second right"*- and so it went on for some time.

"What's the problem?" I asked. *"There's a fire in the Penn Road".*

Suddenly he ordered me to stop, leaped out and sped off into the darkness.

I now had a problem. Not only did I not know where I was, I did not know how to get back to where I had come from - or even what that that last place was called. Unfortunately mobile phones had not yet been invented. I eventually got to the Willcox's house at Ivy Mill a little before midnight.

Having received the necessary security clearances, I was fully integrated into the Terrier project team with particular responsibilities in the field of trials data collection. The conduct of the trials programme was impressive. It involved firing more than a hundred missiles, almost all against a drone aircraft target. I was not at all sure how they achieved what seemed to me very creditable results with officers and men whose basic qualifications seemed to me rather elementary. Looking at the multiple answer test paper for the qualification of Missleman 3rd class, I was a little surprised to find the first question was; Is the Terrier missile powered by (a) Steam? (b) liquid propellant? or (c) a solid fuel rocket motor?" The later questions hardly got any more difficult.

At a much higher level, I was having some difficulty understanding the theory behind a trial plan whose aim was to investigate the accuracy of the missile against the increasing range and altitude of the target. I turned for help to the chief statistician of the BuOrd, one Bill Pabst, whom I had met in Washington. He stayed on board for some time and I got to know him quite well. When I explained my problem, he responded that he also did not understand the plan. "It's sheer corn, Commander, sheer corn." I was relieved.

During those first few weeks, whilst I was thoroughly enjoying myself, I was becoming increasingly aware that I was not getting the sort of answers that I had been hoping for; answers that would assist us at home in the considerable ship fitting and missile development problems that I knew we were having. Too often, the answer to my question was of the character, "Gee, I don't know," or, "We just don't have that problem." Had I come home at this stage, I think I would have tended towards the idea that, "The Terrier project is going very well, but the guys at the front end don't seem to know an awful lot." Later, I came to realise that there was a great deal more to learning about America than just being there.

One eye opener was the trip that I made to the west coast where I visited the Convair Company in California. The company was the research, development and production authority for the Terrier missile. The simulation capabilities that were provided by large scale digital computing seemed to me to be at least a generation ahead of the analogue models that we were using at home. The very extensive development trials facilities at Port Hueneme were also impressive, although sometimes Hueneme was described as "the most expensively instrumented fog bank in the world." They were of an order more comprehensive than those at our disposal at home at Aberporth.

In seemingly next to no time, I was beginning to plan for my return to England. By then, I had I had grown to have a great respect and admiration for the pioneering, entrepreneurial and 'get up and go' spirit that was America. It contrasted with so much of the picture of struggle and decline in post-war Britain. The thought went through my mind that perhaps I should retire from the navy, leave Britain and come to live and work in America - for I was told on many occasions that I would have no difficulty getting a good job in the missile field. I was held back on two counts. One, that I had no 'quarrel' with the RN which had so far given me all that I could have asked for. The other was that I was not at all impressed by the wider educational output of American schools. The manners and behaviour of so many of the young American children that I had come across had little to commend it. I was clear that I would want my children to be educated in England. I did not think, however, that I should be able to afford to live in America and send my children to school in England.

Six months had soon passed. After a final trip to Washington to debrief, I returned to New York to board the Queen Mary for my trip home. My thoughts were now only directed towards being back again with Ann and the two children. The very comfortable four-day voyage seemed to drag at every stage. When I returned to 94 The Brow, whilst delighted and very happy to be back with my family, I nevertheless still found myself, both professionally and privately, somewhat 'off balance' with post-war Britain. I was impatient and a little unsettled. For the time being I was able to remain at Portsmouth whilst GIRDLENESS was undergoing the very early days of her conversion from a merchant ship to a guided missile trials ship.

I attached myself to the experimental department at the gunnery school in Portsmouth which enabled me to have a free hand visiting the many establishments, mostly in the south of England, which were creating the first system of medium-range guided missiles for the Royal Navy. The UK was still at the early stages of the our first generation anti-aircraft missile programmes; 'Red Duster' for the army; 'Blue Sky' for the air force; and 'Seaslug' for the navy. Policy for research and development of these missiles was in the hands of the government's Ministry of Aircraft Production. The research itself was centred at the Royal Aircraft Establishment (RAE) at Farnborough where the development of the Seaslug missile was in the hands of a highly competent naval weapons engineer, Commander Charles Shepherd. The principle contractor for the missile was Armstrong Whitworth Aircraft (AWA). The development of the radars required for the guidance and direction of the system were in the hands of the Admiralty Surface Weapons Establishment (ASWE) at Portsdown. The ship systems for the handling, stowage and launching of the missile were the responsibility of the Naval Ordnance Division (DNO) in Bath – as was a shore based 'model' of the launching and guidance systems which was under construction at the RAE missile trials establishment at Aberporth which I had visited during my long course.

The enormity of the co-ordination task soon became evident to me as I travelled about, trying to get a grip on what was going on – although of course at this stage I was no more than an interested observer. I had also been made aware that not everyone was confidant about meeting the time schedules that had been set, particularly for the missile, whose motor was intended to be a rocket fuelled by liquid nitrogen and kerosene. I myself witnessed an early firing of this motor at the AWA engine test facility, which was a spectacular failure. It was similar to earlier failures that were leading to an overall pessimism in the whole project. When a little later, Ian Wright and I were visiting Aberporth for the first time, the naval ordnance engineer officer there, when told that I was to be the first gunnery officer of GIRDLENESS, remarked encouragingly, *"You must be joking. The first gunnery Officer of Girdleness hasn't joined the navy yet."*

By the end of the year, progress with the ship at Devonport had progressed to the stage where the system was now being fitted, and it was time for me to move down to the Plymouth area. Ann and I were determined to find a place to live outside Plymouth. We were delighted to be able to find a large house on the outskirts of Piympton approached by its own long drive. Chadlewood House had once been a stately home. We were able to rent the centre portion. The house was however somewhat dilapidated. Nevertheless, its rural environment was just what we were looking for and we spent a further very happy two-and-a-half years there. Our landlord and his wife, who lived in the main part of the house, were extremely friendly and helpful. The other third of the house was rented by a civilian engineer who was in charge of the construction of the new Naval Engineering College of Manadon in Plymouth. To the rear of the big house were two small cottages, one of which was rented to a naval submariner. We were a very happy community, to which the addition of our second daughter, Sarah Jane born on the 22nd of Sept 1956, to our family was an added joy.

From my point of view as the trials officer of the ship there was not a great deal for me to do. Most of the work was in the hands of the technical 'wizards'. It was almost a year before the system began to come together. It all seemed to me so very different from my American experience. There were moments of excitement. One was the embarkation of our first live Seaslug missile. The handling gear in the ship was all heavy engineering practice since the missile itself was large and heavy. With its four large 'wrap-round' boost motors filled with solid propellant it was a dangerous beast. The missile arrived from the local armoured depot alongside the ship in the middle of the afternoon and we began the process of fitting it into the handling system. This did not go entirely according to plan but we eventually completed the process by about half past five.

I happened to have a dinner engagement that night and having checked that the various safety devices and alarms were correct, I left the ship in some haste by the forward gangway (I would normally have used the after gangway but I was late). I got home to find an urgent telephone message to return to the ship since safety alarms for the missile compartment into which we had just placed the first missile, were sounding. I made a high-speed return to the ship telling Ann that I would certainly not be back for dinner. Fortunately it all turned out to be a false alarm; but it was late that evening before I returned home. I and the other missile staff were now more aware than before that what we were dealing with was indeed a marriage of new and old technology.

Gradually the process of equipment installation was complete and we moved to the harbour testing phase in which the guidance radar was the key element. The operation of this 901 radar was in the hands of a highly competent naval officer, Chris Field. He and his staff worked very long hours getting us to the stage where we could start trials at sea. Eventually, we had achieved a full complement of officers and men for the ship and were ready for sea.

Our first major sea trial concerned only the missile launcher, a large construction that looked a little as if it had been made as a part for the Forth Bridge. The purpose of the trial was to see what happened when we loaded and fired the first live missile. Whilst we were reasonably confident that the missile with its four rocket motors would leave the launcher and the ship's structure behind it undamaged, there was no certainty. The trials equipment in the ship also involved a complex system of photographic and internal system recording. The conditions for this trial were quite complex. The wind relative both to the ship and to the launcher was closely determined – as for photographic purposes was the direction of the sun. In Lyme Bay it was not easy to achieve all these conditions at the same time. The range of the missile at this stage was only some three miles. Eventually, as trials officer, I was satisfied that these conditions were met and that we were ready to fire.

We were, however, launching the missile in a landward direction. My own radar display, switched to a long-range scale was showing the coast in sharp outline. I told the captain I was ready to fire and he approved. There was a loud whoosh as the missile left the launcher, and as I started to track the missile on my radar screen, I realised that I needed to switch my radar display from long-range to short-range. Having done so, I tracked the missile, which happily flew straight. As the missile 'splashed', I marked the position where it had landed with a large chinagraph cross on my display. The captain was watching over my shoulder and as he saw the position of 'splash' he said, "Christ, Gunnery Officer, that's in the middle of Dorset." I had a moment's panic before I realised that the afterglow of the coastline was still painting on my display and that in fact the missile had landed safely in the sea and not several miles inland as the captain had thought!

As the weeks and months went on, some at sea, some in harbour, the trials programme progressed from stage to stage as was planned. It was often very frustrating when despite every effort the required conditions for the trial could not be met and we were forced to wait for another day. On the occasion when we came to fire the first unguided missile fitted with a sustainer motor, we had a similar experience. In this case, the forecast maximum range of the missile was fifteen miles – and since it had no guidance system we had to have a clear range of fire forty-five degrees either side of the firing line. Fifteen miles was of course over the horizon for the ship and so we were accompanied for this trial by a Gannet AEW aircraft for surveillance.

It turned out to be extremely difficult to find an area of sea clear of all other shipping in order to meet our safety requirement. Eventually, we found an area to the south of Ireland between two lines of shipping which offered some hope of meeting the required safety conditions. Even there, this was difficult. Eventually, I reported that we were safe to fire. On the firing line itself was a merchant ship at a range of about seventeen miles. Thirty degrees from the line of fire was a merchant ship at fifteen miles. The safety conditions were thus met. The captain approved my request to fire. The missile left the launcher and, despite having no guidance system, flew straight. On my long-range radar I tracked the echo of the missile calling out the range as the flight progressed. "Five miles" – "Ten miles, missile flying straight" – "Fifteen miles, still flying." - "Seventeen miles, missile still flying" – "No echo. Presume missile has splashed." The Captain – "Gunnery Officer, the missile wasn't supposed to go that far." "No, Sir. The missile contractor gave us fifteen miles as the absolute maximum."

We ordered the Gannet aircraft, which had been flying, on the disengaged side of the ship to investigate the radar contact, which had been on the firing line at seventeen miles, a contact that was codenamed 'Skunk Foxtrot'. As it flew off in that direction the aircraft reported, "Skunk Foxtrot has faded." In the ship we all looked at each other. Had we been the first anti-aircraft missile to sink a merchant ship? After a short period the aircraft reported that Skunk Foxtrot had reappeared on its radar. We breathed a short sigh of relief and told the aircraft to investigate the contact visually. The next report we received from the aircraft, "Skunk Foxtrot is a fishing trawler, now belching black smoke from its funnel and apparently heading for England at full speed." There was a sigh of relief throughout our ship's operations room. After a short discussion with the captain we decided to send a signal to our shore headquarters at Plymouth. "Trial complete. Missile splash may have been observed close to a fishing vessel which might have reported it as a crashing aircraft." This seemed a sensible way of telling our side of the story first. Fortunately, we heard no more. Anyway, the Suez operation was grabbing all the media headlines.

Eventually, we progressed to firing the first fully guided round which after a number of last minute and very frustrating delays we achieved successfully. The next phase was to conduct firings on the Aberporth range at a drone aircraft. These also were successful. As the trials officer it now seemed time for me to look to my next job.

The development and trials programme had taken a good deal longer than planned and I had now been in the missile business for some three years. A planned relief to take on the subsequent further development trials programme in GIRDLENESS had been selected on two occasions and undergone preliminary experience. Both had unfortunately decided to leave the Navy before they could join the ship. A good friend of mine, Wilf Graham, was therefore appointed and was asked to stay in the ship for six months with me before taking over. In many cases of a general service naval officer taking over a sea job, a turnover period of one or two days is normally considered ample. A turnover of the captain of a ship seldom lasts for more than a few hours. That the two of us had a very enjoyable six months, which included a trip to the Mediterranean to visit the Gunnery Trials ship, HMS CUMBERLAND, without a cross word between us, was to the enormous credit of Wilf Graham who remains a good friend to this day.

My next appointment was to the Royal Naval College at Dartmouth. There was no way in which I was going to work at Dartmouth with my family at Chadlewood House: or at our own house at Portsmouth. So it was house hunting once more. The Naval College had no service housing to offer, a situation that did not bother us, but was most helpful in finding alternatives. We were lucky enough to find a house to rent in a pleasant position in the middle of Dartmouth that belonged to a naval commander, then serving in Plymouth.

Chapter 7

Royal Naval College, Dartmouth - and the Britannia Beagles

"Here he lies where he longed to be, home is the sailor, home from the sea, and the hunter home from the hill."
From Stevenson's Requiem

The Naval College was for me a new challenge. I was now a young lieutenant commander with considerable and valuable experience in the field of Naval gunnery and missilery, with some junior experience in small ships and with considerable knowledge of the Far East. But perhaps not too much else. I well remember that, not long after joining the College, I found myself in the wardroom of a modern frigate that was visiting Dartmouth. After a short while the Captain came in. He was a young commander. I was immediately impressed. He was clearly 'in command' – relaxed, confidant, professional, and very well informed on a wide range of issues. I thought 'can I be like that in a few years time?' I was dubious about my answer - but then I had got quite a few years before I was likely to be of commander's rank.

Ann and I, with our three children, left Chadlewood with much sadness and moved into a very well recommended guesthouse for a few days. We were fortunate enough however to have found a small house to rent in the middle of Dartmouth, not far from the College. It suited us very well. Furthermore, we were fortunate able to find a delightful girl, Margaret Phipps, who has remained a family friend for all these years, to help look after the children. There was excellent private schooling in Dartmouth for children of all ages. So we settled in very quickly.

I had been appointed as the gunnery officer. But I saw my new task as helping to turn young men into embryo naval officers. I regarded the teaching of the cadets about naval gunnery to be but a minor part of my duties – although I did find it necessary to rewrite the syllabus that, in my experience, had become rather outdated. My mind went back to that experience as a midshipman in RENOWN– *"if that young man goes on like he is now, by the time he's a lieutenant commander he'll be a proper bastard[12]."* It was all about leadership and, whilst leadership required that you should be a master of your job, it meant a great deal more than that too.

The system of entry into the College had changed significantly since my own days in the 1940s. For a short period after the war, entry to the College came at the age of fifteen. This was highly unsatisfactory for everyone. Now, young officers came to the College after they had completed their 'A' levels at about the age of eighteen. But it was not only the entry system that had changed since my day some fifteen years before. There was no longer a headmaster. Instead, there was a Director of Studies who controlled a much smaller civilian academic staff. Some of the new entrants had to be brought 'up to scratch' in maths and science and there was still Naval History to be taught; and foreign languages. The old dormitories were replaced by four-berth or single-berth cabins. The cadets were allowed to 'go ashore' in 'plain clothes' from the college grounds in non working hours. The canteen now served beer. It had all changed.

Most importantly, however, the College now owned its own squadron of ships for the sea training of the cadets. Two converted former Algerine minesweepers were permanently berthed in the river at Sandquay and provided facilities for day-running with cadets. A larger squadron of converted type-15 frigates formed the Dartmouth training squadron that was able to accommodate a 'term's worth' of cadets to carry out twelve weeks of continuous sea time, thus allowing the ships to deploy abroad, to the Mediterranean or West Indies.

The new entries to the College each term, were required to take a passing out test on the parade ground at the end of their first two weeks, before they were permitted this privilege of going ashore. This was aimed at ensuring that they knew how and when to salute, to march correctly in column and line, to 'about turn'

---

[12] *See Chapter 2*

without falling over, and generally how to conduct themselves smartly and properly in the best traditions of the naval service at all times. For this test, the parade ground staff would march round a small group before bringing them to the halt in front of me, as the gunnery officer. They would then be called forward one by one to report to me, salute smartly, and announce their name. I would then announce 'Passed' or 'Failed'- for inevitably there were a very few who had two left arms or did not seem to know their left from their right. Not surprisingly perhaps, some of the younger cadets from schools that did not have a cadet force found this quite an ordeal. One boy who, when he came to me and saluted, was so nervous that he could not get out his name, despite prompting. I told him to return to the squad and, when he had remembered his name, to report again. That night, we had a drink together in the pub.

The cadets were now divided into Divisions rather than Houses and I found myself appointed as the Divisional Officer for the Grenville division. That was certainly a full time job but with my family only minutes away from the College, and wives being very much a part of College life, this was not a problem. At the College, the naval officers all worked very hard and played hard as well. At the wardroom guest night on Thursdays, one of the late night pastimes was attempting to write one's signature on the ceiling of the wardroom anteroom. This was a task which required considerable strength – lifting table upon table to be able to reach the high ceiling - and agility to get up there with help from one's friends. The ceiling at that time held the signatures of more than a few distinguished officers who had been invited to the dinner as guests – Prince Philip included - and to be followed in later years by Prince Charles. In one unguarded moment, one of my fellow divisional officers, Jock Miller, who was responsible for the important boating, yachting and seamanship activities on the river, decided to form a 'four o'clock' club. On a guest night no 'four o'clock club' member would go to bed before 0400. Such were the days of youth.

I was delighted at the very start of my first term on the staff to be introduced to the Britannia Beagles. I had been very interested in hunting with hounds since my early days as a schoolboy. It was a particular joy therefore to be invited in my first few days to the Beagle Breakfast. This was an occasion in which the College entertained in the wardroom some fifty of the local farmers, prior to holding, at the Kennels in the College grounds, the annual Britannia Beagle Puppy Show. The Beagle Breakfast was actually a lunch. It had originated in 1884 and in post World War II days, was always held on the Saturday of the Grand National.

Lunch on this occasion was at 1330, so providing time for the officers of the College to have their own lunch beforehand. I noticed the first farmers arriving on the parade ground for this event at a little after twelve o'clock, such was its popularity. Lunch traditionally had as its main course a lamb chop with kidney – with wine, a soup course, pudding, cheese, coffee; and port taken whilst the race was being run. Lunch was therefore seldom over before late in the afternoon. This, however, was not well received by the wives who were also invited to the puppy show due to start at three o'clock – especially when there was a cold east wind blowing over the lower playing field adjacent to the kennels where the puppy show was held.

The Britannia Beagles had been formed in 1878 by a Lieutenant Guy Mainwaring who was serving in HMS BRITANNIA, the former wooden hulled sailing ship of the line that was then used for training young officers. The first member of the pack was called Jim. But Jim was not a hound at all. He was a terrier belonging to the first lieutenant of the ship. Jim had a son, appropriately named Jimson, who ably assisted his father in hunting anything that could be found. This was often a drag consisting of a rabbit skin soaked with herring oil. However, Lieutenant Mainwaring managed to obtain a number of beagles, not all of which were pure bred. One of them, acquired in January 1880, was called Homeless and was acquired from the Battersea dogs' home.

Over many years the pack, hunting the hare, became very popular in the local South Devon area and became a considerable and valuable link between the College and the local community. Recent research has shown that Lieutenant Mainwaring, the hunt's founder, went on to fulfil a distinguished naval career in which he ended with the rank of Captain. His father before him had been an Admiral of considerable distinction. The family home was in Staffordshire at Whitmore Hall to which I was kindly invited in 2006. This is a house of outstanding architectural and historical interest that has been the Mainwaring family home for several hundred years. In the grounds of the estate stands a small church in the graveyard of which is the grave of the founder of the beagles surmounted by a large naval anchor carved in stone. The grave of 'Jim' still stands in the grounds of the Royal Naval College marked by a triangular gravestone inscribed "Jim, first of the pack".

The full centenary history of the beagles is told in the book *Jim, First of the Pack*[13]. The local public attitudes to hunting in South Devon at the turn of the last century is well illustrated by a passage from the diary of Mr W.H. Bartlett of Little Dartmouth, a great supporter of the Britannia Beagles. It reads:

"For 364 days in the year, Bellever Tor stands a solitary mass of rocks, silent and grim, save for the cawing of the crows that dwell in the plantation of the heronry below. Visitors in the summer climb the pile and are ritually rewarded by the beautiful view, which they obtain. Moorland streams meander in all directions, and all around is heather, rocks and gorse.

But on the last day of the Dartmoor hunt week, the last Friday in April, the lovely tor presents a very different scene. From all parts of the moor, streams of people make their way thither. Jogging along on his old grey mare comes a living type of good 'Uncle Tom Cobleigh'. A farm cart with a swarm of robust youngsters sitting on straw rumbles up the hillside. Now a smart dogcart dashes along. Then a coach and four, the key-bugle sounding merrily and echoing back from the rocky heights. Foot passengers, motorcars and cyclists hurry along to the moor. Gathered there we wait for

---

[13] *Jim, First of the Pack, published by J A Allen, London.* ISBN 0-85151-326-4

the hounds. An old gentleman, who has walked from Widecombe, and who has been present at every Bellever day for fifty years, tells in a quaint way some of his reminiscences; and a hearty laugh ensues as a good farmer's wife refuses to allow her robust mate to have a drink from the cider jar. "Wait till lunch time I tell 'e', says she ... and her word is law. *Here they come is the cry and a pretty sight it is to see the hounds, under the care of whips, gently trotting along among the long grass.*"

Over the following years a number of famous people hunted with the Britannia Beagles. These included Prince Edward, Prince Albert, Prince George, Admiral Culme Seymour, Admiral Sir Walter Cowan, Admiral Baird, Lord Cherston and Admiral Sir Charles Lamb. Just as importantly are the names of local farmers whose families have supported the beagles from the very beginning to the present day. They include traditional Devon names such as Trant, Ferris, Pook, Foale, Yabsley, Oldrieve, Bond, Buckpit, Hannaford and very many others, all true countrymen.

The beagles also attracted a good deal of attention in the College journal, the Britannia Magazine. We read some contributions in a somewhat whimsical and poetic style,

The kennel doors were open wide;
He heard a dreadful cry;
And passing by he looked inside
and saw a beagle die.

He came to tea that afternoon
The incident forgot,
But when they gave him stew so soon
It made him think a lot.

It made him grow extremely wise,
"Tis very strange, quoth he,
That on the day a beagle dies
They give us stew for tea".

Following my enjoyable experience with my first beagle breakfast and puppy show, I began to take any spare time that I might have on a Wednesday afternoon after sporting activities within the College were over, to go out onto one of the local farms before it got dark to see what the beagles were doing. At the end of one such day, Bill Huddy said to me, "Why don't you come back to kennels, Sir, and see what happens?" I did and was hooked.

My first memory of Bill Huddy had been at the end of a day's hunting on the Kingswear side when we were calling hounds out of a small, thick covert. We were one hound short and there was Bill calling out "Coot" - "Coot". This confused me, as I didn't think we had a hound of that name. It turned out that the hound's name was actually 'Acute', named after one of the ships attached to the College for sea training. In the almost hundred and twenty five years of their existence the beagles have had only six kennelmen. I learned about hunting from them – but none more than from Bill Huddy. There is an old hunting saying that good hunting starts in kennels. How right that has been proved.

In the early days, the huntsman hunting the hounds was mounted on a horse. He was often the Commander of the College – but for many years between the wars it was a member of the civilian staff, Mr Bashford. The cadets acting as whippers-in were required to run on their feet. Now that the cadets were older and served at the College for two years, the huntsman for the following season was chosen from amongst those who had whipped-in during the previous winter.

In the Christmas leave period the hounds were hunted by the Master, Mr Robin Tonks. After the end of the autumn term, and with the cadets away on leave, I took every possible opportunity to help by whipping in. In due course, he asked me to join the joint mastership. When he retired from the College in 1978, I became senior master.

Stories from the beagles abound. When Edwin Hannaford, who farmed not far from the college and had walked over two hundred hound puppies for the kennels, reached his ninety-fifth year, I went to the nursing home to congratulate him on his birthday.

"Edwin," I said, *"Congratulations on your birthday – but of course you are a young man yet. Farmer Wilf Ferris fell off his horse out hunting when he was ninety-seven."*

"Oh no 'e wasn't," said Edwin *"'e was an 'undred."*

"Edwin, you're not a young man but perhaps your memory is not as good as it used to be. - Our hunt records have him falling off his horse at ninety-seven years of age. I don't think he was a hundred."

"Oh yes 'e was," said Edwin, *"I mind it."*

I responded, *"Edwin you are correct that hounds met at his farm to celebrate his hundredth birthday - and we presented him with a silver salver, but I don't think he fell off."*

"Oh yes 'e did," said Edwin, *"It was a great day and much drink was taken. They put the ol' man up on 'is 'orse and hounds moved off to draw. They went up the lane to go through the big double gates into the meadows."*

"That's right," I said, *"I know it well, we still go that way. But from the records, I don't think he fell off."*

"Oh yes 'e did, sir. 'Is 'orse turned rather sharpish through the gate. But the old man didn't."

I have remained as Master or Chairman of the Britannia beagles now for fifty years supported by the Navy, the College, the farmers and the numerous friends from south Devon. The beagles were part of my life. When it came many years later to my handing over the hunt's primary responsibility to David Bateman, whom I had known from boyhood, I found it a very emotional moment. I well remember standing by the kennels saying, "David, from today these are no longer my hounds – they are your hounds." I cannot deny there were tears in my eyes.

The start of the summer term, 1958 was soon upon us. A major event for which, as gunnery officer, I was responsible was the parade for Her Majesty The Queen to present a new Queen's Colour to the College. Any royal visit entails a vast amount of detailed staff work. The organisation of the presentation of a colour was even more demanding. Sadly, the Queen was unable herself to come on the great day and the colour was presented by the Duke of Edinburgh. It was a day in which heavy rain threatened from the start and it blew a strong gale. Nevertheless it was all a great and memorable success. We had benefited from the previous experience of the Royal Marines when they were presented with a new Queen's Colour on a similar very windy day. At a central moment of the ceremony, when the new colour was laid across a pile of drums, the wind caught the drums and sent them rolling away across the parade ground. We ensured that ours were securely 'anchored'.

A major event of the following summer term was the inter-divisional regatta. The river was not my natural scene and in Grenville division we had no renowned oarsmen, dingy sailors or yachtsmen. Nevertheless, to almost everyone else's surprise, we were the winners. After that, I felt even more deeply about leadership, what it means and how best it can be practised.

A much lesser event was the visit to the College by a Pakistani naval commander who was returning to the Pakistan naval academy. I was designated 'visits officer'. A good programme had been arranged for him, ending with a formal call on the Captain of the College. He was then Captain Frank Hopkins, a renowned wartime naval aviator and a delightful man and one by whom almost anyone would have been proud to be led. He had had a very busy morning. When I entered his office to introduce the Pakistani commander, the captain, with a great smile of welcome and in an accent that I can only describe as being that often used in greeting non-English speaking guests, said In a slow, somewhat accented and very deliberate way, *"Good morning. What have you come from Pakistan to do here in England?"*

In a perfect English accent, the Pakistani commander replied, *"I have been up at Oxford for the last eighteen months studying English language – and am now returning to the Pakistan naval academy to teach English."*

As Frank Hopkins said to me later "If only a hole in the ground would have opened up ...." I was only sorry that there had been no opportunity to brief him in advance.

At the beginning of the following year, I was to receive a totally unexpected surprise. The Navy's system of officer promotion is based on zones. For promotion from Lieutenant Commander to Commander, the zone ran from a seniority of three years to eight years. There were two selections a year, with the result of the selection being announced publicly six months in advance. It was generally rare to find a selection at your first 'shot'. I entered the zone on the 1st of July 1959. To my very great surprise, my selection was announced at this my first shot. I well remember the party. On that same day the Director of Studies at the College, one Joe Stork, a much admired and loved figure, was awarded the CBE. We were all delighted. When I congratulated him, he said to me, "Your promotion means much more than my award. Yours is the start of a career. Mine is for the end of a career."

Although I was delighted with this unexpected advancement, it meant that I was not going to have my full two years serving at the Naval College. I had greatly enjoyed my time at Dartmouth, both from the professional point of view and the domestic angle of my family. However, the prospect of being able to continue to live in Dartmouth was a great joy.

In the earlier part of the year, there occurred another event at the College that was to have great influence on my and my family's life. The College had very good relations with many of the residents in both Dartmouth and Kingswear – in addition to the excellent relations with the local rural community that were underpinned by the activities of the beagles and their supporters – the link between the sea-man and the lands-man.

Through one of these links, Ann and I were invited to a very good cocktail party hosted with much generosity by a Mr and Mrs Paddy Kenyon at their home overlooking the river. During the party, I heard our host say that they were soon to move to London and would be selling the house. As Ann and I left the party, with an uncharacteristic boldness, undoubtedly inspired by the excellence of the party, I said to our host, *"Very many thanks for a wonderful party. I love your house. Ann and I are looking for a house in Dartmouth. But I don't think we could afford yours".*

I thought very little more about it, since we were happy in our present accommodation - and anyway I was very busy. Some months later, my phone at home rang and it was Mr Kenyon. *"I have had an offer for the house. If you are still interested, why not come round and have a full look round."* I had to reply, *"Thank you so much. We really did love what we saw of your house. But I must honestly say that I don't think we could afford it. But perhaps we might come and have another look?"*

We did and fell very much in love with it – but the price did seem beyond our reach. As we pondered the problem during the next couple of days, Mr Kenyon rang again. *"I'm very sorry"* Paddy said *"we forgot to show you the water garden. Please come over again."* We went. Across the road from the house was a gate leading to about a hundred steps that led down to a very small water garden with a steel ladder running down to the river bed and a small shed acting as a boathouse. We were firmly hooked. By selling 94 The Brow at Portsmouth and with a very generous gift from Ann's parents, we decided to make an offer that was accepted. That was one of the best decisions that Ann and I ever made.

Not long after I left the College, a very important new project entered the planning stage. One of the drawbacks of the original College buildings was the lack of a suitable large assembly place. The Quarterdeck was adequate for a standing audience – but even then the acoustics were very bad. At that time, the Chiefs of Staff held quadrennial conferences, hosted by each of the services in turn. The 1963 Unison Conference was the Navy's turn. The Royal Naval College at Greenwich was not suitable as a venue; so led by Admiral Lord Mountbatten, then First Sea Lord, it was decided that a brand new hall was to be built at the College. It stands today, quite near to the beagle kennels, as the 'Casper John Hall' in memory of a great naval aviator and former First Sea Lord.

The building work was completed to time and the very detailed planning began for the assembly there of large numbers of important people, Ministers, Generals, Air Marshals, Admirals and others. It was a highly complex operation – and there had to be a dress rehearsal. One of the lectures was by a very distinguished defence scientist, Sir Solly Zuckerman, who was addressing the subject of the technology of future weaponry. He himself came to give this speech at the dress rehearsal, with the hall full of lesser important senior officers of all three services. I was one of them. Sir Solly described at some length that he did not think that the Russians would invest in orbital nuclear weapons. He pointed out that it needed a lot of energy to get the weapon into space – and not a little to get it back – and anyway, at the critical moment, the weapon orbit might have taken it to the wrong side of the earth.

At question time, the inevitable brigadier, who had not really been paying attention, asked, *"Sir, do you think that the Russians might put a gegaton nuclear weapon into space?* With considerable patience, Sir Solly replied, *"No. I don't think this is likely. As I explained in my talk, it is not really worth it. You are better off with long range ballistic missiles."*

He added, to much laughter, *"You can make love in a hammock standing up – But why try?"* As the laughter died down, the silence was broken by a loud, gruff naval voice from the rear of the hall. *"Is there any other way?"* For this alone, I shall never forget the Casper John Hall where I have since had the great privilege of making several important speeches.

My next appointment was to go back to sea in the business of minesweeping, at which I was delighted for many reasons – and not least because it occurred to me that perhaps I might bring my small squadron of ships into Dartmouth where I now had my home at Stokecliff. In the event, I managed to achieve this – whilst at the same time, creating the precedent of being the first commanding cfficer to knock over a lamp-post whilst berthing his ship at Sandquay. But that is another story.

Chapter 8

100th Minesweeping Squadron and Naval Staff

"You have no right to lead, you only have a duty ......"
Daag Hamerskold.

I soon learnt that my next appointment was to sea as the senior officer of the 100th Minesweeping Squadron (MS100) and the Captain of HMS APPLETON, a 'Ton' class coastal minesweeper. I left the College at the end of the year and started a round of courses, mostly in the Portsmouth area, which were required of every new commanding officer. I also needed a specialist course in mine counter measures (MCM) which was based at HMS VERNON in Portsmouth. I arrived there with the popular definition of minesweeping as a science of vague assumptions based on debateable figures, taken from inconclusive experiments performed with instruments of inherent inaccuracy by persons of doubtful reliability and questionable mentality, ringing in my ears. That sounds just like gunnery then, commented a fellow member of the course,

The 100th Squadron was based at Port Edgar on the Firth of Forth. It was in early summer that I set forth from Dartmouth by car to join my new ship. As I passed through Edinburgh on my way to Port Edgar, which lay just upstream of the Forth road bridge, I stopped with a clear view of the small harbour and my eight little ships in full view below me. The emotional experience of seeing this small force as "my own" was a very powerful one. This was what command was all about.

I went on down to join the base establishment and found a party in full swing in the wardroom. Much later, as I left the party to go to bed, I noticed that it seemed to be broad daylight. Somewhat aghast, I looked at my watch and it was only three o'clock in the morning - but that far north, it was still daylight.

The next morning, dressed in full uniform with sword and medals, I formally joined the ship and took over command. Meeting my ship's company and walking round the ship, together with receiving calls from the Commanding Officers of the other ships of the squadron, occupied most of the rest of the day. I told the captains that we were all off to sea at eight o'clock the next morning so as to get used to working with each other. Minesweeping was very much a 'close company' operation.

The next morning was fine with a flat calm sea. We set off in good order towards the mouth of the Forth to practise close station keeping and the streaming of our mine sweeps. (The magnetic mine sweep was known as 'the loop') My own ship, APPLETON, was equipped with an open bridge and vintage diesel engines. Several of the other ships were of a modernised version with a closed bridge and more up-to-date Deltic diesel engines. In order better to understand these changes, I called the modernised HMS WOLVERTON to come alongside and pick me up so that I could see the improvements at first hand.

The practice of moving people and stores from one ship to another at sea in larger ships is always done by a wire jackstay being rigged between the two ships, over which the transfer takes place. Any direct hull-to-hull contact at sea between steel hulled ships is almost certain to result in dents or other damage. For the wooden built minesweepers this was not a problem. The technique had been established of what was referred to as a 'wash transfer', the two ships coming alongside in direct contact with each other at sea, allowing people to step across as if in harbour. We carried out this manoeuvre without difficulty and having previously turned over command of APPLETON to my first lieutenant – not least to show my confidence in him as a 'driver', I stepped across to WOLVERTON. The two ships then went their separate ways. Having spent an interesting two hours, I was then taken back to Appleton.

We were back in harbour by early evening and I established the procedure that, on every occasion of returning from sea, the accompanying commanding officers would come over to APPLETON to talk through what had gone on. Not everything had gone right on that first day but overall I had been well satisfied. When I asked for comments, WOLVERTON's young CO, Lieutenant Gerry Mitchell, said:

"That was a very interesting manoeuvre that we did today in getting you on board my ship, sir."

"Yes," I replied, *"I'd never done that before – but I learnt about it when I was doing my minesweeping course. I imagine for you that it is usual* practice."

"Well, not exactly, Sir. We normally do that when the two ships are stopped – not, as today, at a speed of twelve knot."

"Ah well – that's how we are going to do it in future. Any other comments?"

"Yes, Sir. You hoisted the flag signal 'Hotel Foxtrot India'. We could not find it in any of the signal books. We were not sure what you meant."

"If you remember, it followed the situation when I got something wrong. I thought you would all know what it means although I agree that it is not in the signal book. It Is a message of irritation and stands for 'Ho, f**k it'. I hope though that I won't have to use it too often".

What I had got wrong was our noon position. It was customary at sea in a force of major warships for the senior officer to signal to other ships of the force his noon position – on the basis that he probably had the most experienced navigator. The signal effectively said, "This is where I am. Now you know where you are". I had told my navigator to send out our noon position – just to show these young CO's what life is like in the bigger ship navy. We were at the time at a longitude very near the Greenwich meridian. Unfortunately, the signal was sent incorrectly. Very soon afterwards, I received a reply from WOLVERTON "Your noon position. *"East is East and West is West - and the wrong one you have chose".* I knew then that I was not going to have a problem with welding my young CO's into a first class team - although they were all of very different characters. I turned out to be right.

I was determined that we should achieve two things during my watch: establish the reputation of the 100th MS as having a strong professional capability; and in the process, have a lot of fun. During the next eighteen months, I believe we did both. There were many mine clearance exercises both of a national and NATO character, the latter being the slightly more demanding. We were as usual particularly close to the Dutch – but found the French a little more difficult. At a combined exercise off Cherbourg in which a Dutch squadron and my own took part, the captains went ashore on the previous evening for an exercise briefing. It was conducted entirely in French. My grasp of the French language was not very good but was enough to get the gist of what was needed. My Dutch colleague, who was word perfect in English, had rather less luck. As we travelled together in a boat back to our two ships I remember him being very critical of the briefing, not least in the linguistics. *"If I can learn focking English, why the hell can't they?"*

NATO was seldom easy. At a more civilised level, I was delighted and privileged to have the famous scientist, Sir Henry Appleton come to visit the ship and to dine with us in our very tiny wardroom.

Our national exercises were usually carried out at weekends with sweepers manned by the various Royal Naval Reserve divisions in the country. They were great – but readily admitted their amateur status. Some were better than others. During one exercise at Portland, the Mersey RNVR Division in HMS Mersey were particularly wayward and sometimes clearly dangerous. We designed a new minesweeping flag signal, "Emergency Mersey Port/Starboard", to be hoisted as a warning whenever Mersey was in the vicinity.

I was determined also that the squadron should demonstrate its capability of being able to deploy far afield, and operate successfully, If required. In January of 1960 I got permission to take the squadron out to the Mediterranean to carry out exercises with the 108th squadron based at Malta. We sailed from Rosyth and passed through the English Channel. By the time we were approaching the Plymouth area, there was a warning of southerly Force 10 gales in the Bay of Biscay. I decided to delay in Plymouth. After thirty-six hours, we pressed on. As we got into the Bay the wind had subsided but the sea had not. It was a very rough passage but our strong little ships performed splendidly. We sailed in open order at ten knots, bouncing about from one wave to another, often disappearing from view of the others in the troughs – but fortunately reappearing shortly afterwards. Even big tankers were slowed to little more than six knots. The only possible danger for us was that, if one got it wrong, and drove into a big wave rather than climbing up it and bouncing off the top. This might lead to damage to the superstructure. The only hiccough that I had in APPLETON was when we fell off the top of a 'small' wave, into the trough of a very big one. There was a 'helluva' of a crash when we reached the bottom! However, wooden ships are by their nature very strong, and we all reached Gibraltar in very good heart and without damage.

We had a great welcome in Malta and had good value and good fun with the 108th Squadron which was based there. The weather conditions for minesweeping or mine hunting were rather more attractive than for most of the time in home waters! The time therefore passed all too quickly before we had to be on our way home. I had promised the Flag Officer Scotland and Northern Ireland (FOSNI) that I would be back in time for a scheduled NATO exercise. We returned to Rosyth on time and in good shape. When I called on the Admiral to report on our trip, he greeted me, *"Well done. I never expected you to get back on time."* I realised that the whole trip had indeed been very challenging for those involved, including myself, when the Admiral added, *"And, either you have lost a lot of weight or you have a very good tailor."*

Another trip on which I took the squadron was to Sweden. There I arranged a visit to Lake Vanern, which lies in central Sweden on the Trolhätten canal joining Gothenburg to Stockholm. It is reached by a series of locks each of which was fortunately able to hold four of our little ships. The last lock raised us to a height above sea level of several hundred feet. I sent a signal to my Admiral in Scotland claiming the world altitude record for coastal minesweepers. I received the reply, *"Approved – mixture of altitude and alcohol may give rise to mixture difficulties – including detonation - take care."*

It was a magnificent visit and my admiral was absolutely right about the alcohol. On the final evening of our visit, we arranged a barbecue on one of the many local small and very attractive islands. One of our sailors, seeing that our cooking fire needed more wood, went rushing off with an axe, into the adjoining wood. There followed chopping noises. Our Swedish liaison officer was horrified. The trees and timber there were strictly protected. I sought out one of our young officers to go off to see what was going on. As he disappeared into the trees, I heard him shouting loudly, *"Put that bloody forest back"*. The spirit of the squadron and the success of the visit were assured. I myself had a ball; including a greatly valued visit to a formal dinner with the Vermlands regiment. They had a very long and strong tradition. Their only problem was that they hadn't been involved in any fighting for over two hundred years.

In June 1960 the squadron carried out a visit to my own home city of Bristol, which was also a great success. Our arrival was quite exciting since we were to be berthed in the heart of the city. This involved a long approach up the narrow River Avon and below Brunel's famous Clifton Suspension Bridge. This presented no difficulty. However, there was a basin through which we had to pass before berthing. This required the opening of a road bridge, and the closing of the road traffic on one of the main roads into Bristol. Thus, I was warned that the bridge could only be opened for a very few minutes. This we had not planned for. I was initially told that we would have to proceed one at time at four separate movements to open and close the bridge. This did not appeal to me at all. A quick voice radio call to my three other commanding officers succeeded in getting the four of us lined up in the right direction so that we could all get through together. *"When I say go, I shall wind up to full revs and make a dash for it, hoping that I can stop in time on arriving on the other side. Follow me as closely as you dare. Anyone who doesn't 'pass GO' in time' goes to Jail'."* We all made it.

My last project was to examine whether we could get a coastal minesweeper through the Caledonian Canal from east to west across central Scotland. In time of war it seemed to me that it might well be an urgent operational requirement to get minesweepers from the east coast to the west quickly, should passage round the north of Scotland be closed to us by gales. I knew the canal was very narrow and carried barge traffic that drew no more water than we did. One potential problem was that the barges normally proceeded at a speed of no more than four or five knots. The slowest that a Deltic-engined CMS could go was about eight knots. My operating authority were thoroughly against this project, quoting in particular the case of an even smaller minesweeper that had gone aground during an attempted passage.

I decided to do a recce by car. It was a thoroughly enjoyable trip and I managed to convince myself that a passage by a CMS was possible, providing there was not too much cross wind – for a minesweeper has much more "top hamper' than a barge. I also discovered that the previous grounding had been due to the captain having passed the wrong side of a channel buoy. Having got that wrong, he was bound to go aground. I returned to Port Edgar to review my planned programme to look for an opportunity to try this passage myself in APPLETON. Unfortunately I was not able to get this into our programme before the end of 1961 when I was due to be relieved. I strongly recommended to my relief that he should give this a go. Sadly, he did not think it was worth it. But, in due course, he was not further promoted. Had I tried it and got stuck in the middle of the canal, I might not have either.

My next job was to be on the Naval Staff in the Gunnery Division, working in the Old Admiralty Building, Whitehall. This was a very different life. We all wore bowler hats to work and carried umbrellas. Working hours were from ten until six o'clock in the evening, although some of the more senior officers worked rather longer. One morning at about half-past-nine the First Sea Lord was talking with his Vice Chief in his office overlooking Horse Guards Parade, and seeing a number of bowler hatted gentlemen wandering in his direction, asked the Vice Chief *"Who the hell are they?"* *"They are your naval staff,"* replied the Vice Chief. *"Well, I suppose we had better not kill too many of them before they can get on the Admiralty Board."*

I had had no training in staff work – but it wasn't difficult to pick up as one went along. I shared an office with two others, served by a civilian clerk. Mrs Cummins was a very pleasant woman who was always helpful, and often kept us on the right track – or rather, off the wrong track. Most of the work was concerned with dockets containing documents, which circulated round all the departments at the Admiralty. Some of them required action. Others were for information only. These were official documents and jealously guarded as such by the civil servants. I was soon in trouble. A docket arrived on my desk on some obscure subject, having passed through many departments, all of which had commented formally on the minute sheet, *"Noted with interest"*. For me, the subject was of no value whatsoever. Accordingly, I added my own comment for the gunnery division, *"Noted without interest"*. It was not long before I was confronted with a small, angry civil servant remonstrating with me for making a flippant comment on his docket. It was, he said, "an official Admiralty document." I don't think I convinced him that I actually meant what I had written.

On a more serious note, I was alone in the office late one evening, when a senior civil under-secretary at the head of our department asked me to come to his office to give advice on a paper that had to be presented to a high level MOD committee the next morning. It concerned the Navy's case for having the Polaris submarine-launched missile as our country's nuclear deterrent, rather than the air launched 'skybolt' missile that the Americans were offering to the airforce. It was a specialist subject on which one of my office colleagues, Michael Simeon, was the expert; but he was away in Washington. Nevertheless, I thought that I had a fairly clear grasp of the strategic issues involved concerning war with the Soviet Union. Not long after I had got to his office, I realised that my well-presented arguments seemed to be getting nowhere. My inquisitor was also getting restless. Turning to me with a rather bored air of condescension, he said, *"Look, young man – you've got it all wrong. We are not fighting the Russians. We are fighting the airforce department."* Such was life in the MoD; and sometimes, still is.

My principal task was on policy for future naval guided missiles. The Seaslug project trials had been successfully completed and the weapon was now being fitted in the operational fleet. One of my problems was to recommend how many missiles, at a cost of several million pounds a throw, we should order. Our budget was such that I was only left to pray that we wouldn't have a serious shooting war in the near future. If we did, we risked soon running out of missiles. Fortunately, our supply was just able to survive its use during the South Atlantic war.

However, I was mainly concerned with drafting the staff requirements for the ship-to-air missile system that would replace Seaslug. The project started off with the title, Project CF 299. It ended up in service many years later as 'Sea Dart', proving its worth in the Falklands Islands war. I can well remember the basic requirement on which I started. It was that the new system should "occupy no more space in the ship than was at present occupied by the then latest 4.5 inch gun turret – and should cost no more than a million pounds". As it turned out this was grossly optimistic, not least because we were always under pressure to meet more and more demanding target requirements. As with other such systems, we were also fielding candidates to meet NATO Basic Military Requirements (NBMR). This inevitably called for higher performances. Frustrating though the work was at various times, I particularly enjoyed our close relationship with the British aircraft industry in the missile field.

Another such system was the Seacat, a short range visually guided missile system being developed by Short Bros in Belfast.. This had gone through severe development problems and was forever near to cancellation. I believed it should continue, and in close alliance with the chief engineer of Shorts started a 'We like Seacat campaign'. At one NATO steering group meeting, there was strong criticism of the system's accuracy and reliability. I pointed to a small window in the wall of the meeting room not more than about three feet square. *"In recent trials,"* I said, *"four out of the five missiles fired from a range of about three miles, if aimed at this window, would have passed through it"*. A long silence ended that discussion. I felt well vindicated when, some twenty years later, the missile system thoroughly proved itself in the Falkland Islands war.

The introduction of the NATO Twenty Projects Programme, which was intended to speed up progress in the introduction of more weapon standardisation between NATO countries, certainly injected more competition; but achieved little progress. However, national future project staff officers became the target for seemingly ever increasing hospitality offered by competing contractors. On our quite frequent visits to Paris, we normally stayed the night in a small hotel not far from the Champs Elysees and dined in a delightful, but not expensive, small café nearby. My French began to improve – but not that much. On one occasion one of my colleagues wanted to order garlic sausage. We tried 'saucisson avec ailes' which somewhat surprised the waitress. After some discussion she showed us a rather nice drawing of a sausage with wings. Saucisson d'ail was what we really wanted! However, the generous hospitality offered by some of the competing missile companies did allow us to sample the delights of the more interesting and expensive areas of Paris.

When NATO headquarters moved to Brussels, it lost some charm but gained somewhat in effectiveness. The scale of the support staff at NATO headquarters, so much greater than that which we saw in the MOD at home, sometimes sprang surprises. I remember as a young commander being served with minute paper by a retired Italian admiral! However, like so many Italians, he was absolutely charming and very amusing. He had been a prisoner of war in Scotland; and had met and became very happily married to the daughter of a member of the Scottish landed gentry. I shall always remember his description of his first meeting with his future parents-in-law. As he walked down the length of the family's baronial hall, he said he could almost hear them thinking,"what on earth does she see in that funny looking little wop".

During this period in London, I was living during the week in digs in Kensington in the home of a former family nanny to one of my colleagues in the gunnery division. I was very well looked after there; and with the opportunity to return to Ann and the children at Stokecliff on Friday night, life had soon settled into a reasonably stable pattern – although leaving Dartmouth on Sunday evening to catch the late train back to London was always a wrench. However, the Cuban missile crisis of autumn 1962 caused me very great concern. I was reasonably happy that Dartmouth would be spared the worst conditions of any nuclear exchange that increasingly seemed to be a possible outcome of the crisis. In this situation, I was certainly not confidant that London would be spared. Ann and I had several discussions on what we might do, or might be able to do, if we became separated. Thank God, the crisis was resolved without war.

My two years on the Naval Staff were most enjoyable and valuable in broadening my grasp of policy issues and the ways of the MOD, of Whitehall - and to some extent, those of Westminster. It was all very different from grasping the practices and problems of seagoing. I admit that I found the issues of the future far more interesting than the more mundane day-to-day issue of the present. But none could compete with the joys of a sea-going command. It was therefore with somewhat modified rapture that I heard that, following a course at the Joint Services Staff College, my next appointment was to be as the Executive Officer (second-in-command) of the aircraft carrier HMS EAGLE.

Chapter 9

Joint Services Staff College - and Aircraft Carrier HMS EAGLE

"A soldier should be sworn to the patient endurance of hardships – like the ancient knights – and it is not the least of these necessary hardships to have to serve with sailors."
Field Marshal Lord Montgomery.

After a spell of leave at home, I was off to join the Joint Services Staff College, situated at Latimer in the Berkshire countryside. The college provided a splendid environment for an officer who had acquired a reasonably broad experience of his own service, to further broaden his horizons and to learn how the other two services lived and worked. At the operational level, Europe, the Atlantic and the cold war had also been out of my sights for too long.

As a result of my recent experience on the naval staff, I was familiar with writing in the style of the MOD 'policy wonks' on matters with which I was well familiar. I had yet to learnt how to write in the context of an operational staff on matters with which I was not familiar. When the directing staff at Latimer presented me as my first task with writing a formal staff paper on something that I didn't know anything about, and for which research facilities were extremely limited, I 'ran out' at this first fence. Fortunately, I was allowed the privilege of writing on something quite different that I did know something about, and could further research.

The course consisted of two major elements – the first was a series of comprehensive and well structured lectures. Our lecturers were top people in the military, politics, industry, technology and international affairs fields. The lectures were normally of forty-five minutes duration followed, after a break, by half an hour of questions. There were very few poor lecturers, for whom it was a struggle to deduce a sensible question. At the other end of the scale, it was not always easy to phrase a first question that was appropriate to the high standing of the lecturer.

However, I frequently found myself in the vanguard of the questioners – but at least my questions were a serious attempt to understand more about what we had heard. Perhaps I was just more argumentative than my colleagues.

The other part of the course was familiarisation visits to the other services. Above all else these were great fun, with each service striving to outdo the others - without appearing to do so. Our visit to the British Army of the Rhine was for me a special experience. I had not before understood how much the Army regiment was a family affair. The wardroom of a well-run warship certainly develops a family atmosphere. In the Army, the continuity within a good regiment encourages relations between junior and more senior officers that were even closer and more informal than we had developed in the Navy. I don't remember where we went or what we did on the RAF visit. The RAF's great difficulty is that they have a small core of operators who are the aircrew – and the rest. The rest comprise the technical, logistic support, base support and servicing staff. At working level, they are responsible through a different line of command. This means that there is little opportunity for the young aircrew to learn and practice the skills of the leadership of men – and women. Nevertheless, as 'aeroplane drivers', the aircrew are generally superb. This division goes all the way up to the top, to the Chief of the Air Staff.

I thoroughly enjoyed both the working and social atmosphere of Latimer and made several good friends in the other services. There were plenty of opportunities for relaxation. I was particularly privileged to be able to do some hunting with the Old Berkley Hunt, with the generosity of the Tetley family, who lived nearby, and mounted me on one of their championship hunters.

By the end of the Joint Services Staff Course, I felt that I had a far better understanding of the broader national and international security issues. I found the excellent lectures given by many distinguished people to be thoroughly good value - but I have to admit that, at the end of the course, I found it very difficult to remember hardly a single word that any of them had said. Nevertheless, the commandant was most generous when he wrote on my report at the end of the course, *"He has the enviable quality of being able to think quickly through a problem and express the nub of it orally in a most lucid manner."* He did not mention my paper work.

The course having ended, I was now due to take up my next appointment as the Executive Officer (Second-in-Command) of the aircraft carrier, HMS EAGLE. She was then undergoing a major modernisation in the naval dockyard at Devonport that was due to complete in mid 1964. This provided me with the privilege of continuing for at least a year to live with my family in my own home, Stokecliff, at Dartmouth, whilst meeting the challenges of what was to be almost a 'new' ship. EAGLE's modernisation was very wide in its scope, including a great deal of rebuilding of the ship's structure below, as well as on and above, the flight deck. These changes would permit the operation of the latest Buccaneer and Sea Vixen aircraft within an overall air complement that include AEW Gannets, Sea King ASW helicopters, in-flight refuelling Scimitars, and plane-guard helicopters. Another major aspect of the modernisation was the first fitting of a new long-range air warning radar together with an automated action data system (ADA) which brought the fleet into the age of digital data handling.

Another challenging aspect of the modernisation was that EAGLE was to be equipped to carry nuclear weapons. This involved complex stowage, security, handling and testing arrangements. However, it was the command arrangements that were later to concern me personally the most. If the ship was ever to be required to launch a nuclear attack, the procedure for nuclear release was highly complex. The first step would have been a signal to the ship to open two highly secure safes containing the authorising codes. These were part of the 'Dual Key' system, which was applied throughout all nuclear procedures. These two safes had six-figure combinations, which on no account could be written down anywhere or shared with any other person. They were to be held separately in the minds of two individuals, the ship's captain, Captain Derek Empson, and myself. It became a nightmare for both of us that, should the order to launch such an attack ever be initiated, highly unlikely though this might be, one of us might not be able to remember the combination which would open one of the two vital safes.

The number and type of officers and men required to operate and maintain all the new weapon systems being fitted in the ship were very different from those of pre-modernisation days. Thus the ships 'domestic' arrangements also had to undergo major reconstruction. This inevitably involved a degree of trying to squeeze a quart into a pint pot. During the modernisation process prior to the ship becoming operational, overseeing such changes became one of my prime responsibilities. The co-ordination of a massive programme of testing and trials was another major task.

The administrative task of managing a ship's company of some three thousand people was particularly complicated by the requirements of the aircrew and maintenance crews of the air squadrons. The latter formed the main armament of the ship. When the ship was non-operational in harbour for more than a short time, they were required to disembark to a shore-side air station. To this extent it was rather like trying to run a vast hotel at which the guests came and went in very large groups.

It was sometimes, however, the smaller problems that were the most difficult to solve. I had considerable difficulty in trying to allocate accommodation for the Royal Marine Band, an important section of the ship's company. They understandably needed their own 'self contained' accommodation. The only space that I could find to accommodate them housed seventeen people – but a Royal Marine Band comprised twenty-one people. However hard I tried, I was unable to convince the Royal Marine School of Music that a band of seventeen people could perform just as well as a band of twenty-one. I can't remember how I eventually overcame this problem – but it certainly occupied a disproportionate amount of my time. The pattern for the new wardroom carpet was another problem. The wardroom would accommodate some two hundred and twenty officers. The range of choice that we were offered was limited and colourful. But who should choose?

Being short of a single volunteer, we hit on the idea of asking a selection from the wardroom officers' wives. We thought that women would be much more qualified than men to make such a choice. The idea failed, with the wives saying with almost a single voice, *"Not us. We are not going to be 'THOSE' wives that chose 'THAT' carpet!"*

After many months of harbour trials and some sea trials, the ship was formally re-commissioned on the 14th of May 1964 under the Command of Captain Derek Empson. I was very proud that my father could attend the ceremony. There were however many sea trials still to be done before the ship could embark our air squadrons and be considered operational. Most of these trials went well. But not all. One of the important trials was to test the launching and dropping of the nuclear weapon that we were to embark. The weapon to be dropped was the 'real thing' except that the nuclear element, which would be triggered by the conventional high explosive charges in the bomb, was removed. The very existence of this trial was of a very high security nature. The Prime Minister himself was to be informed of the successful launch of the aircraft carrying the weapon and of the successful outcome of the drop. This was to be at a weapon range in Scotland. All seemed to go well, the weapon 'prep' was successfully completed, the weapon was loaded onto a Buccaneer aircraft that took off on schedule. We waited to hear from the aircraft that the trial had been successfully completed so as to be able to inform the Prime Minister. The drop went according to plan - but unfortunately the high explosive in the bomb didn't go off! There was pandemonium in the nuclear weapon design world. The first operational trial of this new weapon, vital to the country's strategic posture, had failed. There followed a lot of 'fluttering in the dovecots'.

By the middle of November 1965, with our air squadrons embarked, the ship was ready for operational deployment. Our destination was Singapore where Britain was involved in a confrontation with Indonesia over national borders of the jungle in Borneo. Local and small-scale, military operations, particularly involving Royal Marine Commando forces and Naval helicopter squadrons had been in progress for many months. Now there was some concern that the situation might escalate from confrontation into small-scale war. The presence of EAGLE and her air squadrons in the south east Asia area was to be seen as a deterrent measure.

A few days off Malta allowed the ship and the air squadrons to involve themselves with more complex operations than were possible when operating in home waters. However, we were soon transiting the Suez Canal under the skilled guidance of one of the Suez Canal pilots. Our navigator was able to provide him with the more detailed information of how the ship handled under such conditions, and we made good progress. We had on board the ubiquitous 'gulli-gulli' men. These were the highly skilled Egyptian conjurors that earned their name through the chant that they made as they performed their magic – which indeed it seemed to be. They greatly entertained a large number of the ship's company on the flight deck. Eventually they found their way to the bridge where the captain was sitting in his chair happily monitoring the good and professional team work of his navigator and the Suez pilot. After one slightly anxious moment, our navigator commented, as he was wont on such occasions, on what might be an exchange at a subsequent court martial if the ship had gone aground:

The prosecutor, *"Captain, at this moment when it appeared that the ship was taking a sheer into the canal bank and was likely to go aground, what were you yourself doing?"* The Captain, *"A gulli-gulli man was just removing a chicken from my right ear which I had thought he had just put into my left ear."*

After leaving the canal without incident, we were due to visit Aden but a bomb incident there led to our diversion to Mombassa, where we spent Christmas. This provided relaxation for nearly all in the ship. It was a good run ashore for the sailors. The air group were able to relax. The captain was able to fly up-country for a brief stay at the famous 'Tree Tops' hotel in the Kenyan National Game Park; and I was able to spend many hours relaxing on the glorious local sandy beaches. I also was able to manage a short couple of days' leave in a beach-hut up the coast at Malindi. The only part of the ship's company that lost out, as sadly too often happened, was the ship's engineering department who had to take the opportunity for boiler cleaning. This is never a pleasant task and was made more stressful by the heat of an African summer. This was further aggravated by the need to rectify a problem with several of our large electrical generators, a defect which required assistance from the UK and which extended our stay from four to ten days.

We arrived in Singapore in mid January and berthed alongside in the Naval base, our air squadrons having disembarked to the naval air station at Changi. The atmosphere from a security point of view was in many ways relaxed, for south east Asia was not a war zone for us, despite the Borneo situation and the deep American involvement in Vietnam. Meeting an Australian who had just returned from Vietnam, I asked him to comment on the American 'Hearts and Minds' campaign. He responded, *"I guess that they are working on the basis that if you grab them by the balls, their hearts and minds will follow."*

Nevertheless it was decided that EAGLE should maintain a security status above that which would normally take place in peacetime. The ship being safely berthed, and the captain having left the ship to carry out calls on the local Commander-in-Chief, the off-duty sailors streamed ashore for their first 'run' in Singapore. I was pacing the quarterdeck trying to sort out in my mind whether there was anything more that needed to be done that day. I was disrupted from my thoughts by the officer of the watch bringing to me an agitated engine room rating who told me that he had heard an unusual knocking on the ship's bottom. There had been reports that the Indonesians were training frogmen. The ship's company had properly been informed of this There having been considerable local press comment in the region about the arrival of Eagle, I had to decide rapidly whether or not it was possible that the reported noise was the result of Indonesian frogmen attaching limpet mines to the ship's bottom - or something much less sinister. I thought it unlikely to have been an alien frogman, but with clear evidence of an unusual knocking, I decided to take no risk. The ship was called to a higher state of damage control and I ordered a full 'necklace' search of the ship's bottom to be carried out by our diving team. The result of the search revealed nothing. The incident, however, so soon after our arrival, did emphasise that we were now in a zone that was neither one of peace nor of war.

Singapore, as usual, was hot and humid. This was particularly unwelcome to some of us in the wardroom. When we left the UK, all the 'sergeants' (those of commander's rank, who wore three stripes of gold braid) including myself, agreed to take part in a beard growing competition, to be judged on arrival at Singapore. I was rather reluctant to send my wife a photograph; but when I did so, I was glad that it obtained her seal of approval. "No other women would ever look at you twice, wearing that fuzz", she wrote. The competition was won by the electrical officer, Commander Archie Orr, who grew a splendid pepper and salt coloured set which earned him the title of "The Marble Arch". It was not long before I shaved off my beard because it made my face-mask leak at the sides when I was snorkel diving.

After several weeks in Singapore, we re-embarked our air squadrons from Changhi for operations in the East Malaysia coast area. One of these operations was a major display of naval power for the Malaysian government for which we in Eagle embarked and hoisted the flag of the Flag Officer Second-in-Command Far East Fleet, Rear Admiral Peter Hill-Norton. The ships and air squadrons performed splendidly for a very successful day witnessed by a very high powered Malaysian audience. Operations having been completed, the fleet anchored for the weekend off Pulo Tiaman, a small uninhabited island with attractive beaches. During Saturday the beaches seethed with sailors and beer cans. But there were no disciplinary problems, indicating that moral was good.

The ships however, had not received mail for some days. One of the destroyers was therefore despatched on the Friday night to go back to Singapore to collect the mail. The ship concerned was HMS LONDON, commanded by a senior captain, Captain Joseph Bartosik, a former Polish officer who had joined up with the RN at the beginning of World War II. He was not highly popular with his ship's company – nor with many others also. This task was one that would normally have been allocated to a ship commanded by one of the most junior commanding officers in the fleet - which Captain Bartosik was certainly not. He was not best pleased.

HMS LONDON returned to the fleet anchorage soon after midnight on the Saturday having missed out all of the fun on the beach. In the Flagship all was quiet. The Fleet staff had handed over the duties of the Admiral's duty Staff Officer to one of our own EAGLE duty officers, Lieutenant Commander Tony Malone. As his ship approached the anchorage, Captain Bartosik signalled to EAGLE, "what anchor should I use?" (It was customary at such times that all ships would use the same port or starboard anchor). The signal was received in EAGLE and the duty telegraphist phoned the duty 'staff officer' to ask how he should reply. The duty officer, who had been asleep, in a moment of total folly, unfortunately replied that he should send back "Try a short, sharp, blunt one". When this signal was received in London, the temperature on Captain Bartosik's bridge dropped by several degrees!

The next morning at about half past seven, when I was happily pacing our quarterdeck on a beautiful, clear sunny morning, Derek Empson appeared from below and told me that Captain Bartosik was coming to call on the Flagship at eight o'clock, dressed in sword and medals, to state a complaint. He then recounted to me the exchange of signals that had occurred during the night, of which I was totally ignorant. We quickly and quietly rigged a fire hose on the quarterdeck in case it was necessary to damp down a rather fiery situation. However, in his usual impeccable way, Derek Empson was able to defuse what was potentially a very unfortunate incident. Then we all went to church on board.

From the Singapore area we headed north for Hong Kong for some very welcome relaxation, rest and recreation or "R and R" as it was known. The visit was much enjoyed by all. Our next call was to the Philippines area, which included a short stop at Alongapo. The USN Base there had excellent ship support facilities, and much else in the shanty-town just outside the base. This was much used by the USN for 'R and R' - but in the case of Alongapo it was more 'I and I' - 'Intoxication and Intercourse'. After a wardroom run ashore, I was glad to be able to intercept a photo of myself dancing on one of the night club tables with a somewhat under-dressed local girl, before it reached the editor of the ship's newspaper.

Our operational exercises with the Americans went well, but with the occasional glitch. We were flying an airborne early warning barrier patrol with one of our Gannet aircraft piloted by the CO of the squadron, a very well known Fleet Air Arm character, Butch Barnard. He permanently sported a large black beard. The Gannet, which carried a long-range search radar, was a propeller driven aircraft with two engines driving separate propellers on a single shaft. We had unfortunately failed to tell the US Air Force base at Clarke Field about this sortie. Having detected an unidentified aircraft, the Americans diverted an F15 to investigate.

For Butch Barnard, It had been a hot and rather boring sortie. He had therefore shut down one engine, causing one propeller to stop, whilst cruising happily at some 140 knots on the other. He then took off his flying helmet, opened the cockpit cover and stood up. In EAGLE, we heard the F 15's interception report to his base, which went something like this. *"Am I going crazy? I have made contact with a Royal Navy aircraft - It's flying straight and level at seven thousand feet at about 140 knots - but its engine has stopped. – the pilot is standing up in the cockpit - and I think it must be being flown by God."*

By the time of our return to Singapore, the Borneo situation had stabilised and developed in our favour, so that the ship was cleared to return to the UK. As we passed Aden, we flew a number of operational sorties over the Radfan where ground operations were still in progress. I accepted, unwisely perhaps, the offer of a seat in the back of a Buccaneer due to carry out a low level reconnaissance sortie. Flying at 450 knots at about 100 feet over the arid and seemingly endless, featureless desert provided the sort of bumpy ride that only an aircraft as strong as the Buccaneer could stand – and my stomach could not! Landing back on board was a great relief. I could only wonder why anyone should ever want to own or fight over such naturally hostile and barren country.

We transited on through the Suez Canal for one final visit of the commission to Beirut. This was my first experience of the eastern Mediterranean. But, despite, or perhaps because of, a fascinating visit to the powerful Roman remains at Baalbek. I was left with the feeling that there seemed little hope of the Middle East problems being solved in any rational way. Regretably, I have not since changed this view.

We had had quite an exciting entrance to the quite small port, for EAGLE was a big ship. By local regulations we were forced to take a pilot who insisted on taking charge of the berthing operation. He was used to handling merchant ships and tankers for whom the engine movement "full-ahead" or "full-astern" was frequently used. Such ships had little power and so that full-ahead had little immediate effect. In a warship, the full-ahead or full-astern order is only used in an emergency and with the power of a large warship can have dramatic effects. When as we moved gently towards the berth, the pilot suddenly ordered 'full-ahead'. There was consternation on the bridge. Order followed counter-order as the Lebanese pilot and our navigator exchanged heated words in broken English as to who was in command of the berthing operation. Fortunately, order was restored in time to prevent the ship knocking a large hole in the jetty ahead.

After brief stops at Malta and Gibraltar, we arrived back in Devonport on the 24th of May where, with much sadness, I turned over to my successor, David Smith[14] and left the ship. I was deeply

---

[14] *Later, one of the Elder Brethren of Trinity House.*

moved and grateful for the comment of my Captain, Derek Empson, whom I had respected, admired, and with whom I had greatly enjoyed serving. He wrote on my 'flimsy',"*I count myself lucky indeed to have had as my second in command the most outstanding officer of Commander's rank that I have ever come across*". I was equally delighted, though surprised because this was my first shot in this promotion zone, to be told that I was to be promoted to the rank of Captain.

Chapter 10

Recruiting and NATO Defence College, Rome

"Don't take life too seriously. You'll never get out of it alive."
'Bugs Bunny'

My surprise at my early promotion encouraged me to make an early visit to my 'appointer' to see what my next job would be. Despite my recent time in EAGLE, I hoped that I might again go back to sea. *"We are planning to make you DDNR (O),"* said my appointer, *"How does that suit you?"* *"I've no idea,"* said I, *"I don't even know what the letters stand for."*

I discovered that I was to be the Deputy Director of Naval Recruiting (Officers). Although disappointed not to be back at sea, this sounded interesting and the sort of job that might provide opportunities beyond the normal call of naval life. So I accepted 'with pleasure'. I probably did not have much choice anyway. As it turned out, this was an inspired piece of appointing. I was at that time almost certainly the youngest post captain in the Navy – some might have remarked "and the least widely experienced at sea too" This was possibly also true. But In this job, my first job as a Captain, I was clearly not going to be under pressure. I thus had time to find my feet as a Captain. For this, I shall always be grateful.

The appointment provided me with an office in the Old Admiralty building just opposite the room where Admiral Lord Nelson was laid to rest before his burial – so I felt in good company. I was provided with a car. My task was to encourage young men to apply for entry as officers into the Royal Navy. Entry into the WRNS, the Women's Royal Naval Service, was separately handled. There were two forms of entry to a full naval commission, a direct entry from school to the Naval College at Dartmouth after successful completion of 'A' level exams; and a university cadetship scheme for those who had obtained provisional acceptance at university, in which the Navy paid university fees in return for limited training and service commitments. Other short-term commission entries were available for some specialisations, such as aircrew and the Instructor Branch. I had a small team of officers scattered round the country who did most of the visiting of schools and universities to advise on what the Navy had to offer. In addition to their supervision, I inherited the personal task of visiting all the major public schools, a commitment that I did not change.

At this time, the number of young officers that we were entering into the Navy broadly matched the requirement. Provided that a potential candidate had the necessary academic and medical qualifications, selection was in the hands of the Admiralty Interview Board, at which we sought to maintain and improve the standard of our entrants. The procedures were not too dissimilar to those that I had gone through some twenty-five years before, except that they now included practical initiative and leadership tests. One of the board members was always a headmaster and he was often the key to answering the question that was set by the interview, "Has this boy got the personality, the qualities and character that we are looking for?" For those who were borderline cases, the question became "Has he got these qualities but is, perhaps, not able to show them to us here?" It was a difficult conundrum and one that board members often spent a long time discussing. I myself sat in on the Interview Board from time to time so that I was able to tell future candidates the sort of procedure that they would be undergoing and to get a feel for the standards that the board were setting.

The assessment of motivation was one to which the interview board paid much attention. My boss, the director of naval recruiting, Rear Admiral Courtney Anderson, who was born in Southern Ireland, was responsible for the recruitment of naval ratings and artificers. As a result of his own experience at the age of thirteen, he tended to be cautious over the issue of motivation. His father had taken him to see a British warship that had berthed in a nearby Southern Irish port. They arrived at just on eight o'clock to see the ceremony of 'colours' (the daily hoisting of the White Ensign). As eight bells were struck, the quartermaster on watch saluted and reported to the officer of the day, *"Eight o'clock, Sir"*. The officer of the day replied, *"Make it so"*; and the ensign was then hoisted. *"Dad, Dad,"* he exclaimed excitedly, *"They even salute each other when they tell the time."*

Later that day when they returned to the ship, he managed to look through the wardroom scuttle (porthole) where tea had been laid and there were 'sticky cakes' on the table. It was a Tuesday. *"Dad, Dad,"* he said, *"look, they must have sticky cakes for tea every day of the week."* This was clearly the life for him - and in due course he became an Admiral.

Like a number of Irishman that I have met, Courtney had the great ability to produce the apt and telling phrase at the right moment of a discussion. A small but complex issue had arisen in our department. We were very properly handling it at our level. However, the Second Sea Lord's office, to which we were responsible, got involved and took the matter into their own hands. It then all went pear shaped. At a subsequent meeting with the Second Sea Lord, Admiral Sir Frank Twiss in the chair, this matter was on the agenda. The Chairman complained about the unfortunate outcome of this matter. *"Second Sea Lord"* said my boss, *"what can you expect when the level of decision rises above the level of comprehension."* That ended that agenda item.

All three services were understandably ever seeking higher quality. To help achieve this, and to broaden the base of our advertising, the Government's Central Office of Information (COI) was investigating the cost effectiveness of placing full-page recruiting advertisements for officer entry in the Sunday newspapers' colour supplements. These would complement the smaller 'coupons' inserted in daily newspapers; some of which had rather unimaginative titles, such as "Join the Navy and see the world". This was an expensive exercise, the cost being about £5,000 per entry. It did, however, have had a considerable public impact and significantly increased the number of applications for officer entry.

The COI had recommended, a small advertising agency, to which I thereafter paid not infrequent visits. I did not get off to a good start. At our first meeting, having met the director, I was being taken round talking to the various members of staff. I met one from whose neck was hanging an impressive row of cameras *"You must be the chief photographer?"* I said cheerfully, *"No"* he replied a little sharply, *"I'm the Creative Director."* Ouch!

This was a new world for me. Curiously I found the agency very reluctant to move outside the very traditional picture of what a naval officer should be and do. We spent much time encouraging the agency to be more adventurous. On one occasion when, together with my boss, we were viewing a particular campaign intended to illustrate the physical challenges that life at sea could offer, various proposed advertisements were shown to us. One of these was a picture of a naval officer in oilskins on the bridge of a destroyer in heavy weather with waves breaking over his head. It had the caption *"Dog watch, dog tired"*. This drew from my boss the response; *"It looks to me more like morning watch, morning sickness."* As we got to know each other better, however, we established a very good relationship with this agency.

At the same time, we started the process of creating the first University Royal Naval Unit (URNU). Whilst we had long had a graduate entry scheme for those that had completed their university degree as well as the University Cadetship scheme, we did little to engage the interest in matters of the sea of those who were already at university. We were impressed by the undoubted success of the Army units at Oxford and Cambridge, not only as a means of recruiting future officer cadets but in bringing to the university community a better understanding of what the army was all about. We set about developing the naval equivalent with its own small seagoing craft flying the white ensign and under the command of a young lieutenant commander. We chose Aberdeen University, whose Military Education Committee was keen to support this initiative. It was soon apparent that the 'call of the sea' was still strong and that the value of creating a wider understanding of maritime matters by getting undergraduates to sea was of wider and additional value than that of just recruiting additional future naval officers. There are today, some forty years later, fourteen URNUs.

A crowning moment of the recruiting visits, which my boss and I made, happened in Belfast. We were there with the object of appointing one of three candidates for the job of careers officer in that city. The candidates were always chief petty officers from the local area who, if selected, were promoted to lieutenant in the naval careers service. The Admiral, who had been born in Southern Ireland, asked a final question of the second candidate, *"How"* he said, *"would you best describe the Reverend Ian Paisley?"* In a memorable response the candidate replied in soft Irish brogue, *"Well, Sir. I think you could best describe him as being like a French letter on the prick of progress."* We had no trouble in selecting him - and he did a fine job thereafter.

From my own school visits I found the boys interested in joining the Navy varied widely in their character and their motivation. But I don't think that there was a single boy of whom I had to tell his headmaster that he was very unlikely to pass the Admiralty Interview Board; and perhaps, therefore, he should look elsewhere. My school visits also involved me in all sorts of outside activities; playing tennis with the boys, hunting with school packs of beagles and, in one case, an attempt by the air section of the Cadet Force to get me airborne in their unit's glider. This was launched, not by a winch, but by dragropes manned by the cadets. Unfortunately my weight was too great and the exercise ended up with the cadets exhausted and myself not yet airborne. At least I was spared the ignominy of crash landing. It was at this school that the careers master, a monk, seized a bottle of sherry from his study cupboard, slipped it under his cassock saying, *"I had better put this in here in case we meet too many boys on the way to the Common Room"*. The enthusiasm of almost every member of the staff of all the schools that I visited never failed to make a good impression on me.

During this period, working from the MOD in London, with my home in Dartmouth, I was faced with a problem of finding accommodation during the middle of the week. The Ministry of Defence ran a list of suitable names and addresses from which I chose a flat in the Bayswater Road. Its owner was an elderly lady, Mrs Jean McLean. On most evenings of the week, by the time I had finished in the office, or returned to London from a school visit, it was nine o'clock or later. By this time she had gone to bed. She was though, by disposition, somewhat nervous and there were occasions when I would return to find her in the sitting room with a glass of whisky in her hand. It was one such evening when I returned, having seen a film about Russia, Dr Zhivago.

Jean McLean had been the first wife of Sir Robert Bruce-Lockhart who had been our man in Moscow during the Russian Revolution. He had subsequently written a well-known book entitled 'Memoirs of a British Secret Agent'. Jean McLean herself maintained a close interest in the events of that time. She told me on a number of occasions that she had written a letters to very senior levels at the Foreign Office in order to express her concern that some apparently unconnected incident might compromise the source of funds that had been covertly used during the Revolution more than forty years before. The name Bruce Lockhart was also quite widely known. Logie Bruce-Lockhart was headmaster of Gresham School. John Bruce-Lockhart had a distinguished career in the Foreign Office at a senior level. Members of the family in more recent years had also been involved in the intelligence world.

I was at this time honoured by being asked to join the Board of the Royal United Services Institute. In this position, I was asked to chair an RUSI open meeting, which would be addressed by John Bruce-Lockhart. It had the title 'The relation of government with secret intelligence services'. This scholarly exposition had been given before to senior service audiences at the staff colleges; but never before in public. There was therefore considerable press and public interest. A large and distinguished audience was expected. I felt nervous and was at a loss to know how best to introduce the speaker, whom I had not before met.

On the previous night, I happened to be reading Gerald Durrell's book, "Esprit de Corps". He was telling the story of a naval attaché in a Balkan country that had virtually no navy. Becoming a little bored, he took up a correspondence course in transcendental meditation with a swami in the Edgware Road. Several months into his course, he received a telegram from his swami saying that he had made such impressive progress that his swami was planning to fly to the Balkans to meet him. The naval attaché was somewhat perturbed at this, fearing that the arrival of his swami at the embassy might embarrass his ambassador. He therefore consulted his friend, the embassy's first secretary. *"Don't worry,"* he said, *"Just pretend he is somebody important like Noel Coward or Bruce-Lockhart."* This gave me a perfect introduction.

To return to the film Dr Zhivago, which she told me that she had seen and much enjoyed. I asked her whether it reflected some of her personal memories of Russia and she confirmed that it had indeed. I asked her further whether she kept in touch with any of her or her husband's friends and colleagues who had been in Russia at the time. *"Oh yes,"* she said, *"I quite often see ...".* Here she mentioned the name of a lady who was still well known in London society. *"She was the woman that my husband was in bed with when he was arrested by the Bolsheviks. I know she was sleeping with at least two other men in Moscow at that time."*

This was one of a number of very interesting conversations that I had with her about Russia. They were particularly helpful to me because I had been invited by the Royal Navy Club to preside at one of the club's regular dinners, at which some historic naval event was celebrated. It usually seemed to be some battle against the French. But whatever the occasion, the president was invited to speak in some detail about it. My invitation was to speak on 'The part played by the Royal Navy in the Russian Revolution 1918-1920'. This was a subject upon which I knew little. The principle that I often use in delivering an after-dinner speech, is to refer briefly to the subject in hand; and then digress so as to deliver a related message that I think is important and relevant. I thus wrote to the Naval Historical Branch asking them to draft for me a few introductory comments about the RN's part in the Russian Revolution. They seemed not quite to understand what I wanted because what I got back from them was a long reading list of books and documents that I might wish to study.

A further very interesting late night discussion with Jean McLean encouraged me to base my speech on a wider account of the events of those years than I had intended.

Her own story followed. In 1916 the Royal Navy had towed four small submarines across the North Sea to carry out operations against the 'Reds' ships in the Baltic. She was then living in St Petersburg. "There were four young captains" she told me, whom she had got to know. "They had a very difficult time. But they were wonderful and behaved impeccably – except one of them had a little affair with me."

With the help of Jean Maclean's fascinating stories and much independent reading, I was able to base my speech around the fact that the Royal Navy was then fighting on no less than five fronts. We were fighting in the north in the area around Murmansk. We were fighting in the Baltic Sea. We were fighting in the Crimea area of the Black Sea; and had established sea control in the closed Caspian Sea. Guns were sent across by rail from Baku to be mounted on merchant ships in the Caspian by whose use we established sea control there. We were also fighting in the Far East from Vladivostok. In 1918, a 6inch gun and four 12 pounders from the cruiser HMS SUFFOLK were mounted on a train, and manned by British sailors. They then proceeded some two thousand miles inland to be used against Red Russian forces in the area of the Urals. They operated gunboats on the Kama, a tributary of the Volga river, in a highly adventurous and hair raising way, fortunately with only one casualty. By the summer of 1919, the fight was lost and gunboats sunk. In due course, the detachment arrived back in Vladivostok having rescued their guns and transferred them to the White Russians. This was the beginning of my own deepening interest in Russia leading subsequently to the close relations that I after leaving the Navy, developed with Moscow and some senior members of the Soviet hierarchy. These events are described in my Book Three.

By the end of two years of recruiting, I was keen to get back to more conventional sailoring. But it was not to be. My next appointment was to the NATO Defence College in Rome where officers from fourteen countries (fifteen NATO members minus the Greeks) and all three services, together with military related civilians, were instructed in the ways of NATO. This was normally a prelude to subsequent appointment to a NATO staff, a prospect upon which I had some doubts. However, I had no qualms about accepting this appointment to Rome as I was told that it would be followed by a sea appointment "in command".

Six months in Rome provided a marvellous opportunity to take my wife Ann with me and to have the three children join us for the summer holiday. My wife and I drove through France to Rome to arrive in the spring, a glorious time of the year when it was possible to spend the morning skiing in the hills near Rome; and then drive down to the coast and spend the rest of the day swimming and sunbathing on the beach.

Ann and I spent the first few days at a hotel which was conveniently near to the college at EUR, the southern extremity of the city, and adjacent to the offices of the United Nations Food and Agricultural Agency (FAO). We were lucky to find a very pleasant flat in rural surroundings only a short distance south of EUR, suitable for the children and ourselves. The rural life there reminded me of ages past - a shepherd with a long crook tended his sheep all day across open land. I was never quite sure what he did with them at night.

The summer in Rome can be extremely hot and we were delighted to meet a former naval colleague, John Ray, who, having been Assistant Naval Attaché in Rome, had decided to leave the Navy and to settle in Italy. He and his wife bought a piece of uncultivated hillside some twenty-five miles to the east of Rome near Castel di Decima. Close at hand were the ancient ruins of Horace's villa (Villa d'Horazio); and the local hilltop village. They camped there a while whilst they decided what to do with their new property. When the rains came, they soon found that their land was in the path of a torrent of fresh water from the hills above them. They decided that they would harness the water, having first built a locally appropriate house, and would then run a fish farm, breeding trout.

John, and Brenda his wife, were extraordinarily kind to us 'Brits' on the NATO course, and we were regularly invited to spend the weekend there, relaxing in the cool and the quiet of the hills. We spent many hours digging fishponds and humping concrete blocks – but they were very happy hours – and days.

The course itself, like that at the Joint Services Staff College, produced many very good, and some not-so-good, lectures from influential figures in the military and political world. But for me, the opportunity to live, work and socialise closely with officers and their wives from a wide range of differing nationalities and backgrounds was by far the most valuable feature of the course. There were of course 'Pooh traps'. In the early days, we nearly lost an American officer who, whilst exploring Rome, found himself in the middle of what he took to be a large, partly empty parking lot. Then, as he put it - *"A policeman blew a whistle and the whole goddamn parking lot got up and drove straight at me."* He had been in the middle of the Piazza Venetzia. A very good friend of mine in the Royal Marines also nearly got arrested. He was 'caught short' in the middle of Rome and sought a public convenience. One was in sight marked "Signori" at one end, and "Signore" at the other. Not being quite sure at which end he should enter, he asked a Carabinieri. He was very nearly arrested.

Ann and I quickly had to learn about Italian driving. I had brought from home a new and quite fast car. However, my driving had never before met such a challenge as that provided by drivers in Rome or on the anulari – the Rome ring road. The NATO Defence College being situated on the south side of Rome, the dual carriageway from Naples ran through EUR towards the centre of Rome. On this final stretch, there were numerous traffic lights. The Italian habit when stopping at such lights was for the driver in the front position of the fast lane to watch the pedestrian 'walk' signal, and as soon as it changed from green and started to flash red, he would fully rev his engine. When the road signal then changed to green, he would let in his clutch sharply, so as to get away at high speed in front of other cars. On this occasion I was in the second car of the middle lane. The car at the head of the fast lane, a Ferrari, was revving its engine to the maximum. The light turned green. The driver let in his clutch sharply. Unfortunately he was in reverse. There was a loud crash as he hit the car behind. Fortunately, because of the short distance that he could travel, nobody was seriously hurt. But, mamma mia, you have never seen the commotion that followed. I was only sorry we could not stay and watch.

I found Italy a fascinating country, and one that I loved. Not everyone shared my view and one of my close English friends on the college directing staff was not infrequently heard to complain that Rome was full of lovely little restaurants in outstanding and historic surroundings - serving quite ghastly food. Italian pasta dishes are not all to everyone's taste. The first few weeks of the course were very hectic, from sightseeing in Rome to socialising within the course on every possible occasion. The last six weeks of the course were similar with an impossible programme to visit all the places you had not yet visited; and attend all of the various national farewell parties. Our farewell course ball was to be held at the Palazzo Barberini, which in a very well-appointed and historic setting, provided a very suitable venue. In a very Italian way, it seemed to be run on the basis of a marriage between an officers club and a NAAFI canteen.

As one of the organising committee, I asked the college authorities for a staff car to take us to the Palazzo Barberini in the centre of Rome so as to make the detailed arrangements. About thirty minutes after the requested time, a car came to where we were waiting. But the driver immediately disappeared. We had asked if another driver was coming, *"No. You asked only for a car."* Rapid enquiries to the college seeking approval for one of us to drive the car received a firm no. Eventually we obtained a driver. Such was life in Italy.

The Palazzo was approached from street level by a long and steep set of stone steps. One of the detailed arrangements we wished to make was for the Senior National Naval Attaché to greet our guests formally at the head of these steps on their arrival. For many years, all the naval attaches had been of captain's rank, and their seniority was measured by the length of their service in Rome. However, very shortly before the party, a certain Latin American country broke all the 'rules' by sending as their attaché, an officer of Flag rank. He took his new duties very seriously – but unfortunately, he spoke no Italian. He insisted that, nevertheless, he would 'do the honour' of greeting our guests.

As is often the practice in Rome, this was a very long and protracted process, during which one of our colleagues kept him going with ample supplies of vino. It was after midnight when the last guest arrived. It happened at just the time when one of the early arrivals was about to leave. The Admiral would not desert his post, insisting that he must also say 'thank you for coming and goodnight' to every one on leaving.

By about four o'clock in the morning, when the last leavers were about to depart, the Admiral was very full of vino; and hardly able to speak his own language, let alone Italian. He was eventually persuaded that his duty had been well and duly done, and that he himself could now go home. Someone fetched his cap which he managed to balance on his head, whilst he set off very unsteadily in the direction of the revolving doors which guarded the exit at the top of the long stone steps. Unfortunately, the doors were revolving slowly in the wrong direction. The door caught him fully in the chest, knocking him backwards onto the floor. Willing hands dashed to his aid, helped put his hat back on and dusted him off.

He then gallantly set off for another try, holding his hands well in front of his face. Unfortunately on this occasion, the door was slowly revolving in the correct direction. This time, he passed through the doors without his hands meeting any resistance, and reaching the top of the steps, he tripped - and fell head over heels to the very bottom. His hat rolled into the road. Again the 'willing hands' ran down the steps after him to put him back on his feet again. Fortunately, his chauffer driven car was just nearby and they managed to get him, hat and all, safely into the car to take him home. By the time, we had left Rome a few days later, he had not been seen again.

In the middle of the course, there had been extensive visits to other NATO countries, with opportunities at weekends in between to visit other parts of Italy. For our trips abroad, we flew in an ancient, propeller driven aircraft provided by the Belgian government. It meant some very long periods in the air. To get to America took us almost a whole day, having had to make a refuelling stop in the Azores. The weather there for landing was appalling but we got down safely – just. Wherever we visited there were inevitably highlights. When we were taken for a visit the American Air Defence Command (NORAD) headquarters at Colorado Springs, we discovered that the annual defence budget for this headquarters alone was greater than the whole of the annual Turkish defence budget. When it was noted in the local press that there were no Greek members of our course, a leading member of the local Greek community invited us all to dine as his guests at his well-known restaurant. He was a first generation American who had made his first million dollars. He had begun this by sending a box of his homemade chocolates to the White House. Fame and fortune followed. We soon discovered that, whilst enthusiastically embracing the democratic process, he did not fully understand the responsibilities of freedom that go with democracy. His restaurant was not licensed, so the Coca Cola bottles were all filled with Metaxas brandy, which he downed with astonishing rapidity. Despite his most generous hospitality, no one wished to follow his enthusiastic call for us to follow his example, which had quickly emptied his restaurant of all other customers. He did this by hurling a tray loaded with glasses of brandy to smash against the wall whilst shouting at the top of his voice, *"If I want to say President Nixon, you are a bastard, I say*

PRESIDENT NIXON YOU ARE A BASTARD." It was not without some difficulty, that we managed to extract ourselves without causing offence.

The highlight of our visit to Germany was an evening spent with colleagues at a nightclub in Munich. Sometime in the evening, Ronnie Harcus, one of my British friends, had collected two good-looking girls. We joined forces with other course members at the nightclub. Fortunately for us the two girls departed on their own before the evening, at which we had been drinking champagne and dancing, equally vigorously, had ended. It was at this stage that some of our colleagues discovered that the nightclub was charging an extortionate price for the champagne. We certainly had insufficient Deutsch marks with which to pay – but I had a credit card, which was accepted. When we returned to Rome and recounted the events to our wives, and admitted its cost, they merely said, *"well that's another hat for me"* ... and, *"I'll have another handbag for that."* Fortunately, we didn't have to pay up to our wives as the bill that I had signed never showed up on my credit card statement. Nor, as I at one time feared, did we receive any blackmailing threats.

For seminar work, the course was divided into syndicates. At the end of the course, each syndicate was required to make a presentation on some aspect of NATO's political or military affairs. One member of our syndicate was an elderly and very senior officer of the Italian cavalry. He spoke little during the whole course and seemed to understand less. The two NATO languages of French and English were clearly alien to him. He always wore dark glasses and never drank alcohol. In our syndicate presentation, it was a little difficult to place him in the cast for our scenario. This was based on the visit by an African Potentate and potential ally, to NATO and the Warsaw Pact so as to be briefed on the military capabilities of the two sides. We first acted a scene in Moscow and then the similar scene in Brussels. We thought that his lack of a NATO language would be minimised if he took the part of the African potentate.

Our scenery was changed by replacing the bottle of vodka that was on the table in Moscow, with one of coca cola, which was on the table in Brussels. My role in Moscow was as Mr Brezhnev. Our first rehearsal did not promise well. As the potentate and I sat down together to talk about the Warsaw Pact, on the table between us, there was a large bottle, clearly labelled VODKA. For the rehearsal it was filled with water. I poured out two 'stiff' glasses and proposed a toast to the victory of Warsaw Pact forces. Both of us emptied our glasses. I then said to him in slow, deliberate terms, *"Your Excellency, what have you come to Moscow to do?"* He looked at me and said in halting English, *"What do I say now?"* This was not an encouraging start. Somehow, however, we managed to get through the rest of the scene.

The following day for the real occasion in front of an audience of some hundred members of the course and the directing staff, I had filled the bottle with real vodka. Having greeted his excellency, I filled his glass and mine and offered the toast by emptying the contents in one go and throwing the glass over my shoulder in true traditional Russian practice. The Italian colonel followed suit. There followed an astonishing transformation. He shook his head and took off his glasses. His eyes shone bright red; and he broke into passable English with a story that was quite long and very funny. This performance brought the house down. I don't think he ever spoke English again – or drank vodka.

The opportunities of travel round Italy was such that I shall always regard the country with great affection; and my children learnt from it too. They learned that you never buy anything without asking for, and getting, a discount – a "sconto". A sconto for NATO was a popular ploy. The children also learned other lessons. While travelling on the metro from EUR into Rome in a crowded carriage, my daughter Sue felt somebody pinch her bottom. She immediately thought it must be her brother who was standing close behind her. She whipped round sharply, ready to give him a clout; but found herself confronted by a gorgeous young Italian boy, to whom her bottom was just too attractive not to be pinched. They stared into each other's eyes for what seemed an age before she turned back and blamed her brother. But Italy was like that - it was part of its attraction.

I have remained a strong supporter of NATO and the NATO Defence College as an 'Ancien'; although the style, the character and the site of the college in Rome has now changed enormously, as have post cold war developments in European security. I am, I believe, the only student of the college who has become one of the three Supreme Commanders of NATO and I now regard myself privileged to hold the position of the President of the UK NATO Anciens Association. I am, however, now deeply concerned at the implications both for NATO and for European security, of the present Alliance involvement in Afghanistan. I address this matter in the final chapter of Book Three.

Ann and I drove back through France to England in the early autumn to return to our house in Dartmouth; and for me to start a series of courses prior to taking command of HMS INTREPID. My instructions required me to proceed to Singapore and recommission INTREPID for further service in the Far East. I was to travel by air from RAF Brize Norton, in company of a good friend, Captain Hugh Jannion. He was to take command of a Leander-class frigate, which was at that time deployed in the Persian Gulf. Our flight was due to take off late in the afternoon. It didn't – and as the hours progressed, so the delay lengthened. It was eventually clear that we would not depart before early the next morning. I was allocated a twin-bedded room for the night; and for the first, and last, time I slept with a Group Captain. Unfortunately, he snored.

Hugh Jannion had a delightful wife who had come to bid him farewell. She was however a rather emotional person. When told that the RAF could not make arrangements for her to stay overnight so as to see her husband off in the morning, there was something of a scene. Navy- Air Force relationships fell to a very low level.

Our aircraft eventually took off early the next morning. As the two most senior officers on board, we had the privilege of two seats adjacent to the passenger door, so allowing us unlimited legroom. Flying with us was a young attractive and uniformed RAF public relations girl who had been involved on the previous evening with the fracas over Captain Jannion's wife. Our first stop was Bahrain. A well-known fault of the VC10 was that condensation at high altitude could cause ice to form on the inside of the aircraft. On landing in hot climates, the ice could thaw quickly, with a cascade of water falling in the vicinity of the passenger door.

On this occasion, as the aircraft came to a halt, this cascade of water landed in the middle of Hugh Jannion's lap. Moments later the RAF public relations girl, unaware of this accident, went to Captain Jannion to say, *"Captain, at least, I can now say that you have had a good flight."* *"Certainly not."* he replied.

"Oh dear, Captain Jannion, what's wrong now?" said the girl with resignation. *"Look at this."* he said, pointing to a large wet patch in his crotch. *"When I walk down the steps, and my officers here to greet me see this, what are they going to think?"*

The three of us laughed heartily. I proceeded on to Singapore.

CHAPTER 11

HMS INTREPID

"In war, to ignore a threat is often to create an opportunity."

Corbett

I arrived in Singapore on the 4th of December 1968 to be met by the previous captain of the INTREPID, Captain Tony Troupe He had bad news. The ship was non-operational. He explained that the day before, a young mechanic engineer had gone berserk in the ship's engine control room and smashed several panels of the control gear. It would require a week or so to repair. But such is life. The rating was court-martialled and sentenced to a short period of detention. I was subsequently asked whether I would have him returned to the ship. Having read his naval service documents I had no hesitation in saying yes. By the time I left the ship some two years later, he had fully re-established himself and I was delighted to be able to promote him to the next professional and leadership level as a Leading Hand.

The Navy prides itself on its 'divisional system' to provide supervision and guidance to every junior member of a ship's company. Sadly, in this case, the system failed. Why or how was not easy for me to ascertain as it was all in the ship's previous commission. We were now in a new 'commission' with many changes of officers and men. This was all part of my challenge. INTREPID was re-commissioned on Saturday 14th of December, by which time the dockyard repairs to the Engine Control Room were complete. At the commissioning service I suggested that everyone should set himself the task of achieving something personally worthwhile during our time in the ship.

Five days later, we put to sea for a few days 'shake down' exercises in the local area before returning to Singapore naval base for Christmas. On Christmas day The Area Naval Flag Officer, Rear Admiral Derek Empson, my former Captain IN EAGLE, kindly invited myself and all the other commanding officers of ships in

Singapore at the time, to Christmas lunch. My morning task was to walk round my own ship to say 'Hello and Happy Christmas'. Rum was still being issued at that time. 'Tot time' was normally at twelve noon. On Christmas day tot time was informally brought forward somewhat. I started my rounds at about 1000. When visitors are asked to a naval mess deck, it is traditional that they are offered a drink of rum, either 'sippers' or 'gulpers' - the difference being obvious. Regrettably I was offered either sippers or gulpers in almost every one of the approximately fifty-two messes in the ship. I did not manage to get off the ship for lunch at Admiralty House until well after 1300; and with much difficulty I remained just coherent. Fortunately I did not fall in my soup but I have to admit that I do not remember very much else about lunchtime - except that it was great fun and very much enjoyed. The morning remained rather a blur – but I regarded it as a welcome and encouraging but challenging introduction to my new ship's company.

INTREPID, a ship of cruiser size with deep displacement of about 17,000 tons, was of an unusual design, formally designated as an LPD (Landing Platform Dock). The ship's design was highly flexible, with its primary task being to put ashore an embarked military force of some four hundred troops and their vehicles; and to continue to support them over the beach. At the stern, was a large dock area which, by flooding or emptying a number of large internal tanks to the sea, would allow large landing craft, loaded with tanks or heavy stores to be readily transferred between ship and shore. Smaller landing craft were carried at davits designed for over-the-beach landing of men and light equipment. Above the dock was a helicopter platform from which we could operate Wessex helicopters to carry men, or heavy supplies in cargo nets slung below the aircraft. The co-ordination of all these operations could be complex and required considerable practice. I was aware that the successful outcome of such an operation was dependent on good planning, strict timing, and the need for initiative and firm leadership at all levels. I therefore gave high priority to these characteristics in all that the ship did.

At the New Year, we were back at sea to continue our series of shake down exercises and to join the Commando Carrier, ALBION, for amphibious operations in the Penang area. However, since our military capabilities were not in high demand in the Malaysian area at this time, we were able also to devote time for 'showing the Flag' more widely in the Southeast Asian region.

On the 21st ofFebruary we embarked the Commander Far East Fleet, Vice Admiral Bill O'Brien for a visit to Borneo. Our first visit was to Brunei where formal calls were to be made on the Sultan. Since Intrepid was too large to go up the river to the Brunei capital, Bandar Seri Begawan, the ship anchored offshore in the Labuan anchorage. On arrival, the admiral and I helicoptered ashore to land in the grounds of the residence of the British High Commissioner. The admiral paid his formal calls whilst I visited the naval base. I was impressed by the Sultan's large, fast patrol craft and the enthusiasm of their local crews.

That evening, the High Commissioner had arranged a large reception in the grounds of the residence. It was a splendid affair with wide local representation. The High Commissioner himself, together with his wife, acted as our hosts – as did his wife's sister. As the evening progressed it increasingly seemed to me that we were presented with a ménage-à-trois. The next day's programme involved helicopter flights to a native long house in the jungle and to a visit to Seria, the oil-producing centre in the south of Brunei. As the evening turned towards the morning under a warm, clear, tropical sky, I found my dancing partner, the High Commissioner's wife's sister becoming increasingly amorous. Her nails dug deep into my hand as she whispered in my ear "You will sit next to me in the helicopter tomorrow, won't you?" I was extremely glad that I was not due to spend the night at the residency and was booked in to a hotel nearby.

The next day's programme was fortunately completed without too many incidents. The seating in the helicopter had been pre-arranged. The visit to the long house in the middle of the jungle was fascinating and the visit to Seria went well except when a fake bomb was found in a helicopter that we were about to use for carrying a close relative of the Sultan. This incident, resulting from the misplaced initiative of one of our Royal Marines to exercise our internal security procedures, was bad news – but we managed to recover from the incident without too much political damage.

The two-day visit being completed, we re-embarked the Fleet commander-in-chief whose impression of the set up at the High Commission had not been dissimilar to mine. In few, but very effective words, he summed it up in the terms, *"That was sheer Somerset Maughan, sheer Somerset Maughan."* Fortunately, he was able to make his impressions clear to the Foreign Office, at a time when Brunei was unusually high on their agenda, since the Queen was to make a visit there in a couple of months time. Shortly afterwards the High Commissioner retired and was replaced by a friend of mine, Peter Gautry, who had been with me in Rome as a member of our course at the NATO Defence College.

Our next visit was to Kota Kinabalu in East Malaysia, the capital town of British North Borneo. Jessleton, as it was called in former days, is the scene of many second world war graves, both Australian and British. It was here that Countess Edwina Mountbatten, wife of Admiral Lord Mountbatten of Burma, had been taken ill during an official visit in 1960 and had died. Having completed his formal calls, Admiral O'Brien's programme for the afternoon, in which I was to accompany him, involved a journey inland to visit a Malaysian tea station, which we reached after a long, dusty and distinctly uncomfortable landrover ride. The tea station was interesting but hardly dramatic. What was however dramatic was that nearby, in the shadow of Mount Kinibalu, we came across an extraordinary war memorial. It took the form of two parallel concrete walls, perhaps ten feet high, several hundred feet long and thirty feet apart, between which lay a shallow trough, designed to be full of water. At the far end was a high curtain wall of stone obscuring any further view. However, as one advanced towards it and came close to the end, a clever design opened up to reveal the majestic outline of Mount Kinabalu silhouetted against the sky.

This was the memorial to the approximately one thousand people who died in what is known as the Sandakan March. Sandakan, a town on the north coast of Borneo, had been used by the Japanese as a prisoner of war camp for British and Australian troops who had been captured, and for former British colonial residents. It was the scene of appalling atrocities. In 1944, as the American forces drove west across the Pacific, the Japanese decided to move some one thousand Australian POWs south and west from Sandakan down to the Jessleton area. The march took them through virgin jungle during which very many died. It came to an end at the foot of Mount Kinibalu, when the handful of survivors could go no further. To stand within the walls of this memorial, which lay unfinished and apparently uncared for, being gradually devoured by the jungle, was an enormously emotional experience. It seemed to represent the uselessness and tragedy of the death of so many innocent men, women and children[15].

The following year, when INTREPID had returned to the southeast Asian area following a refit in England, the ship was involved in another visit to Brunei, to exercise with the Sultan's navy. This comprised several British built high performance and well armed fast patrol boats, commanded by a British soldier. It was also planned that we would carry out amphibious counter insurgency exercises involving an embarked force of 42 Commando and elements of the Royal Brunei Regiment and the Gurkhas.

The first serial of the exercise programme was to be a night encounter exercise with one of the Sultan's fast patrol boats. I found it quite difficult, however, to envisage a scenario that would represent a challenge both to my own ship and an attacking patrol boat in such a one-upon-one encounter on the high sea. I therefore decided that, since I would have time-in-hand before the scheduled start of the exercise, I would try to liven it up by approaching the designated exercise area to the south of Labuan island, from the north. Since INTREPID would have previously

---

[15] *Further information on the Sandakan atrocities can be found on the internet with a Google search "Sandakan"*

departed from Singapore, I confidently predicted that the enemy would expect me to be coming from the south.

To implement my plan to approach from the north meant that I had to navigate a somewhat narrow and shallow channel between Labuan Island and the Brunei coast. This was a route that was not normally considered suitable for large ships. At least by this plan, so I argued, and by using the advantage of our embarked helicopter for visual search, I should surely gain the benefit of surprise.

The exercise was due to start at 2000. At about half- past- eight, with the ship fully darkened, and the sun having set nearly an hour earlier, I was just exiting the Labuan channel heading south. Ahead of me, I could make out on radar the navigational buoy that marked the southern entry to the Brunei River and the Labuan anchorage. The buoy was also marking the northern limit of the exercise area. My helicopter was some fifteen miles ahead looking for the 'enemy'. Suddenly, INTREPID was illuminated in the very bright light of two rocket-launched flares. I was astonished and no one in my operations room team had any idea of where the rockets had come from.

My first thought was that I had taken a 'sucker punch' from the enemy craft that must have been secured to the navigational buoy, which my radar was showing ahead of me. I cursed myself roundly for not having ordered my helicopter to 'sanitise' this buoy; for attaching themselves to a navigational buoy was a trick that the Germans had frequently used in the latter stages of the small ship battle in the English Channel in 1944. For me, a minor veteran of those days, this was a major misjudgement. I cursed myself again.

However, the true story was rather different. The Brunei patrol boat had been due to leave harbour at 1800 so as to enter the exercise area by 1900 and deploy to the south at high speed hoping to ambush INTREPID as she entered the exercise area at the southern limit. Unfortunately her sailing was delayed by an engine fault that took some time to put right. Already two hours late for the start time of the exercise, she left her berth at high speed heading for the open sea and the exercise area. She had just cleared the entrance to the Brunei River and turned south, when the captain noticed in the darkness that there was the stern of a large vessel carrying no lights, very close ahead. It was not long before they realised that, although it seemed unlikely, it was probably INTREPID. Dropping back several hundred yards, he fired two illuminating rockets - and lo and behold, there we were. The encounter exercise was over – before it had even begun. The exercise was thus somewhat of a failure, but I had to blame myself for trying to be 'too clever by half'. Nevertheless, we all agreed that it had been fun – and that we had gained experience from it.

Following our visit to Kota Kinabalu, we were due to visit Hong Kong. Unfortunately on 'flashing up' the next morning, a serious explosion occurred in one of our two boilers. Luckily nobody was hurt. But with only one boiler in service the ship could not be considered fully operational. We limped off, heading for the nearest dockyard repair facilities which, fortunately, were at Hong Kong,

Because of our reduced manoeuvring power available, we entered Hong Kong harbour from the west and after passing Green Island, signalled for the tugs, that had been offered to assist in our berthing at the naval dockyard. I was not particularly pleased to receive the offer because I was quite confident to berth on the outer arm without tugs but I felt it unwise to turn the offer down. We proceeded at slow speed towards our planned berth. As we neared the dockyard and were passing the crowded Hong Kong-Kowloon ferry piers, I was forced to slow down almost to a stop, there being no sign of the promised tugs. It was a foul morning with low visibility and a fresh wind from the northeast. As we waited, I noticed that we were beginning to drift down rather alarmingly towards the ferry piers. I could see a difficult situation rapidly developing. Despite the advice of the Chinese pilot, who was quite useless, and kept on telling me that the tugs were just about to come, I decided to go ahead without them.

The ship was now in a position in which the only way of clawing back upwind so as to make a reasonable approach to our berth was to order engine revolutions for high speed. Gradually the ship gathered way and I began to be hopeful that we could berth on the outside of the dockyard arm as planned, and not get pushed down by the wind to get stuck in the narrow entrance to the dockyard basin. With the delay in waiting for the tugs, which never came, this at one time had seemed a distinct possibility.

As we now approached our proper berth, I realised that the ship was going too fast and that I might not be able to stop in time so that we didn't demolish the entrance to the China Fleet Club that lay across the road at the end of our berth. The situation required drastic measures. I ordered, *"Full astern both engines - stand by both anchors"*. I had not heard, before nor since, of such orders being given whilst berthing. But I was in luck; and without having to drop either anchor, the ship came to a stop in almost exactly the right place and parallel to the berth. At this stage I was still biting my nails. My wife, who had just before arrived in Hong Kong, was watching from the jetty. As I staggered over the brow onto the jetty to greet her, my nerves were still twitching. *"Darling,"* she said, *"that was marvellous. But I thought you were going to do what you normally do with the speedboat at home - ram it straight into the jetty." "Yes, dear, so did I."*

Our boiler was repaired most efficiently and in time for us to take part in a planned HK local amphibious exercise. Apart from one slightly scary incident when it appeared that one of my large landing craft was about to unload its tank-like large recovery vehicle onto a communist Chinese beach, the exercise went well. It was a great joy to be together again in Hong Kong with Ann and to be able to see our many friends there and to revisit our old haunts. But the end of March was soon upon us. Ann flew home to collect our three children from school. In INTREPID, we set course for Singapore, the first leg of our long trip home via the Persian Gulf, Durban, Gibraltar and due in Plymouth on the 12th of June. When leaving the Gulf, I decided to take the ships company on the scenic route which took us through a very narrow and deep channel between two islands that was seldom used by other than local craft. The navigator and I studied all the local data before deciding it was both feasible and safe. I have to admit that as we approached it, it did seem narrower than I had expected. The only mishap was one sailor who had been asleep. He woke up, and looking out of his scuttle, and seeing land seemingly only a cricket pitch away thought we were about to hit one of the islands at twelve knots, and fell out of his bunk.

Having spent five happy days in Durban, we rounded the Cape and headed north, I was studying the chart of the South Atlantic and noticed that the very small Island of Saint Helena, of which I knew little, except that it had something to do with Napoleon, lay very close to our planned track. I asked to see the large-scale chart of the island. Studying it, I began to think that I was living in a much earlier 'pirate' age. The chart showed a place on the island named "Spy Glass Hill" and another "Two gun Point". Having a little time in hand, I decided that we should make a brief stop there. A signal to the Foreign Office quickly received approval. The view of the island on arrival did not disappoint. It seemed to rise many hundred feet vertically out of the sea. Around the edge of its 'roof' lay what seemed like an arid brown 'circlet'. Inside it was a roof of lush green vegetation.

We anchored off the landing place at Jamestown very close to the shore since the depth of water ran down very quickly to several hundred fathoms. A small number of the ship's company were able to get ashore to walk round the quaint little town that seemed to rest on a ledge at the bottom of almost vertical cliffs, and provided the only access to the Island. It was indeed the Island's one link with the rest of the world, for there was no terrain suitable for an airport. Once a month, a single supply ship would call there.

I was transported to the top of the cliffs – I can't remember how – to make a call on the Governor at Plantation House. He had very kindly arranged a visit for me to Longwood, the estate in the middle of the island where Napoleon Bonaparte had been imprisoned following his capture in 1815 after the battle of

Waterloo. The estate had been declared to be the territory of France; and it remains today the residence of the French Consul to St Helena. A highly knowledgeable guide, who was an expert in the fascinating history of the island, accompanied me[16].

We returned for tea at Plantation House which was not only the home of the Governor and his family – but also of Jonathan, a giant tortoise (Testudo Gigantica), who was then reputed to be over a hundred years old. After tea, as we played croquet on the lawn, Jonathan joined in enthusiastically – only, he would place his very large and heavy frame on top of any croquet ball that came his way! In view of his age, and the belief that whilst there was such a tortoise at Plantation House, St Helena would always be British, I was glad to be able to arrange for him to be given a successor, who was in due course delivered to the island by a ship of the Royal Fleet Auxiliary.

INTREPID arrived in Plymouth on the 7th of June, having had to conduct full power trials on the day before with thick fog in the channel – not the most comfortable situation for the captain. The ship was almost immediately taken in hand by Devonport dockyard for a nine-month refit. It was to be almost exactly a year before she would be ready to head back again for the Far East. I was particularly delighted to be home for these winter months as I was able to hunt the Britannia Beagles twice a week for the whole season. In the spring of 1970 at the end of the hunting season, I invited all the BB puppy walkers and many of our hunting farmers to lunch with me in the ship, together with their beagle puppies. The oldest of our supporters there was Mr Edwin Hannaford, aged ninety, from Lower Norton Farm, near Dartmouth. He told me that he had only once before during his life been to Plymouth. He also found it difficult to comprehend that I had brought the ship back from Singapore. It was a great day.

---

[16] *I thoroughly recommend Gilbert Martineau's book "Napoleon's St Helena", published in Britain 1968*

With our dockyard completion date slipping to the right, as refit dates then seemed almost inevitably to do, I began to be a little anxious as to how much more time at sea I would have before my time in command, where I was extremely happy, would be up. This anxiety was partly allayed by my being told that I would stay in the ship until the end of the year. This started my mind turning to what I might do next. I had five years to go before I reached the top of the Captain's list, when it was either up or out. An appointment that many of my peers valued was to the year long course at the Imperial Defence College – often irreverently referred to as "that high class prep school in Belgrave Square". This did not appeal to me. I had listened to a large number of high quality lectures from important people, both at Latimer and Rome – and I still could not recall what almost any of them had said. I was more interested in doing my own thinking. I had though just become aware of an MoD 'University Fellowship' scheme, whereby senior members of all three services were permitted to spend a year at university undertaking research. This did appeal to me and, after making various enquiries, I decided to apply.

Before we sailed to return to the Far East, we were delighted to have the privilege of hosting on board a 'Top of the Pops' broadcast, featuring a song and dance group, Pam's People, a delightful group of six very pretty girls. This event brought the normal business of the ship almost to a halt for several days – but was a marvellous boost to the ship's company's morale – including that of her captain. On the 23rd of June 1970, we sailed from Plymouth for trials in the channel.

One major item of new equipment that had been installed during the refit was the first ship-fitted digital satellite telephone system. We had had a team of the 'wizards' who had built this system come to sea to complete the final setting up the equipment as an operational system. However, the aerial had been positioned by the dockyard on the foremast where it could not complete a full 360-degree rotation. It had an approximately forty five degree 'blind arc'. The MoD saw this as a serious tactical limitation on the system. This cast a shadow over the project team's professional competence. The Devonport dockyard was therefore looking at every possibility of moving the aerial to a better site. Not only did I not wish to return to the dockyard to have this work done (re-wiring et al), but I also saw the present arrangement as a positive advantage to me, the captain. If I should find myself in a situation with some senior officer ashore telling me to do damn silly things that I, the man on the spot, had no intention of doing, then I could avoid any argument by saying, *"I'm very sorry; but I have now got to alter course quickly in order to avoid hitting another ship. That will take my satellite aerial into a blind arc and we will both be cut off – good bye."* I did then not even have to alter course. I could just switch the equipment off. Nelson never found his blind eye any disadvantage. During my command, the aerial remained firmly where it was!

By Sunday afternoon, most of the satcom wizards had flown ashore. Only one remained, who came to me and asked if I would like to speak on the line to Singapore, where there was a special receiving station, to sample the remarkable quality of the voice transmission. He said, *"You are through to the Headquarters of the Far East Command at Phoenix Park."* I picked up the handset and said,

"Can I speak to the duty staff officer at the headquarters please?"

"Sorry, Sir, I don't think he's here", came the reply, very loud and clear.

"Well, can I speak to one of the other staff officers?"

"No Sir, I'm sorry, I think I am the only person here."

"Well who are you?"

"I'm the duty messenger."

"But are you not at the headquarters of the Commander in Chief, Far East Command?"

"Yes, Sir. Where are you?"

"In the middle of the English Channel"

There was a long silence. *"Can you say that again, please Sir?"*

"In a warship in the middle of the English Channel"

Further long pause. I continued, *"And you are sure that there is no one else in Phoenix Park."*

"Yes, Sir, I am sure."

"But why are you the only person there?"

"It's a holiday, Sir. It's Labour Day." I gave up. But the quality of the voice transmission was outstanding.

Some days later, we left the channel, and after a fair weather passage across the Bay of Biscay, we arrived at Gibraltar to pick up the Flag Officer Gibraltar. He was also accredited as Naval Attaché to the King of Morocco. We were to take him to Casablanca, from where he was to go to Rabat to present his credentials to the king. On arrival, there was considerable interest in the ship's visit; and several local requests to look round the ship. These included the Moroccan Navy, the local port authority; and the Soviet naval attaché. Very quickly, the ship's visit programme became complicated, not least because at a recent Russian Naval visit the British assitant naval attaché had been invited to tour the Russian warship. We could then not reasonably not invite the Soviet attaché and his party to tour INTREPID. But the Soviets did not want the Moroccans informed that they had been invited. And they both wanted to come on the same morning. We eventually had to draw up a somewhat complicated plan for them both to be on board at the same time, without either knowing that the other was there. It even worked.

Another very early visitor from ashore was the local British Mission to Seamen parson – an elderly, earnest and delightful man, who was on our invitation list for our evening reception. The Soviet naval Attaché and his assistant had also been invited. Before the party started, the commander, Chuck Giles, very properly warned all the officers about security, bearing in mind the presence of the Russians. Having greeted all our guests at the head of the gangway, I joined the party on the flight deck. After a short while, I noticed the British Mission to Seamen parson on his own with nobody near him. I summoned one of the midshipmen and asked him to go over and talk with the parson. Not long after, I again noticed the parson on his own. I despatched another young officer to 'take him in tow'. After this had happened yet a third time, I said to another of the Midshipmen,*"Why won't anyone talk to that parson over there?"* *"Oh"*, he replied, *"he's a Russian agent."* *"Don't be silly"*, I said. *"That's the British Mission to Seamen padre."*

The full story then emerged. Shortly before the start of the party, our electrical officer, who was also the security officer, was watching over the ship's side and observed an elderly gentleman cycle slowly and sedately up the jetty towards the ship. He stopped just short of the gangway, took off his bicycle clips, parked his ancient bicycle and straightened his dog collar'. Jokingly, the security officer, who had recognised him from his call on the ship earlier in the day commented flippantly to a midshipman standing at his side *"Oh, we need to watch him. He's one of the Russian's most dangerous agents."* This remark was rapidly passed round the other young officers. Unfortunately, the remark was not taken in the humorous context in which it was intended. When I later apologised to the parson for the apparent lack of courtesy by my young officers at the beginning of the party, he was delighted with the story and commented that it was the most exciting thing that had happened to him during his last twenty-five years at Casablanca.

Whilst the programme for visitors to the ship was just a little bit difficult, it was as nothing compared to the complexities of getting, or not getting, the Admiral and his delightful French-born wife to Rabat for calls in the Royal Palace. By the time the ship had to leave two days later, they were still at Casablanca. However, on the evening before the ship's planned departure, the Admiral, his wife, the Flag lieutenant and I received a very rare and most welcome invitation to have dinner with the harbourmaster at his home. We were warned that it would be a major gastronomic event. Indeed so it was. We were most warmly received by our host and made very comfortable on mounds of soft cushions. As we lay thus, drinking whisky served by very delightful young Arab girls, I thought "This is the life for me"!

Then the first of the twelve courses on the menu arrived. On a most handsome large brass dish were twelve beautifully cooked pigeons. They were delicious and almost a meal in themselves. Unfortunately and unbeknown to me before we arrived, the Admiral had developed a bad stomach-ache. As it was clearly impolite to refuse food, I was designated to eat for him. I can only say that I did my best.

The main course was a 'meshui' – that is a whole roasted lamb that was to be eaten using only one's fingers. I was just a little concerned that, acting as I was for the principal guest, the Admiral, I might be offered, as is traditional, the eye. As the Admiral viewed this magnificently cooked carcass from the front end, he asked our host whether it was a male or a female lamb. From where I was sitting at the other end, it was all too clear what sort of beast it was. It was a young ram. I was then even more concerned at what delicacy I might be offered.

In the event, and to my relief, both ends of the lamb were left intact and we feasted on the delicious flesh from its flanks – and there were still four courses to go. By the time that I had finished eating for myself, my country and my admiral, I could hardly get up from my nest of cushions. It was, however, one of the most unusual and finest banquets that I have been privileged to attend. Next morning, we sailed for Capetown. I ate only indigestion tablets for the first forty-eight hours.

By the time we reached Capetown, I thought I had recovered. But I was to be proved wrong. At our reception there, I managed to prise a very attractive young lady guest out of the hands of my young officers to take her to dinner. It was a very pleasant evening, during which she invited me for a game of squash the next morning. I accepted with much pleasure. I didn't consider myself of the same standard at squash as that to which I aspired to on the tennis court – but at least I had not been beaten by anyone on board. However, as soon as we got on the court, I realised that I was not as fit as I thought I was. It also became rapidly clear that she was very much better than I. Nevertheless, although my morale was somewhat dented by an almost whitewash, I much enjoyed the game - which was probably more than she had been able to do. However, my morale recovered slightly when she told me that she had recently been coached by, and played with, Jonah Barrington, one of the top squash players in the world. She was a sweet person and invited me to let her know when I was again visiting the Cape so that we could play again. It was not to be.

Our next stop was at Mauritius, where I made my first call on the Prime Minister, Dr Ramgoolan, who was elderly and of Indian birth. I did not find small talk with him very easy and so broached the subject of the Mauritian economy and tourism. He made a short and informative response, and we talked about the price of sugar; sugar being a major export for the Island. My mind then wandered back to tourism and to an incident at Capetown where one of my ship's divers had been arrested for taking a large crayfish from the sea bottom- which was against the law in that area – *"And how about the fishing?"* I asked.

Immediately I realised that it was about the most tactless remark I could have made, because I knew that Mauritius was then having a furious row with the British Government on the subject of fishing. The issue involved was that of the granting, by the Mauritian Government, of a licence for Soviet fishing vessels to operate from the island. For the Mauritians, this was an economic issue and most welcome. London, however, was convinced that the Soviet vessels would be more involved in intelligence collection than fishing. However, Prime Minister 'Ram' took my indiscretion in good part.

My call ended with him expressing his sorrow to hear that, on that day, all sailors in the Royal Navy were to lose their traditional daily tot of rum. I well understood the reason for this decision by the

Admiralty Board but nevertheless felt that it did not take into sufficient account the harsh conditions for sailors on the lower deck, particulatly in small ships. My next call was to the Governor who was a former senior British Trade Union Leader, now finishing his days in a splendid colonial mansion set in a glorious maritime setting. He too sympathised with my concerns about the loss of the Navy's tradition of the rum ration.

The next day, the ship was visited by the Island's Chief Excise Officer, who brought two cases of white rum with him as a present to my sailors from the Prime Minister. I thanked him warmly. After we had left harbour, I decided that we should open a bottle to try it for taste. It was certainly different. One of my supply officers said, rather unkindly, that it reminded him in appearance, smell, consistency and taste, of the spirit that we used to put in our office duplicator machines. What then were we to do with it? I then remembered that my good friend Hugh Jannion, when captain of a frigate in the Persian gulf and facing a similar situation, had welcomed the wardroom's proposal to use it as a base for a cocktail to be served at the reception that they would hold at the next port visit. When the day came, the captain went ashore in the afternoon to do some local shopping. Whilst he was away, the wardroom steward, realising that he did not have a receptacle large enough in which to mix the cocktail, asked the captain's steward whether he could use his bath for this purpose – there were only showers in the rest of the ship. The captain's steward said he was sure that the captain would not mind.

Hugh Jannion, having returned to the ship rather late, had to change quickly into uniform for the reception. Seeing that his steward had kindly laid out his clothes, he nipped in to his bathroom. Seeing that the bath was full, he jumped in – and very quickly jumped out again! Not a word was said to anyone else; and the party was a great success. But as Hugh Jannion commented afterwards, he "never got crutch rot again."

We then called at the Seychelles islands to refuel from an RFA tanker. Some while before, another RFA tanker had sunk there, having ripped out her bottom on a steep pinnacle of rock. This was not marked on the chart, although apparently local fisherman had known of its existence for many years. I was glad that I had not been aware of this incident when I had taken departure from the Gulf through the very narrow channel some twelve months earlier.

We called briefly at Gan before arriving in Sigapore early in September. One of my first commitments was to call on the Army Commander in Chief, Far East, General Sir David Fraser at. his headquarters at Phoenix Park. I sensed that my reception was a little short of being a warm welcome. When I described to him the ship's amphibious landing and support capabilities, he responded in the sense that those capabilities were not much use to him in the Far East. However, I was aware that his nickname was 'Fraser, the razor'– so I cheerfully remind him that we would be around if he needed us. I thought better of telling him the story of my first digital phone connection from the English Channel to his Headquarters on Labour Day.

Not long after, the General's time as the CINC FE was complete. As part of his farewell, he came to the naval base to say thank you for their support in the particularly difficult circumstances of the Borneo confrontation to a large gathering of all three services, gathered on the flight deck of HMS ALBION. It was a good 'soldierly' speech, though perhaps a trifle long for most sailors. As we all departed back to our ships, I overheard one sailor say to his chum *"Hey Chalkey, I never knew we were commanded by a f***ing General."*. This reminded me that, for most sailors, soldiers and airman, the only 'higher authority' that they normally recognise and respect, other than 'Queen and Country', is their own individual unit commander.

In early September, with the headquarters of 3 Commando Brigade embarked, the ship departed for Borneo for further exercises with the Brunei armed forces. On completion, we returned to Singapore for a brief maintenance period before setting off on the northern circuit, Hong Kong, Korea, and Japan. The highlight was to be a visit to Hiroshima, the first visit there by a foreign warship since the dropping of the atom bomb some twenty-five years before. This was clearly going to be a very sensitive occasion, for Hiroshima had now earned much respect in the international community as the 'Peace City'.

The evening before, as we passed through the Shimonaseki Strait, our elderly and much respected character and doctor, Commander Jack, asked me if he could speak to the ship's company. I agreed of course, but I wondered what he was going to say; perhaps his usual warning to the ships company about venereal disease. *"However, much you think she looks so good, that doesn't mean she must be 'clean',* he used to say. *"But It takes a doctor with his stethoscope to be sure". "So,"* he went on, *"if you see me go ashore with my stethoscope round my neck, you know where I am going."*

On this occasion it was all very different. He told, in fascinating terms, the story of a great schoolboy friend of his and the extraordinary escapades that they got up to together as young men. He himself became a medical student. His friend, Leonard Cheshire, joined the airforce. In due course, with a fine wartime record of bravery and success, his good friend was duly promoted to group captain. One day he was detailed to join the crew of an American B29 named 'Enola Gay' tasked to bomb Hiroshima. In the bomb bay they carried the atom bomb. What he saw and experienced that day, totally changed his life. The war being over, he committed the rest of his years to the care of the lives of others. He was unceasing in his efforts to raise funds for his "Cheshire Homes" which became a byeword for charitable care throughout the UK. It was a truly memorable and totally appropriate speech – and the ship's company listened to every word.

This introduction made a very significant contribution to the undoubted success of this visit, in which I was delighted to be formally welcomed to the city by Miss Hiroshima 1970. Very many of the ship's company visited the Peace Museum and I was able to have a memorable meeting with Mayor Yamada, who was the accepted leader of the World Campaign for Peace. The visit was not without its lighter moments. Following our formal reception in the ship, the wardroom officers decided as a group to visit a Japanese bathhouse. It did not go quite right. Having relaxed in the hot communal bath, they were expecting to have a skilled massage from pretty Japanese girls. Instead, in the words of the commander, they "had little Japanese men running up and down their backs with hob-nailed boots on." However, I and the captain of our accompanying RFA, were offered more personalised treatment - which sounded promising. In the event, we were left to bathe together, but entirely on our own! Nevertheless, it was a memorable visit.

The end of my time in command was fast approaching and after returning to Singapore, I was greatly looking forward to my last visit which was to be to Perth in Western Australia. The juxtaposition of our Hiroshima visit and our forthcoming visit to Perth held particular poignancies for me, having been there when the bomb was dropped. I would, so I hoped, be able to view the beginning of the atomic age through 'both ends of the telescope'. I had already sent ahead my young Royal Marine officer to Perth as iaison officer to pave the way for the visit; and had received his first report. It was a local greetings card, on the outside of which, was a very attractive picture of the local beach, emblazoned with the words *"Come to Sunny Perth"*. You turned the card and inside was printed *"The land of sex, sin and sand"*. You turned the page again to find written prominently *"You never had it so good"*. And on the back were the words *"Or so Often"*. That sounded a very attractive prospect! But it was not to be.

In mid-November, a series of cyclonic storms had led to tidal waves and flooding of very large parts of the Ganges delta with destruction in Bangladesh on a massive scale. INTREPID's visit to Perth was cancelled with the ship being sailed soonest for the Bay of Bengal where she would act as headquarters ship for the very large international relief effort that was being mounted. It was agreed that the handover to my relief, Captain William Staveley, should be advanced and would take place before the ship sailed on the 20th of November.

On the eve of the handover, I went for my last run ashore in Singapore. Returning to the ship at about midnight, I was as usual greeted by the officer of the day. I paused at the top of the gangway and asked, as was my wont- *"All well?"*

"Not really, sir."

What do you mean – not really?"

"Well sir you know that we had a draft of sailors arriving this afternoon by air from UK. One of them went missing."

"So what?"

"Well sir, he was later apprehended by the naval patrol in Sembawang village"(a run ashore spot for sailors just outside the gates of the Naval Base)

"So what?"

"Well sir, it seems that he was very drunk and had got himself into a serious fight with some of the locals. The naval Provost Marshal says that if we hadn't rescued him, they might well have killed him."

"How the hell did he get in such a lot of trouble in such a short time? Has he been out here before or something?"

"I don't know, sir, he is a very curious looking chap. He's got long hair and is very unkempt looking."

"But how did he get on the aeroplane, if he was looking like that?"

"I don't know, sir. But the NPM says that we have got to send him home again before he gets into any more trouble."

"OK"

"But that, sir, means that you have got to see him as a defaulter tomorrow morning."

"Why?"

"Well sir, the NPM says that to send him home on today's flight, he has to be charged with an affray and with departing from his flight without permission. So we have arranged for you to see him as a defaulter at 0900."

"Do I really have to?"

"I think so, sir. The Master of Arms is very keen that you should."

"OK then. Goodnight."

I went to bed feeling rather cross. I had never enjoyed 'defaulters', which some miscreant once described as "imposing injustice with partiality." Just before nine o'clock the next morning, the commander reported to me in my cabin. *"Your defaulter ready, sir"*. As I left the cabin to enter the small compartment across the passage, I noticed a tall and very scruffy looking individual flanked by two patrolmen. When I got a closer look as he was brought in front of me at the table, I was astonished. He was slovenly, unshaven, and had filthy looking hair down to his shoulders.

"Off Cap" ordered the master at arms.

He turned to glare at the 'Master', took off his hat and threw it over his shoulder.

The master at arms read out the charge. *"Do you understand the charge"* *"Naaa."* responded the defaulter as he turned back towards me. I noticed the Regulating Petty officer, standing at the other side of the table, take a small step forward – probably, I thought to try and protect me if the defaulter took a swing at me.

As I looked at this extraordinary creature straight in the eye, I found it difficult to believe what I was seeing and hearing. Then I noticed that the colour of his hair did not seem quite to match his sideburns. Looking again at his hair, I suddenly thought 'he's wearing a wig'. As I looked even more closely at his face, I seemed to recognise his features. I was beginning to smell a rat.

"Haven't we met before." I said.

We stared at each other for several moments. Then I saw a small smile come over his face.

"Are *you by any chance one of my Chief Engineer Artificers?*"

The 'spoof' was out.

But the 'play' was not complete. The doctor came in to explain that the fracas in Sembawang village had been about a woman – and that the defaulter needed to be castrated. The padre said that he thought he should be excommunicated. The engineer officer came in to day that despite all that had happened, he was an excellent worker in the ship - and so on.

As I returned to my cabin, the Commander told me that as he and the master at arms had been waiting outside my cabin for the start, the master had turned to him and said *"What, Sir, shall we do if the 'old man' doesn't think it is funny?"* The next time that the defaulter and I met was some thirty years later when we were together at an HMS COSSACK reunion – and I did not at first recognise him then either!

I left the ship riding in the 'bucket' of the Beach Armoured Recovery Vehicle. I was very sad to leave. But I was happy and confident that the ship's company I was handing over to my successor would be able to meet any unforeseen challenges that the Bangladeshi disaster might throw at them. I took an early flight to Kuala Lumpur, from where I travelled north by car up to the Cameron Highlands for a few days leave at what had been a rest station for the Malaysian State Railways. It was close to the jungle, and in almost every way ideal for winding down – except perhaps that the somewhat primitive nine hole golf course finally confirmed that, whatever prowess I might have at other ball sports, I was never going to become even an adequate golfer.

Chapter 12

Oxford and Flag Rank

"For I also am a man subject to authority, having under me soldiers: and I say unto one "go" and he goeth; and to another "come" and he cometh."

St Luke 7 v. 7-8

Following my application for a year's Defence fellowship at Oxford University, for which the alternative would have been as a student on the year-long course at the Royal College of Defence Studies. I had meanwhile given much thought to what I wanted to do at Oxford. Unlike some of my predecessors there, I did not want to write a book. I wanted time to think about some of the wider issues than those that inevitably dominate the lives of those serving in front-line operational forces. I was becoming particularly interested in the relationship between political and military decision- making.

The British serviceman's allegiance is to "Queen and Country". 'Accepting the Queen's shilling' involves a discipline that brooks no challenge to a lawful order. A serviceman may be ordered by his superior to risk his life, or even to give his life, and there is no lawful right of refusal. He cannot say, "But thank you, no. It is too dangerous." or "Yes, I will do it later; but not now." He has no lawful right to refuse. Under the Queen's Regulations and Admiralty Instructions (QR&AI), such an order can only be given by those in the chain of military command. That of course does not include any member of the Government, not even the Prime Minister or Secretary of State for Defence – nor any civil servant. What then is the relationship between political control and military command in the use of armed force? To throw light on this problem of the structure of political control and operational command, I wanted to look at several past operations, where political and military considerations were closely involved, to see how this relationship worked in practice; and to examine the implications for NATO operations.

The war in Iraq has since raised such issues at the highest level. It is public knowledge that in the run up to the Iraq war, the Chief of Defence wrote formally to the Government seeking reassurance that the proposed action against Sadam Hussein would not contravene international law. The Attorney General's reply has never been made public. Nevertheless, there are a number of senior political and military figures that believe that the action to go to war was illegal. Others, of whom I am one, take the view that the political decision-making process leading to war was deeply and disgracefully flawed, reflecting no credit on the Government, or Parliament. The catastrophic situation in Iraq and more broadly through the Middle East, at the time of the execution of Sadam Hussein, was almost entirely predictable – and was indeed predicted. I address these issues and their implications for the future in Book Three.

Following the provisional acceptance of my application for a year at university, I was invited to London to face an MOD interview board of senior civil servants and the three Service Secretaries. I was at this time of my career more used to being an interviewer rather than an interviewee. I thought I was quite clear what I wanted to do. I was rather less clear about how I was going to do it. But within a time span of a year at university, this did not worry me too much; and I would certainly not be unwilling to take advice. Much of the time of the interview was taken up with the questions as to which university I wished to go, and whom I thought might be asked to supervise my study. This had already been provisionally agreed, so was not too difficult. I was therefore somewhat taken aback when at the very end the military secretary, a senior army officer, went through the various issues that I had stated on my application that I wanted to study and said, *"And at the end, I imagine you would wish to draw conclusions?"* *"Yes, of course."* I replied. *"What then are the conclusions that you are going to draw?"*

I was somewhat non-plussed by this. I could only respond *"If I knew that, I should not be asking for a year at Oxford to study the problem."* On that note, the interview ended.

I was particularly delighted to find a place at Oxford at University College. The master of the college was Lord Maud, whom I greatly admired. The bursar was a retired naval officer, Peter Gretton, a most distinguished anti-submarine group commander in the Battle of the Atlantic in the Second World War. My supervisor was to be Michael Howard, the very distinguished military historian, a Fellow of All Souls.

I rapidly discovered that the pace and form of life at Oxford was very different from anything I had known before. I was privileged to be in *status professori* rather than *status studenti;* but nevertheless it was different. The college was most welcoming and I began to learn the form. At dinner in Hall each evening, the dons assembled in the anteroom before proceeding to join the high table. I discovered that there was a strict order of seniority to be rigorously adhered to. I certainly had no idea that, in the academic world, there was such a rigid pecking order. However, this suited me well, since I was the junior don and the senior (and only) naval officer and, in my book, I came last on both counts. The shuffling for order took some time, which usually allowed me to have a second gin and tonic.

At that time, one of the issues which was perplexing the colleges of the university was the admission of women to the traditionally men's colleges. It was a matter of heated discussion, in which views were deeply divided. There were three general views – the first that women should be admitted; the second that women should not be admitted; and the third that women might be admitted, but not yet. University College generally lay in the third category.

On one evening at high table I was sitting opposite a young psychology don whose lifestyle was, at least on the surface, very different to that which I was used to – in as much as he carried a handbag and wore earrings. We were discussing over dinner the admission of women. "I think it would be terrible" he said, "It would be the end of rowing." I could not respond to that. It seemed to me that there were many facets of the argument, for and against, but I had not foreseen that one. I could perhaps have imagined such a response coming from a very elderly don sitting in his armchair in the Oxford and Cambridge Club in London – but not from the young academic sitting opposite me.

After a short spell living in digs, I was allocated a very adequate room at the rear of the college. This was very convenient to me as it was close to the real tennis court, a game that, as a member of Queen's Club, I had learnt in London and much enjoyed. It is quite unlike lawn tennis in almost every way; including that it can only be played in an indoor court yard built especially for the game. The game is also not very interesting to watch, unless you know a great deal about the rules and the scoring system. It is a game that is a great test of character. In brief, there are two opportunities of winning or losing any point. And the win or lose decision may rest with the honesty of either player when he has to 'call' your shot better (you win), or worse (he wins), in relation to how far it bounces, on the second bounce from the rear wall of the server's court in relation to your own shot.! This procedure involves the players having to change ends. The court then rings with cries such as "better than four yards", or "worse than two and a half", as the former receiver calls his opponent's shot. The opportunities for a little cheating are legion. The game is also one of very considerable skill in being able to impart spin to the ball. The court is also surrounded by hazards that can make the ball fly off in all sorts of different directions – or just drop dead. If you know the rules thoroughly, it is fun. If you don't, it is usually total confusion!

My programme at the university was nobody's business but my own. I determined that I would share in university life as much as possible. I therefore went to occasional lectures, spent time browsing in the Bodlean, played tennis, helped exercise and hunt the Christchurch beagles, and joined the small group of young naval officers who were at the university in *status studenti* at the East Gate pub on Thursday evenings. On Friday afternoon I went home. In my spare time, I researched my subject – not infrequently in the MoD archives in London.

My first task was to select the first military operation that had political overtones, to see if and how the element of political control inter-acted with the military decisions. I chose the situation in 1963-64, relating to the British military intervention in the insurrections that threatened the governments of Tanganyika and other East African countries following their earlier independence from Britain. In the one amphibious operation, 45 Commando RM, embarked in an aircraft carrier, was despatched from Aden in early 1964 to land at Dar es Salaam. I was astonished to find in the Ministry of Defence, archives, a substantially full record of all the signals that were sent within the force and between London and the force throughout the operation, which was a complete success. It was a story that could have formed the basis for an interesting book in its own right. Despite its eventual success, it went through some difficult phases – such as on the second morning at sea when the senior officer of the Royal Marines had to tell the Force Commander that they had forgotten to bring their small arms ammunition. A whip round of the ammunition outfits of the small ships of the force fortunately found enough rounds to cover at least the early phases of the operation.

The operation was completed in about three months. In the event very few shots had to be fired. I was fascinated by this story and became the greatest living expert on this particular operation. However, after a while, I realised that I had made little headway in what I was really concerned with, which was the interplay of the political and military factors. I had to recall the American expression "If you are up to your arse in alligators, it is easy to forget that the reason you are there is to drain the swamp".

In the middle of the summer I was somewhat rudely awakened from the tranquillity of academic life. I was called to London to see the naval secretary. To my complete surprise and astonishment, he told me that I was being selected for promotion to Rear Admiral with effect from January 1st, 1971. In the normal course, promotion to Flag Rank came only after eight years service as a captain. It was then 'up or out'. I only had five years seniority as a captain. He explained that the First Sea Lord, Admiral Le Fanu, was concerned that, in the process of selection at the most senior level of the Chief of Defence, it was very difficult to provide the series of senior appointments that would permit the candidates to have gained a sufficient breadth of experience when it came to selection for the very top jobs. He had therefore decided to dip down the captains' list. Since it might be seen to be inequitable to choose only one, two were to be chosen. I was lucky enough to be one. The other was a good friend of mine, Jock Miller, who was just a little bit older and more senior than I. I was told that on no account was I to speak to anyone on this before the official announcement was made.

Not long afterwards, however, whilst walking down Whitehall I happened to run into Jock whom I had not seen for some years. We looked closely at each other with a look that hopefully said, "Do you know what I know? And do you know what I think you ought to know?" The answers were "Yes". We talked about what we each would like to do in our next job as an admiral. My choice was to go to sea. His reply, which surprised me, was in the sense that the last thing he wanted to do was to go to sea again. I did not understand this, particularly because he was a specialist seaman officer - a 'salt horse'. I was unfortunately rather dismissive of his doubts. In the event, he did get a seagoing command as a Flag Officer; but after about a year, he had to be removed from his appointment for health reasons. This was a tragedy. It was only then that I recalled our conversations in Whitehall and realised that his doubts reflected his concern that, by going to sea, he would find himself in command of captains who might now have far more sea-going experience than him. He was retired from the Navy, and not long after died a sudden death at a formal dinner at which Princess Anne was the guest of honour. This was a further tragedy.

I had further surprises in store. The naval secretary sent for me again to discuss my next appointment. The First Sea Lord, he said, was planning for me *to be DGFS. "How would that suit?"*

This 'title' had a vaguely familiar ring about it, but I had to say, "*I am sorry, I don't even know what the letters stand for.*"

He told me that I was to be the Director General of Fleet Support. I was now not much the wiser. It transpired, however, that he had got it wrong and the proper title of my next appointment would be the Assistant Chief of Fleet Support (ACFS). The Chief of Fleet Support, Vice Admiral Sir Alan Trewby, a distinguished engineer, was a member of the Admiralty Board and responsible for all aspects of the material upkeep of the fleet, including the five Royal dockyards. I was not inexperienced as a customer of the dockyards – but was usually critical of them for delays to completion of their work on ships, delays that seemed to be the rule rather than the exception. Nevertheless, I looked forward to changing sides and now becoming a provider of support.

Not long after the announcement of my new appointment, Alan Trewby was hospitalised. This was the second occasion that a boss of mine had suffered such a mishap. I had only to hope that it was not my appointment that caused it. The effect of this was that his Assistant would take over full responsibilities of CFS; and I would take over as the Assistant as soon as practicable.

At this stage of my Oxford study, I had had time to do all the thinking and reading that I required. All I had left to do was to set out my ideas on paper. I cheerfully said that I thought I would be able to do this in about six months, whilst at the same time carrying the full responsibilities of my new job. I therefore agreed to take up my new appointment in the late autumn. In the event, my paper entitled "The Management of Force"[17] was not finally completed and reviewed until I was once again at sea in the spring of 1976.

In that paper, I set out the problems involved in the interplay of political and military factors for the command and control of military operations in the context of NATO. I was delighted to

---

[17] *A copy is retained in the Eberle papers lodged with the Liddel Hart Military Archives at Kings College, London*

receive a personal letter from Admiral of the Fleet Lord Mountbatten warmly endorsing the results of my labours, describing my paper as "of great interest" and commenting that he "would have liked to go a lot further in reorganising the MOD, and the three service ministries and Chiefs of Staff". He said he regarded his reforms, made when he was Chief of the Defence staff, "as a first step"; bearing in mind that he was already "extremely unpopular with the conventional admirals, generals and air marshals." I also subsequently received a personal endorsement of my work from Admiral Ike Kidd USN, then the Supreme NATO Commander Atlantic, describing it as the best paper he had read on the command of NATO military operations. I was later to observe in NATO operations in the Balkans the impact of the practical problems that I had tried to address. It was regrettably clear that little if any progress towards their solution had been achieved in the meantime.

The problem of being an "assistant" or "deputy" is that your job is what your boss says it is. However, in my case, as Assistant Chief of Fleet Support, I had two clear areas that were entirely my responsibility. The first was the Fleet Maintenance Organisation. At each of our dockyards, whose principal workforce was entirely civilian, we also had developed a series of Fleet Maintenance Units (FMUs), manned by naval officers and ratings under the command of a naval captain. These were responsible for the upkeep of the Fleet in between ships' refits, the latter being the responsibility of the dockyards. Normally, ships' refits occurred about once every three to four years.

A matter which was initially of concern to me as ACFS was the potential impact on the tasks of the Fleet Maintenance Units of the new ships coming into service which would be fitted with gas turbine engines for their main propulsion rather than the steam turbines that had previously powered our major warships. If the failure rate of these new engines in their new marine environment, was greater than had been forecast, then engine changes between ships' refits could bring a sharp drop in operational readiness of the Fleet and a very formidable new load on our FMU's, with engine changes having to be undertaken at very little notice anywhere around the world. In the event, my fears were unfounded. The change from steam to gas, an initiative which had been the brainchild of Sir Alan Trewby, was an outstanding success.

The change from steam to gas also required major changes in the maintenance procedures within the ships themselves. In the steam era, maintenance often required large spanners and heavy hammers – and if these fell in the bilges during use, that was often where they stayed. For gas turbine maintenance, as the Royal Air Force had learnt, it was very important that there should be strict control over any tools that came near a gas turbine engine. A small spanner left inside such an engine could prove very costly! We therefore now had to imbue our steam-trained mechanic engineers with a new philosophy of tool control, where every tool had its place in the tool kit – with the kit being checked at the end of every stage of maintenance. At the same time, we were introducing into the fleet a new much improved system for identifying and obtaining the spare parts for all naval machinery. They were to be listed and identified in new documents called a Parts Identification List (PIL).

It became fashionable for maintainers to ask of their colleagues, "Are you on the pill?" I wanted a similar catch phrase with which to introduce the new tool control system. I wanted to refer to it as the Task Integrated Tool System (TITS). Some measly-minded civil servant, without my knowledge, vetoed this.

A second area of my department's work was that of the Naval Air Repair Organisation (NARO). Under the direction of a senior naval air engineer, NARO directed the work of a number of air repair yards in appropriate parts of the county. The latter were under naval command but were manned by a very professional and mainly civilian work-force. They carried out the repair and maintenance of all naval fixed wing and rotary wing aircraft and overhaul of their engines. The organisation was efficient and effective.

One of our repair yards, Sydenham, was in Belfast. There were, as always, strong pressures within the MoD to reduce costs – and one of the savings measures for the following year's defence budget was the closure of this yard. We in the Navy were strongly against this, for there was no operational justification for its closure. I had visited the yard myself and was impressed by the commitment and performance of the workforce. I also noted that on the adjacent airfield there were an exceptionally large number of hares. This I found interesting, because recently I had seen a similar large population on the Dutch airfield at Schirpol. Why did hares find airfields so attractive? On leaving, I discussed the matter with the airfield maintenance staff, musing that the Irish hare was of a different sub-species to the English hare and commenting that it would be interesting to see if the two would interbreed.

Back in London, the battle to save Sydenham continued. Sadly, the Navy lost and ministers directed that the yard be closed. I was designated as the one who must break the news on site before the formal press announcement was to be made. Accordingly, I again flew to Belfast. On arrival, I was greeted with a strong demonstration with the chairman of The Trade Union Whitley Committee telling me in his strong Irish brogue that, "You have achieved today what the bombers have failed to achieve in the last twenty years - A WALK OUT OF THE WORKFORCE."

It was a very emotional moment, not only for the workforce, but also for myself. Nearly all of the employees had worked in the 'naval family' for many years. They had been loyal and effective. I knew that in the prevailing situation in Northern Ireland, there would be some who would almost certainly never get another job. Despite this, my meeting with the trade unions was restrained and workmanlike. The die had been cast; and they and I knew that sadly there was nothing effective that could now be done.

After lunch, as I walked towards my aircraft which was ready to depart, a workman came slowly towards me carrying a stout cardboard box. I admit that I felt just a little anxious; but as he came close to me, he said, in a broad Irish brogue, *"We were up at four o'clock this morning to catch these for you, sir. I'm not sure whether they are rabbits or hares. But you are very welcome to them - and you can forget about any paper work."* "I took the box and looked inside. There were four half grown leverets. Having thanked him most warmly, I handed the box to the WRNS cabin crew. *"Please take great care of these. Apart from you and I, these are the most valuable cargo on the plane."*

Immediately after arrival home, I set them free in an appropriate place on a local South Hams farm. I shall never know whether those leverets survived and bred. I rather suspect not. But I shall forever remember the kind-heartedness of those Irishmen.

It was in my 'watch' as ACFS, that the naval catering scandal was unearthed. The caterer of a ship was authorised to purchase the items of fresh provisions direct from a shore side civilian supplier. For a big ship the quantities were large. It transpired that widespread fraud was being conducted by the supplier manipulating the quantities or quality of the provisions being delivered, relative to those entered on the invoice. This was concealed by the payment of substantial kick-backs, in cash personally and privately to the ship's caterer, who was of course responsible for checking and entering the delivery in the ship's provision account.

This practice had become so widespread for so long that it became accepted by caterers throughout the Fleet as standard practice. It was of course thoroughly dishonest and illegal. Then one honest man blew the whistle; and a thorough investigation revealed the widespread nature of this practice. There followed a number of civilian court actions and naval courts martial that naturally attracted much attention in the national and local press. This caused a dent in the public perception of 'Honest Jolly Jack', and did the Navy no good. It was a shameful episode.

A senior member of the Navy Board commented, "I am astonished that the naval catering branch managed to 'keep the hat on' such malpractice for so long. If I have a particular matter in my office that I would prefer to keep private, I normally find that, in a very short time, it has become common knowledge throughout the MoD."

A major task of my department was in the field of administrative automatic data processing (ADP). The Navy, the Army and the Air Force, each working independently, had already introduced the new technology of digital data processing in the fields of personnel management and stores control. The systems were in general were working well and the field was set for further expansion.

The Government, noting the potential for all government departments, had set up a Central Computer Agency (CCA) in order to provide a single point of expertise and experience and advice. The MoD, following this lead, decided that there should be an Administrative ADP Working Party to coordinate its policy and practice throughout the three services and their supporting civil agencies. For reasons that I did not fully understand at the time, and still do not understand, I was made chairman of this committee. One of our first tasks was to communicate with the major international computer companies to obtain their advice as to the general direction in which we might proceed. Without exception their forecast for the future was that the cost of computing hardware would decrease with the increasing power of computers, and that software would become cheap. This was a clear victory for the 'maxi', rather than the 'mini'. It pointed strongly to the development of large computer bureaux that would centralise computer power for all MoD users via a country-wide network of high speed data links.

It rapidly became clear that for the prime reasons of security and capacity, it would be necessary to have a number of such large bureaux throughout the country, all linked with high speed data links. The CCA supported this policy and the construction of the first of these central bureaux was approved at Devizes in Wiltshire. It was known as Bureau West. The principal naval bureau which was then in successful operation nearby in Bath, was under the charge of the Director General of Stores and Transport (Naval), a department belonging to the Chief of Fleet

Support. It was not long before conflict arose between the two establishments over the question of where further naval applications then in development should be run, Bath or Devizes. The decision clearly had local staffing implications. It also had wider implications for the principle of the 'maxi bureau' concept.

Within the local staff of these two bureaux, ill feelings began to grow. Fortunately the managers of the two projects, a Dr Nutter and Dr Wright, were made of sterner stuff and successfully promoted cooperation and competition between the two establishments. A part of the agenda was the organisation of a road relay race between Bath and Devizes for members of the two staffs. This received considerable support, encouraged by a handsome trophy for the winner that was named the 'Wright Nutter' Cup. The origin of this little problem was, of course, the totally wrong short-term prediction of the computer industry that it was the 'maxi' that would at that time clear the board.

Nevertheless, although very small computers, such as laptops, were then not even on the far horizon, my department was closely involved in the use of administrative ADP in operational ships, with an internally generated project known as the Ship Upkeep Information System (SUIS). Despite very strong project leadership, the system became too ambitiously complex and fell the victim of financial pressures.

A government agency with which I became involved was the Property Services Agency (PSA). As ACFS, I was responsible for the Navy works programme. With major shore training facilities and five naval dockyards, the naval programme ran in excess of one hundred million pounds a year. The PSA was responsible for its implementation. In addition to the Army and Air Force, the PSA had many other large government customers. The customer-supplier relationship was an important one.

I had already had some difficulty with our relationship with Ove Arrup, a well renowned architectural group, over their proposed design of a new ship refitting dock at Portsmouth dockyard. Their design, which was elegant and innovative, had been accepted.

After construction was complete, Ove Arrup asked for naval support for submitting this design in some prestigious European architectural competition. I refused on the grounds that, in practice, the design had turned out to be far from satisfactory. The maintenance teams in the refitting ship and in the dockyard just did not like it. Despite some pressure at the highest level, I refused to change my mind. "I accept that it is elegant, innovative and looks great," I wrote, "It just doesn't work very well." That ended the argument as far as I was concerned.

Good customer-supplier relations are important to both customer and supplier. It was very appropriate therefore that the then chief executive of the PSA, Sir John Cuckney, called a large-scale conference to discuss the PSA-customer relationship. I attended representing the navy. Despite the attendance of the departmental minister, the conference did not go well. After a little while, it seemed to me that the customer was being largely ignored in the discussion. It became clear that there was a fundamental divergence of view within the agency between its two disciplines. There were the 'professional' professionals - the architects; and also the professional administrators – the civil servants. The architects said that they did not understand why the agency required professional administrators – administration was part of the training and practice of architects. The professional administrators said that they did not need architects within the agency. They could go out to contract to get all the professional architectural skills that were needed. In this internecine struggle, the customer hardly got a look in!

This event brought home to me in this, my first senior level job in the Ministry of Defence, how lucky we were not to have a problem of this order. Within the MoD, we had the professional professionals, who were the serving officers; and we had a large cadre of civil servants who were the professional administrators. On the whole we got on very well together and worked well together, a relationship that had developed over many years. There were nevertheless occasional small exceptions.

In my earlier job on the naval staff, the Navy Department had been housed in the Old Admiralty building in Whitehall. Now all departments of the Ministry came under one roof of the large building which stands, figuratively of course, on the opposite side of the road to the Treasury, the Foreign Office and No. 10. In the centre of this building are four large conference rooms labelled Historic Rooms 1, 2, 3 and 4. Soon after the Navy had moved to the other side of the road, I had attended a meeting in one of the historic rooms on some rather boring subject chaired by a particularly dull and elderly civil servant.

He wasn't doing very well. My mind wandered. I am an inveterate note-passer at meetings. Having surveyed the room with some care, I passed a note to my unknown neighbour on my right, "Do you know what is historic about this room?" "Not really" he scribbled in reply. I tried again, "Could it be the Chairman?" I asked. He responded "Possibly," to which I added, "I rather think not, because he's hysterical rather than historical." I thought no more about this when I left the meeting, leaving my note on the table. The next morning my secretary came in with this piece of paper in his hand and said "I have an infuriated civil servant in my office outside who wants to know if this is your handwriting." I looked at it closely and said, "I think it's a very clever forgery." I learnt something about the civil service from that; and also that I should never leave my notes on the table.

Whilst the job of ACFS had not perhaps been the most exciting, and was not the sea job that I had hoped for, I believe it was an inspired piece of appointing for me. I was not particularly stretched, and on this my first job on the Flag list, I had had the time and opportunity to acclimatize myself to the ways of the Ministry of Defence at the higher levels. I enjoyed it because that is what life is all about.

Chapter 13

At Sea again - FOST and FOCAS

The personal problem with reaching Flag Rank is that thereafter, further promotion is on the basis of 'up or out'. I was delighted therefore to hear that I would get another job – and that this would be as Flag Officer Sea Training (FOST) at Portland. This was a task very much to my own heart. The FOST organisation was responsible for the basic and advanced operational training of all the Navy's destroyers and frigates.

Its origin was in the work-up base at Tobermoray in World War II, which provided operational training for the many small ships that carried out convoy and anti-submarine operations in the Atlantic. It built up a fearsome reputation, with the training staff seemingly bent on showing the captain that his ship was hardly in a fit state to go to sea safely; and certainly not to join in the war. It was a hard, critical but necessary routine – there was a war on. Tobermoray's post-war successors, the training staff at Portland, whilst carrying out a similar task in peacetime, succeeded in changing that reputation to one of an organisation that was there to assist and support the ship in trying to reach the highest levels of operational readiness; and was not there just to find fault and to criticise. Nevertheless, FOST remained a challenge for commanding officers and their ships' companies at every level of the ship's organisation, for peace or for war.

My immediate predecessors had made great strides in this constructive approach, and I was determined to continue it. Of course it was necessary to stretch the ship's company and to give them confidence that they were capable of dealing with any problem that they might face. The key to the operational efficiency and effectiveness of any ship was the commanding officer. The FOST training organisationwas therefore led by the commander Sea Training (CST). He was supported by a substantial staff of experienced senior ratings, known as the 'Sea Riders'. They were themselves experts at all the varied tasks that are required to run a fighting ship. They were there at sea every day instructing and encouraging the ship's staff. The CST's role was central. Being of commander's rank, like most of the commanding officers, he was able to talk to them as a friend as well as a critic. I was particularly lucky in having an excellent CST, Commander Barry Wilson.

When I visited a ship at sea, which I did as frequently as possible, I regarded my role as to sit and listen, so that I could present to my CST a separate view of the ship and how it was being run. I therefore spent the vast majority of my time at sea, either on the bridge, in the operations room or walking around talking to sailors. I also enjoyed occasionally taking part in one of the set piece exercises that ships were required to undertake. One of these was a simulation of a colonial island, suffering severe internal problems, where the Governor had sought the assistance of one of HM ships to help restore stability and security. In such a situation it was necessary for the governor formally to request military assistance. In the exercise, therefore, a member of the staff, taking the part of the governor, would board the ship to discuss the situation and agree appropriate action.

For this one occasion I decided to take the part of the governor. My personal assistant, a very pleasant, very attractive and most efficient Wren officer, asked if she could come with me as the governor's lady. I agreed to that, and that she would take her little cairn dog with her. I abandoned my naval uniform and put on a tailcoat and top hat. Mary dressed accordingly. The three of us survived the boat journey to the ship and mounted the ship's ladder. I had not informed the commanding officer that I was personally taking the part of the governor and it was not until my PA and her dog got to the top of the ladder that he fully realised who I was. We then went down to the wardroom. This move was not a great success because Mary's dog crapped on the wardroom carpet. We retired to the captain's cabin. All was then signed and sealed, and Mary, dog and I prepared to depart. I had agreed that the ship's first action was to mount an armed guard on my residence ashore - which for exercise purposes was my office.

As we went ashore, the ship had acted speedily, and an armed sentry barred the entrance to my office. As I approached he ordered me to halt in the approved manner, and asked for my identity. I said I was the governor, Sir James Eberle, and showed him my identity card. He then asked Mary for her identity. She had not foreseen this problem and had left her identity card in the office. I sprang to her assistance and said firmly to the sentry *"That's all right my man. She is my lady and I have her identity card here."* In my pocket I always had a second identity card that I had had made to test the vigilance of sentries. On it was a photograph of a gorilla and it was in the name of 'A Terrorist'. I showed this to the sentry. He looked at the photograph on the card; and then, looking at Mary, said, "Yes, Maam, that'll be alright." My PA nearly killed me when we got back inside to the office, for she was indeed a most attractive looking girl.

One of the particular pleasures of the command was that we also undertook operational sea training tasks for the Dutch and German navies. This added a particular spice to the task of the Sea Riders. Most of the Dutch spoke fluent English; the Germans didn't. Much of the German equipment was also somewhat different to that of the RN and the Netherlands' Navy. Nevertheless, the principles remained much the same.

Some of the exercises that we mounted were essentially initiative tests. These were locally known as 'FOST funnies'. The occasion was a summer's evening on which my staff and I were taking part in a very pleasant reception on the sports ground adjacent to the base. Towards the end of the party, I decided that it was an opportunity for me to practice fly fishing, a discipline that was to be required of me in a forthcoming field sports event. As a target for my fly, I was using a circular life buoy. Unbeknown to me, one of my staff sent an immediate signal to a German ship alongside the pier, saying that there was a madman at large on the playing fields who was trying to catch fish on dry land. The German sense of humour interpreted this rather more seriously than as a FOST funny. In a very short time a landrover appeared at high speed and, before I really knew what was happening, I was bundled to the ground by two hefty German sailors and strapped straight-jacket-like into a Neil Robertson stretcher. It took rather a long time to persuade the Germans that this was an exercise that was now over.

I believe we provided a very good service to our NATO partners – but it was one sadness for me that we never persuaded the US Navy to send one of their ships for work-up. As usual the Dutch were particularly good value and generally extremely efficient. I was delighted therefore when I was told that the Inspector General of the Dutch Navy, Prince Bernhardt, the husband of the Queen of the Netherlands, was to visit Portland to see the Dutch ships performing under the FOST organisation. He was coming on his own and had asked to stay overnight at my house.

The admiral's house was of a modern, modest nature but fully adequate for its purpose. As a still rather junior admiral I was a little nervous at having a member of a royal family to stay in my house. The time of the visit was the spring. As I returned to my house one evening in my car, driven by my coxswain, I remarked that it was a pity that HRH was coming at a time of the year when little grew in the bleakness of a Portland winter. In the summer, my garden could look quite nice – but not at this time of year. My coxswain, whom I knew as Chief Petty Officer 'Pertwee' (adherents to the BBC radio programme The Navy Lark will understand the significance of this) was a marvellous man who looked after me in every way that he thought appropriate for an admiral. He was 'Mr Fixit' personified. I never asked him if he had an Uncle Ebenezer – because I knew he must have. I had, for instance, to be very careful not to comment favourably on almost any attractive object which we passed within the naval base or in some other officer's garden; because the next thing I knew was that it had been 'rescued' into my own garden.

About two days before Prince Bernhardt was due to arrive; I noticed my garden was ablaze with colour. *"Coxswain,"* I said, *"What's all this?"*

"Well, sir," he replied, *"I remember what you said the other day about the garden – and I've got a friend in the Parks Department at Weymouth."*

After a short discussion about the permanence of all these plants he said, *"They are all planted in pots sir, and when Prince Bernhardt leaves they can all be returned to Weymouth."*

"Thank you, coxswain that's splendid - but what is it all going to cost me?" *"That's all right sir,"* he said *"A couple of bottles of whisky will put that right."*

I can't remember whether Prince Bernhardt commented on the garden or not. I expect he did; but if he didn't I'm sure I told my coxswain that he had.

Although I was able to do a little bit of appropriate entertaining in the house it was little more than a place for me to rest my head during the week. We deliberately kept the weekend free for all the ships to relax after a hectic week – and I was able to go home to the farm on Dartmoor. Apart from VIP guests such as Prince Bernhardt and Princess Margaret, who came accompanied by her two young children for them to spend a day at sea, I was able to accommodate overnight quite a large number of other interesting visitors. One of these was one of the BBC's top outside TV presenters. He was good fun and we gave him a very good account of our work. Having spent the day at sea with him, we sat up late in my house discussing the world and what he had seen during the day.

Not unreasonably, and from time to time, he referred to television programmes, to which I was forced to reply, "I'm sorry, I didn't see that – I don't have a television." In a very nice thank you letter that I received some days later, he wrote, "I didn't believe you when you said you didn't have a television – but I have to admit that I searched your house before I left and you were speaking the truth. I hadn't imagined that there was anyone in England that didn't have a television set in the house." Such was the pace of life during the week at Portland.

On many occasions I would go to sea overnight and was thus able to take part in some outside activities during the day. I kept a horse at the nearby Royal Armoured Corps camp at Bovington, which ran an Army Saddle Club. From time to time, therefore, I was able to have a day's hunting, usually with the South Dorset hounds. My PA, Mary, knew nothing about horses or hunting and asked me if she could come with me one day, driving my landrover. I was delighted and determined that she should enjoy it and hopefully be impressed. We drove to Bovington. I hitched up my trailer and loaded the horse.

Off we set towards the meet. In the middle of the camp there was a deep dip in the road at the bottom of which was a military police post. Happy to be on time and 'on course', I drove down the hill towards the police post. As I was nearing the bottom, I was somewhat surprised to see one of the military policemen making rather peculiar and urgent looking signs in my direction. I continued on, to start mounting the hill the other side. We had gone only a couple of hundred yards when I remarked to Mary, *"My landrover's pulling very well today."* I then happened to looked in my mirror and, to my horror, there was my horsebox some fifty yards behind me heading in a somewhat different direction. This was not a good start to the day or to my wish to impress. The trailer had disconnected itself because I had failed to screw down the hitch. Fortunately the safety wire had done its job and put on the trailer's brake. The trailer veered gently into the side of the road waiting for me to recover it. The rest of the day went well – but I don't think Mary trusted my ability outside the Navy any longer.

The effective movement of key Sea Riders from ship to ship was only made possible by the major use of helicopters from the nearby Portland Naval Air Station. I myself used them a great deal and from time to time was able to get some experience in the front seat alongside the pilot, which I greatly enjoyed.

However, for most of my time I was dangling from a wire from the rear cabin up or down to the deck of the ship below. One visitor, who had not before undergone this experience, remarked later that he found it an interesting phenomenon as he dangled in mid air, that the diameter of the wire attaching him to the helicopter, seemed to decrease as the height of the helicopter above the ground rose.

I was not however subjected to the experience of my successor. Relaxing in the rear cabin after a long day at sea, he sensed the helicopter coming to a low hover. They were then some ten miles south of Portland Bill. He was rather surprised when the air crewman started trying to push him out of the open door. He did not react well to what he thought was an exercise, perhaps a FOST funny. Admirals were usually excused FOST funnies. However, he realised that something else was amiss when the air crewman jumped out with him, to be followed rapidly by the appearance of the helicopter's rubber dinghy. They were glad to see the helicopter move over before it fell into the sea and turned upside down – helicopters have a habit of doing this when they fall in the sea. The pilot fortunately also got out. When the three of them had sorted themselves into the dinghy the admiral, seeking to relieve any tension, asked the air crewman how long he thought it would be before the duty air sea rescue helicopter came to pick them up. The air crewman replied, *"I'm sorry, sir, we were the duty air sea rescue helicopter."* Fortunately it was a warm, calm evening and they did not have too long to wait.

The normal period for a ship's operational sea training (OST) was seven weeks, at the end of which a ship was assessed as either very satisfactory (v.sat) or satisfactory (sat). In my time I had never to consider a failure. The passing out test took place every Thursday in what we called "The Thursday War". This was a full-scale operational exercise with all the ships at Portland involved, and included air, surface and sub-surface operations. It was demanding – but there were many commanding officers that would say that, although they had not looked forward to the day, they did actually enjoy it. It was in this sense, the achievement of well-justified self-confidence, which gave me personally the greatest satisfaction.

I left Portland riding in uniform on the back of a horse, which to my complete surprise had been arranged by my staff. I cheerily waved farewell, happy that my time at FOST had been both a thoroughly enjoyable and rewarding experience; and happy also that my next job was to be at sea as the Flag Officer Aircraft Carriers and Amphibious Ships (FOCAS). Junior Flag Officers were fortunate to get one sea job, let alone two. This appointment also carried with it a NATO command role within the Atlantic Strike Fleet as NATO Commander Carrier Strike Group 2 (COMCARGRU 2) – later to become COMASWGRU2.

I was the first non-aviator to be appointed as FOCAS, an essentially aviator orientated job. Inevitably there were a few old time pilots who saw this as a seriously retrograde step due to my lack of time in the cockpit. My achievement of a provisional pilot's licence on Tiger Moths did not, understandably, seem of much relevance. I had as my chief of staff a very experienced and widely respected aviator, Captain Lynn Middleton. At Fort Southwick at the back of Portsmouth I had a shore headquarters with full and effective staff support. I was also privileged to have the use of a flat in one of the nearby forts. This was very convenient. However, being responsible for the operational efficiency of all the ships of the squadron – the big ships did not go to Portland for sea training - I fully intended to spend most of my time in the aircraft carriers and amphibious landing ships of the squadron, at sea. Having recently commanded HMS INTREPID, one of four major units in the amphibious fleet, I was reasonably happy that I was familiar and up-to-date with most, if not all, aspects of amphibious operations.

Having settled myself in with my shore based staff at Fort Southwick, I hoisted my Flag In HMS EAGLE for the quadrennial major NATO live maritime exercise. The UK Carrier Strike Group, was to operate as part of a major NATO strike force carrying out flight operations in the north Norwegian Sea. This was an area of key strategic interest in the event of war with the Soviet Union.

EAGLE was positioned some way to the south of the two US carriers operating combat air patrol (CAP) and anti-submarine warfare (ASW) flight operations.

I was aware that our presence in this area might well provoke a Soviet response. As we continued to steer north, reports started to come in from the US carriers ahead of us of Soviet long-range reconnaissance aircraft in their area. Not long after, a large force of Soviet anti-ship missile armed aircraft was reported closing on the force from the north. All this represented a scenario, which we had frequently 'gamed' on the tactical exercise floor. I was not overly concerned – not least because my EAGLE force was still some way outside the missile range of the Soviet aircraft. Nevertheless, it became increasingly apparent that the Americans were not at all sure that the Soviets were regarding this as an exercise. In due course, the Soviet strike aircraft turned north for home without firing any missiles; and a sense of greater calm prevailed.

I was more than a little surprised at the American reaction that seemed to me to be somewhat over the top. From subsequent discussions, it became clear that the Americans must have been monitoring and reading the air-to-air and air-to-base communications of the Soviet strike aircraft. Whilst I am in no doubt that it was not the Soviet intention to go to war in this situation, the realism with which they conducted this exercise was such that it raised doubts in the minds of the US Force Command that it might perhaps be for real. In the British Force I had neither the equipment, nor the trained operators, to undertake such a communication monitoring task.

I next flew my flag at sea in HMS HERMES heading for the Mediterranean where the ship, in the role of a helicopter assault ship, was to take part in a major NATO amphibious exercise, 'Deep Express'. The exercise was to take place in September 1975 in the Aegean Sea. It was to be the largest amphibious landing since D-Day with a task force of thirty five ships with about five thousand men from five different nations. Prior to the exercise, the Task Force gathered off Anatalya in southern Turkey.

As a consequence of the bad relations between the two NATO allies, Greece and Turkey, it had not been possible to agree on an American command for this operation in such a very politically and militarily sensitive area which involved an amphibious landing into Turkish Thrace.

The command task therefore fell to the UK. I was left carrying the baby. However, I became increasingly concerned at the very primitive command arrangements – 'perspex and chinagraph' in my flagship. Accordingly, and being personally ready to grab opportunities if they present themselves, I signalled to the US Sixth Fleet commander, Admiral Fox Turner, in Naples, for approval to exercise command, and fly my flag, from one of the suitable US warships due to take part. I was very pleasantly surprised to get early approval and allocating the USS JOSEPHUS DANIELS (DLG27) for this task. I was even more surprised, but delighted, to be told that an officer from the DANIELS would be coming on board HERMES to brief me.

During the afternoon, I was made aware that there was an urgent requirement to return one of our sailors to the UK on compassionate grounds. Due to congestion at the small local airfield, there seemed little hope of getting him away quickly. Nevertheless, I asked our naval attaché from Ankara, who was with me, to take the man ashore and see what he could do. Some hours later, the attaché returned to the ship and told me that the man was now on his way to the UK. *"Well done"* I said. *"How the hell did you manage that? I thought that all the flights were fully booked." Yes sir, they were."*

"Well how did you get him away?" "I persuaded the authorities to take off another guy, an American."

"How did you do that?" "I had more whisky than he had!"

The briefing that I received from the young officer from the USS DANIELS was short, professional and fascinating. He told me that he had approval from Washington to brief me on some special equipment fitted in the ship. In short, what he described seemed to me to be a ship-borne tactical version of equipment capable of carrying out many of the local intelligence tasks performed in Britain by the GCHQ Cheltenham. GCHQ Cheltenham, which I had visited on a previous occasion, is best described as the British listening centre for intelligence in the field of international political and military communication, including code breaking and links to facilities for direction and position finding. The US shipboard equipment was codenamed 'Classic Outboard'.

Many years before, at the end of the war in the Pacific, I had been aware of the 'Y' organisation that intercepted and monitored Japanese naval communications. Following the war, it seemed to me that the Navy abandoned such intelligence-gathering at the tactical level. I was most recently made aware of our lack of capability in this field by my recent experience in EAGLE in the North Norwegian Sea.

I boarded the JOSEPHUS DANIELS that evening, hoisted my flag, and prepared to get to grips with commanding this large force. It became immediately clear to me what an extraordinary capability 'Outboard' had, and its value to a force commander. During the following three days that I spent in DANIELS, my initial view was totally confirmed. This was the sort of tactical shipborne intelligence capability that I had long felt represented a major deficiency in the British Fleet's armoury. As soon as I had returned home, I took the unprecedented step of wring a letter direct to the First Sea Lord – I also copied it to my C-in-C - explaining what I had seen. This triggered one of the Navy's most rapid acquisition programmes to fit six of our most modern frigates with 'Classic Outboard'. This programme, in terms of cost and complexity, was second in size to that for acquiring the Polaris missile system.

In retrospect, I pondered for some while the extraordinary rapid response by the US Commander 6th Fleet, not only in granting my request for a US flag ship; but also in allocating the JOSEPHUS DANIELS for the task. I was sure that he could not have done so without approval from the US Navy Department in Washington which was not well known for its speed of response in such matters having strong security overtones.

Such enquiries that I was able to make indicate a story along the following lines. The USN in Washington had been trying obliquely for some time to alert their opposite numbers in London as to the progress that they were making in this field. Sadly, the message kept falling on deaf British ears. When my request for a USN flagship was received from the US 6th Fleet Commander, the Navy Department responded in the sense 'let's give the Brits just one last opportunity to understand what we have been trying to tell them obliquely for so long. If this Brit admiral does not get the message by riding the DANIELS, then the Brits aren't worth bothering about.' I cannot be certain that this represents the full story. But at least it reflects what actually happened – and the Brit admiral did get the message.

The exercise had gone well and I returned with the force to Istanbul where we were all very well received. A liaison officer had very kindly arranged some horse riding for me. I went ashore in my barge to the pier where I was to meet my host. I found the pier to be thronged with sailors of several nationalities. There then appeared through this multitude, a large car from which stepped the most gorgeous looking young lady, beautifully dressed in a finely tailored riding habit and jodhpurs. She was my host. The roar of approval from the assembled sailors as I got into the car with her was spontaneous and almost deafening.

We motored some way through Istanbul in the direction of the Black Sea before stopping to find three very fine looking Arab horses attended by a number of grooms. I 'hopped' on board the most handsome and beautifully turned out horse that I was offered, whilst the lady, with much assistance from several grooms, mounted the other. We set off, together with a mounted groom, at a gentle pace along the shores of the Bosphorous. Conversation was not easy for she spoke very little English. After a little while the gorgeous mounted lady said that she was tired and ought to return. I was delighted to be invited to go on with the groom and the two of us had a glorious ride at an exhilarating pace along the very beautiful Bosphorous shoreline. We returned for tea with the good lady, which was a very pleasant experience.

But I never got to the bottom about who she was or how she came into the picture. I trust that my fulsome and well meant letter of thanks for her hospitality reached her.

The few days of rest and recuperation allowed me the opportunity of studying at first hand the extraordinary World War I story of the Gallipoli Campaign. It is a quite remarkable story of a truly gallant failure in which ANZAC troops fought with outstanding bravery in the face of Turkish troops defending their homeland and national honour; and of a great deal of incompetence on the Allied side. I was left with a question that I could not answer. If we had won the campaign, would it have been worth it?

My next sea visit was to HMS INTREPID that was carrying out a training task in the Mediterranean for young officers from the Britannia Royal Naval College. Having traversed the Ionian Sea, we berthed in the Grand Harbour at Venice. After making my formal calls, I took advantage of an offer by our naval attaché to take me over a battlefield in Northern Italy, where my father had fought during the later stages of the First War. My father had written a remarkable personal account of his experiences in France and Italy throughout the four years, published under the title "My Sapper Venture"[18].

With his book and some of his wartime maps in my hand we set off to pick up the trail. An early overnight stop was at Bossano, the site of the famous Alplini Bridge over the Brenta River. Its fame rested on the gallant defence of the river-crossing by the Italian Alpini who had held off an Austrian attack in the nineteenth century. Our hotel was at one end of the bridge. At the other end of the bridge was a well known grappa bar, which the naval attaché suggested we visit. I had first met grappa, when I had been at the NATO Defence College in Rome. It is a favourite post-prandial Italian drink, somewhat like absinthe, neither of which I liked. However, this was a Nardini grappa bar; and Nardini grappa is famed throughout Italy as being the very

---

[18] *Pitman Publishing ISBN 0 273 31745*

best. As we sat having a beer, the attaché said to me, *"Look at that elderly man over there. That is Senor Nardini himself, the head of the Nardini family. Would you like to meet him?"* We went over and the NA who, having an Italian wife, spoke perfect Italian, explained briefly about our tour. He beckoned us to follow him to his spacious office below, where he sat down behind a large and beautiful antique desk. I produced my father's book in which he describes the occasion when his battalion of the British 48th Division was visited by the general of the 6th Italian Army, of which the 48th were part.

Senor Nardini became deeply interested. After much discussion and study of the book, Senor Nardini said, *"I was the driver of the car that brought the General for that visit, which I still remember."*

Leaning over, he pulled from the bottom drawer of his desk, a small triangular flag. *"And that"* he said *"was the flag that was flying on the general's car, of which I was the driver, on that day."*

It was a remarkable and deeply emotional moment. We thereafter drank enormous quantities of grappa, which, on that occasion, I even enjoyed. I shall never know how we got back that night across the Alpine bridge to our hotel.

This was an amazing start to a memorable few days. We were able to locate to within a few hundred yards a trench where my father had been when the sappers held off an Austrian counter-attack. We travelled up the road where my father described that, on the final day of the war, they had to hitch up two teams of horses to each tool wagon because of the steepness of the hill – and where they passed what my father called the 'last pub in Italy'. This was where the Italian general was negotiating the Austrian surrender with the Austrian General.

I had of course read my father's book when it was published in 1973, with a general appreciation of the horrors of that war, particularly in France. I knew that he had written it drawing almost entirely from his own letters and diaries written at the time. I also knew that after the war, he never returned to the battlefields in France or Italy. Yet almost every step of our visit seemed to provide confirmation of the astonishing accuracy of his day-to-day account of events as revealed by his book. The book became alive – he was alive and he was there with us, telling us what he saw, what he did and what he felt. It was an astonishing and deeply emotional experience. I was determined that I should do a similar tour of 'his' war in France.

In the spring of the following year, I went to the to the West Indies to join HMS BULWARK for a series of amphibious training exercises in the Netherlands West Indies. For me, this was a quiet period in which I was able to make considerable progress in writing my history of the Britannia Beagles. I was also able to join the landing parties ashore on several occasions and practice my long out-of-date military skills - like throwing hand grenades. I noticed that on this occasion my personal staff had found something else of interest to watch from a very safe distance.

Having carried out an Operational Readiness Inspection, I took the force to Kingston in Jamaica for an informal visit. The British High Commissioner there, John Drinkal, helped us greatly to ensure that there was virtually no troubles with the ships' companies when ashore, despite a somewhat highly charged local political atmosphere in some areas of the island.

On the Sunday, several of my officers and I had been invited to the North of the Island, where facilities for the international holiday trade had been developed, to have lunch with the former head of the Jamaican Armed Forces, who was the owner of a sheep farm there. We were very warmly entertained and following a very good meal, we were taken on a tour of the farm. In one of the lambing sheds, I saw in the corner a ewe obviously in great difficulty. I asked what her problem was and was told that she had a breached birth and would soon be dead. I was not very happy with this attitude, and knowing quite a lot about lambing down ewes from my own farm on Dartmoor, I managed to pick her up upside down and in due course with some help to deliver a live lamb. This 'good news' story somehow got into the local press and seemed to attract more attention than the presence of the whole British naval task force!

I transferred my Flag to HMS INTREPID to take the High Commissioner for an informal visit to Port au Prinz in Haiti, to which he was also accredited. Haiti was in its usual state of political chaos. it was also the time of '*carnival*', which was in full swing. I later learnt that some of Intrepid's sailors had joined the festivities thronging the square in front of the Presidential Palace. To their surprise they found a clear sector right in front of the palace from which they were able to join the singing and dancing. It was not long before they discovered why this particular space was vacant. At the apex just inside the palace grounds was a machine gun, behind which several soldiers were observing the crowd menacingly.

Some of the ship's officers told me that they had found themselves with the 'tout macout' - effectively a semi religious terrorist group – in some sort of ceremonial rite which involved the killing of a pig – unfortunately, this was achieved by the chief 'witch doctor' biting out its neck with his teeth. Their consensus was that this would not have been approved by the RSPCA.

The High Commissioner and I were taken off for a tour of the northern part of the island which had recently been savaged by a hurricane. Large areas were still flooded. In a disparately poor area, the plight of the survivors was desperate. Sadly there was nothing we could do about it. It was a very salutary experience for us both. INTREPID sailed the next day bound for Vera Cruz in Mexico.

In the arrangement of such visits, the British Embassy in the country concerned, is always consulted and is most helpful in making the arrangements. For this Vera Cruz visit, I responded to our Mexico embassy that I would be very happy to have a game of polo – or 'horse hockey' as it was occasionally referred to by sailors. On arrival on the 4th of February 1976, I went first to call on the local general. In most countries one would first call on the local governor or mayor – but in Mexico it was different. The military came first. I arrived appropriately dressed in full admiral's regalia. He greeted me warmly. He was a small man and wore glasses. He had a modest office. He told me that he was very cross. He had been delighted to hear of my interest in playing polo, for he was a polo player; and had set up a game for me. Unfortunately, when the proposed programme was sent to Mexico City for government approval, he was told "no polo". The British admiral might fall off his horse and be injured – and they would be to blame – so, NO POLO. I thanked him very sincerely for his effort on my behalf and added that there were very many other very interesting things to do and see – which indeed there were.

We had a very pleasant call with a good interpreter, as I do not speak Spanish and he did not speak English. When I got up to leave, the general advanced towards me, put his hand on my shoulder and appeared to pull. I was not familiar with the Mexican habit of 'embracer' and thought that he wanted to turn me round to show me something out of the window of his office. As I turned round, I unwittingly and unknowingly knocked off his spectacles with my epaulettes so that they fell to the ground. I was left looking out of a window, through which I could see not very much. I then realised that the general was not with me. As I turned round to see where he was, my left knee caught him full up his backside as he was bending down to retrieve his spectacles. He, being off balance, went flying across the room onto his face. As my Flag Lieutenant remarked to me later. "Admiral what happened? I saw the Mexican general come over to kiss you – and the next thing I saw he was flat on his face on the floor!." Fortunately, the general took it all in good part – and when he returned my call on board, we drank a great deal of malt whisky together.

The only disappointing thing for me from this visit was that I had hoped to be able to buy a donkey-sized saddle for my wife. She was not fond of horses and thus did not come foxhunting with me, which, in addition to beagling, was a favourite winter activity of mine. She had said, however, that she might come foxhunting if she could come on a donkey – but we needed a saddle. I was hoping to buy one in Mexico. Unfortunately, I could only find a horse-sized one. It seemed that in Mexico, if you could only afford a donkey, rather than a horse, then you constructed your own 'make-do' saddle. I was therefore able only to buy a horse-size one; but more of that later.

Our next visit was to Corpus Christi in Texas. To get up the river to berth, we had to pass under a high, modern and elegant road bridge. Initially, it appeared that our mast might be too high for us to get underneath. But careful calculation suggested that we should, at the time of our arrival, have about five to six feet of clearance. This is not very much when the height of the tide can vary from its predicted level by at least this amount. However, the navigator was confident that it would be close, but OK. So I agreed with the captain that we would have a midshipman on the radar platform at the very top of the mast, holding a six-foot long broom handle, with which would tap the bridge as we, hopefully, passed underneath. The person who, up to the very last minute, was not at all sure that we would pass clear underneath was the midshipman at the top of the mast The navigator's calculations were however correct. The visit was a great success with warm hospitality being shown to the ship's company. More than eighteen thousand visitors toured the ship.

For myself, I took two days off to go up country. I had on this occasion asked to visit a farm. Rather than visit a nationally well-known holiday ranch, the nearby BIG K, I accepted the kind private invitation of a local rancher. I flew upstate and was met by my host, who told me that he farmed a thousand head of Her'ford-cross Droughtmaster cattle on several thousand acres. The latter are an Australian breed from a Bramah Cross, which adapt well to the very dry and hot Texan environment. His stocking level was approximately one cow to an acre. He also had a herd of Buffalo on his property.

As we drove around the property on a hot sunny day, the mass of Her'fords was a wonderful sight. The cattle looked in prime condition, almost indistinguishable from a first class English herd of Herefords that any farmer would be proud to own. We were accompanied by his neighbour who had a uranium mine on his ranch. They were discussing a local court scandal where a man was suing a nearby neighbour for the "alienation of the affection of his wife". The court had unexpectedly reached its verdict that afternoon. *"How did they find?"* asked my host. *"Somewhat surprisingly, they found for the applicant"* came the reply.

"How much did they find for?" asked my host. *"I hear that it was two hundred thousand dollars"*

"Gee, that's mighty expensive pussy." But that's Texas!

I had a fascinating time, including a visit to a nearby county store. It was as if in a time warp – having hardly changed in the previous seventy years. The very elderly owner had never in his life travelled outside the county (an area not dissimilar to one of our larger British counties). Being in the store, it was all too easy to imagine that one was back in the cowboy days of the early part of the century.

INTREPID sailed for her return trip to the UK. En route we called at Bermuda for two days. Bermuda was the home of Sir William Stephenson on whom I wished to call. I found out that we were there on his birthday. I had come to know the name through a book that he had written entitled *A Man Called Intrepid* and had previously written to him with birthday wishes for his 80th birthday when I was captain of the Intrepid.

Sir William Stephenson had been a major senior figure in the intelligence world during World War II. He served for a considerable part of the war as the British Intelligence Coordinator in the United States. It was a fascinating story – as most intelligence stories are. It had encouraged me to read other accounts of World War II intelligence operations from which I found that there seemed to be two quite different versions of what clearly was the same event. I could not bring myself to believe the author of one or the other was being untruthful. I had come to the conclusion that intelligence operations are so heavily controlled that two people can be deeply involved in the same issue without any knowledge that the other is also involved. I had found that the views of Stephenson and Popov, another key intelligence personality, were not infrequently starkly different. On one particular intelligence operation, it seemed to me that the situation could be compared with two people looking at a penny from opposite sides. They both see the same coin. But, from one side it appears to be a picture of the Queen. From the other it is of a portcullis. The two pictures are entirely different but it is the same penny.

It was a great privilege to be able to call on Sir William personally and present the congratulations and compliments of the ship's company of INTREPID. He was delighted and we had a long and thoroughly interesting and enjoyable talk. This meeting sharpened my own concerns about the handling of more current intelligence matters. I became fascinated with the difference between the use of intelligence for tactical purposes and strategic intelligence. The problem with all intelligence is that there is a fundamental conflict between the interests of the provider of intelligence and that of the of the user. The intelligence provider is very often dependent on a covert source, the security of this source being of prime interest and great importance to him. If his source is compromised, further intelligence may well be lost. The provider therefore puts a great value on maintaining his source and often feels that revealing information that he acquired from that source might put the source itself at risk. On the other hand, the user of intelligence may not fully appreciate that the use of the information with which he has been provided may compromise its source. There is therefore a potential conflict of priority between the value of the informer to the intelligence officer, and the value of the information that the informer may reveal, to the potential user. It is often difficult to achieve a balance between these two priorities. This balance is particularly difficult at the higher levels of political intelligence.

It is at the MI6 (or the Secret Intelligence Service as it is more properly called) level that such sensitivities are at their most extreme. It is only recently that the name of the head of the SIS has been publicly revealed. He was traditionally always referred to as 'C', whether in conversation or on paper. I had the privilege on one occasion of lunching with C at one of his establishments. In conversation before lunch I had said to him, *"One thing I don't understand about you lot is why you permit those who oppose you to survive. Take the case of Philip Agee."* Philip Agee was an American who was a very serious thorn in the side of the CIA. There was little doubt that he was responsible for breaking the cover of a considerable number of CIA agents and indeed the death of some. *"Surely"*, I said, *"Philip Agee must at some time cross the road in front of a bus? Why does he always have to get to the other side?"* C smiled. *"One day, I shall write a book, perhaps a novel, and it will start "it was at lunch that the admiral suggested..."*. Some years later when we met again I asked him about the book. *"I haven't started it yet."* he said.

Two examples of the conflict of interest had come to my personal attention. The first was in my time on the naval staff when we were drawing up the staff requirement for the surface to air missile replacement project for Seaslug. The performance of the new missile was very dependent on the target characteristics of Russian aircraft and missiles against which we were trying to defend. On certain of their missiles we had to make intelligent guesses in an area where small differences could result in big increases of complexity and cost in our defensive systems. It was by pure chance that, on a visit to our naval technical intelligence staff on a quite separate matter, I discovered that the information that I needed on Soviet missile characteristics was actually known. This had never been passed on the user because of the sensitivity of the source.

The second example occurred later when I was making a visit to the GCHQ at Cheltenham. In the course of a general briefing I discovered that the broadcast schedules of certain Soviet radio broadcasts to their submarine fleet were known. This knowledge had never been passed to my operational Fleet staff. It could however have been of vital tactical importance. Russian submarines whilst 'deep' could not have received such broadcasts. This was where detection by our own anti-submarine forces was most difficult. To have known when Russian submarines were likely to be 'shallow' would have allowed our own limited ASW forces to be deployed at times when their chance of success was greatest. With limited ASW forces at our disposal, this information would have allowed our ASW commanders to maximise their effectiveness. As a result of this experience, I was able, when Commander-in-Chief, to achieve far greater cooperation between the strategic outlook of Cheltenham and the tactical requirements of the operational fleet.

It was only much later when I visited the Bletchley museum, Bletchley having been the centre for all UK code breaking operations in World War II, that I began to appreciate how this divide between strategic and tactical intelligence had arisen In the early days of the war. The development of the means for breaking the German naval code (Enigma) used in the control of their submarines had been at the centre of Bletchley's operations. The output from Bletchley made an invaluable tactical contribution to the winning of the anti-submarine war in the Atlantic. The security involved in maintaining the integrity of such code breaking was of the highest order. Similar security was necessary during the cold war when new and highly sophisticated intelligence gathering measures were brought into play. The distribution of the information that they provided was severely restricted on a need-to-know basis, covered by imaginative codeword procedures.

My first girlfriend in 1944 had worked at Bletchley as a Wren and I never had any idea of what she was up to. Later in the war when the Atlantic battle was almost won, code breaking there concentrated on a different German network, which was the link between the German Central Staff and their major theatre commanders. This information was then clearly of greater strategic rather than tactical value. Thus the culture of Bletchley operations switched from the tactical to the strategic. When the war ended and Bletchley was closed and the task taken over by GCHQ Cheltenham, that strategic culture went with it. I hope that I may have played some small part in restoring the balance between the two.

In times of peace, the majority of strategic intelligence is of a political nature and highly politically sensitive. If the Government is involved in important international negotiation, perhaps on trade issues, it is of enormous value if its negotiators know in advance the negotiating position of the other side. I myself on one occasion received such a piece of high-grade intelligence. I was conducting a negotiation with a very senior European naval colleague whom I knew and respected, on a very operationally sensitive issue that had both political and naval overtones. I was told that on his shortly coming visit to Britain "he was going to give me a very hard time on the issue". In the event it was all sweetness and light and we were able without difficulty to arrive at a mutually satisfactory outcome. Given the circumstances, it seemed likely that this intelligence came from a bug. Perhaps he had only been trying to pacify a difficult political master of his own!

INTREPID, having sailed for the UK, I remained in Bermuda over the weekend, staying at the former residence of the Resident Naval Officer, and sunning myself round the edge of his swimming pool, whilst awaiting a flight to London.

Having arrived in the UK I was able to go home to the farm for a quick weekend before returning to my shore offices at Fort Southwick where some urgent business demanded my presence. I arrived at the farm in the late afternoon to be greeted by my wife who said, *"Put on your wet weather gear – we must go and get the lambs in as the weather is deteriorating fast."* It was getting dark and there was a very cold wind. Much of the ground seemed like liquid mud. As always in such situations neither the ewes nor the lambs seemed to want to pay any attention to what we were trying to do, which was to get them in to the dry and warm. I thought how stupid I was as I lay in the sun the previous day in Bermuda to be so anxious to get home!

I then embarked in HMS ARK ROYAL, which was due for an extended deployment in the western Atlantic, a period which covered the American bicentennial. ARK ROYAL that was commanded by a good friend of mine, Captain Wilfred Graham, was due to represent the Royal Navy at the American bicentennial celebrations on the 4th of July at Fort Lauderdale, Florida.

The ship possessed a puppet also called Wilf – Wilf the puppet came before Wilf the Captain. The Captain became 'Big Wilf' and the puppet was 'Little Wilf'. Little Wilf had his own closed-circuit television programme every Saturday night in the ship. He was immensely popular and often very funny. All the senior members of the ship's company had their own nicknames. The master at arms being bald, was named Kojak. On arrival I was Big Jim.

On Wilf's first Saturday show after I had joined he referred to my arrival adding that I was most welcome now that my balls were at the top of the mast. A Rear Admiral's flag was the Saint George's Cross with two red circles. He went on to comment, *"and have you seen that hat he wears? He looks like a f***ing jockey."* I did not wear a normal naval beret but preferred an American model. During the week I was asked if I would do an interview with Little Wilf on the Admiral's bridge. Of course I agreed. The young naval airman who ran Wilf arrived on the bridge with his puppet and the appropriate equipment. I started off by explaining what I did and why I was in the ship. I also talked a little about the ship's general programme. As the interview was coming to its normal end, the puppet turned to me and asked, *"Could I borrow your hat, Sir?"* *"What! After what you said about it last week on your show?"*

"I said you look like a jockey." *"No you didn't. You said I look like a f***ing jockey."*

"That's sailors language, sir." *"Alright, Wilf. You may borrow my hat."*

I turned to little Wilf and put my hat on the head of the puppet. Looking first at me and then at the camera, Wilf asked, *"How do I look?"*

I replied *"You look like a f***ing jockey."* *"Oh,"* he responded, *" I thought I looked like a f***ing Admiral."*

I was not going to win that one!

I also had trouble not long after with my non-uniform dress habits. I did not wear the normal shoulder boards with my tropical rig. I preferred to use the silver stars on my shirt collar that represent Flag rank in the United States Navy. In the very early hours of one morning, I was wandering around the ship at sea talking to the middle watchman, and went into the engine control room where a small number of senior engine room staff were gathered. I asked them about their problems. In a perfectly tactful way they described one issue of which they were critical. I told them that I knew and agreed about this and had administrative action in hand to improve the situation. They looked a little bemused. *"Who are you?"* they asked. *"I am your Admiral."* I replied. *"Oh"* one said, *"we thought you were the padre."*

As a result of catapult problems, ARK ROYAL was forced to spend some time at Norfolk, Virginia for repairs. She also visited Mayport where I rejoined the ship. Political America was in turmoil for the first time in some years, Jimmy Carter, a Democratic President had been elected. The Yankees were out and the first president from the south was going to overturn the Washington mafia. Our British consul general from Atlanta had kindly come down to meet the ship and he was rightly insistent that I should come up to Atlanta for a few days to meet some of Jimmy Carter's former colleagues so as better to understand the revolution in the White House that the southern Democrats were threatening. I flew up to Atlanta on the Saturday afternoon. My first appointment on Sunday morning was to go to the service at the downtown Fifth Ebenezer church. The consul and I were, I think, the only white members of a very full congregation. The preacher was a young pastor from North Carolina who was the son of Martin Luther King. He preached a sermon with enormous youthful, southern and evangelistic vigour, which must have lasted the best part of three quarters of an hour. But it seemed like only five minutes. Our dear vicar at home would preach for ten minutes and it seemed like half an hour. This was certainly a new experience for me, and one I valued.

The next day my first call was a breakfast meeting with Frank Lloyd Wright, one of America's most famous architects. My knowledge of architecture whether British or American was regrettably minimal. I did however regard the Tricorn building in Portsmouth and the Stock Exchange building in London with disdain. The latter reminded me of a ship's engine room inside-out. Nevertheless it was a fascinating meeting with my host who was highly critical of the impact of British planning and building regulations on good architecture. He said he would never again accept a project in Britain for this reason.

It was perhaps no coincidence that I had been booked to stay at Atlanta's Peach Tree Plaza Hotel, the first 'inside-out' hotel, which I found impressive. However I wasn't quite sure about the outside lifts. I was reminded of my first visit to the top of the NatWest Tower in London for a meeting in the boardroom there. The walls were floor-to-floor glass. On arrival, my host called me over and said, "Do come and look from here at this magnificent view of the city." I said "no thank you" and stood firmly in the middle of the room. "I can see it all from here." My visit to Atlanta was much appreciated and I learned a lot about America from it; although in years to come the revolution in Washington's affairs that the southern Democrats were proclaiming was certainly not clear for all to see.

Later in the deployment, we joined up with one of the large American carriers, the USS FRANKLIN D ROOSEVELT. She was flying the flag of my American opposite number, COMCAR, GRU 1, Rear Admiral John Dixon, USN. We agreed that we should do some 'cross decking' – that was her aircraft landing on ARK ROYAL'S flight deck as our aircraft landed on the FDR. I saw this as an opportunity for me to do some flying from the back seat of a Phantom. On the 6th of June 1976, with the CO of the Phantom squadron as my pilot, we were catapulted off Ark Royal and joined the landing circuit of the FDR. It had been agreed that we would do one or two 'rollers' – a 'touch and go', before carrying out an arrested landing. As we came in for the first touch and go I was intrigued that I could not see the 'meatball' on the FDR's mirror landing sight – but made no comment so as not to make a fool of myself. We pulled away and came round for another go. Again no meatball, but we touched smoothly and the pilot opened the throttle and again pulled away. I heard the pilot call the flight deck control. "Next time would you please switch on your meatball?" There followed a short embarrassed silence followed by "Wilco".

I had planned this sortie so that I could meet and talk with John Dixon – but I had hoped to surprise him and directed that the FDR should not be informed until our final approach when I asked my pilot to call saying, in good Americanese, "two stars in the groove". We landed and I got out only to learn that John Dixon was not there. He was at the controls of one of his aircraft that had just landed in ARK ROYAL.

My next American experience was of the ship's presence at Fort Lauderdale in Florida for the American bicentennial. Fort Lauderdale was anyway a favourite visit for the aircraft carrier squadron and was regarded as one of their American 'home ports'. The bicentennial ball to which I was invited was indeed an experience. There were of course many beautiful, attractively dressed young women who would gladden any sailor's heart – and certainly did mine. However, I was even more fascinated by the large numbers of expensively dressed elderly ladies whose main occupation seemed to me to be trying to give the impression that they were at least half the age that they actually were. I found it really quite bizarre.

For the great day itself there was to be a major parade. I felt very privileged to be asked to take part in the parade, riding in a famous Indianapolis 2000 racing car. I was fully 'booted and spurred' in uniform, with medals and decorations. The car was clearly used to travelling at a hundred miles an hour and more. The walking pace procession of which we were a part was not something it was used to - so that, at one stage, I and my fellow passenger had to get out and push. I can't quite remember how we restarted it but we got to the saluting base in good time where I was due to join the mayor on the platform. I greatly appreciated this honour and much enjoyed the long procession with bands and representative groups from all possible walks of American life.

Having passed the saluting base, the thousands of marchers were marshalled into a very large park. At the entrance to the park there was a cowboy sitting deep into the Western saddle of his horse watching the world go by. I saw my moment to solve a problem, which had developed from my purchase of a Western saddle during my earlier visit to Mexico. I had tried to use it on one of my horses but I could not work out how the girth worked. It seemed to me that the buckle on the end of the girth for attaching it to the saddle straps was upside down – and I could find no apparent way of fixing it. Here, I thought, was a chance to find out from a real cowboy how the cinch of a Western saddle worked. At an appropriate moment I wandered over to him. He appeared to be almost asleep. I put my hand firmly on his knee and said in my best British voice, "Excuse me, old boy." He looked down in total surprise for he had clearly never before seen a British admiral in full regalia. When I added, "I just wanted to see your cinch," a look of total amazement came over his face. I only wished I had had a camera to record that moment. When I explained a bit more closely my problem, he could not have been more helpful. He showed me the cowboy's way of doing the cinch in what can best be described as the 'quick release mode'; and how also it could be more securely fastened. I was most grateful and he remained most astonished.

Early in the following year I again returned to the Caribbean to carry out operational readiness inspections, this time in HMS FEARLESS. The inspection being completed we proceeded for a visit to Cartagena in Colombia. Leading up to the visit, I had asked the embassy there if I might be able to play tennis, and received the response that the Commander-in-Chief of the Columbian Navy would himself enjoy a doubles match. I signalled my acceptance with much pleasure. The embassy responded with a signal saying that the Columbian admiral was a "good" tennis player. This was fine by me, for I had been playing tennis for the Royal Navy for some twenty years; and one of the FEARLESS officers was also a navy player. Two further signals from the embassy described the Columbian C-in-C as "Very good" and then "Very good Indeed"! I began to wonder whether perhaps the admiral was competent rather than good; but had a partner who was very good indeed.

In the event, when my partner and I won the first set, I got the clear impression that it would not be a good thing if we also won the second set. So, we didn't. The idea of throwing the final set appealed to neither my partner nor I. But it was not now easy to get back into the match. Neither of us, though, was prepared to loose our own service and after a long set, we declared honours between the Royal Navy and the Columbian Navy to be even. Such was 'tennis court diplomacy'.

It was not long before I was greeting my successor. I had enjoyed my appointmant as FOCAS immensely, but it was time to move on. I had now been promoted to Vice Admital and appointed a member of the Navy Board as Chief of Fleet Support. I realised that this was not just a further promotion. I was going to move into a new phase of my life, where I was no longer directly, closely and personally involved with the effectiveness and operational capabilities of individual ships, and the welfare and efficiency of their officers and men. I was moving onto a much broader canvas. I was still determined that life should be fun. But, perhaps, a rather different type of fun – and so to Book Three.

In the year 2002 I had the privilege, as a Knight Grand Cross of the Honourable Order of the Bath, of having my banner installed in the King Henry the Seventh Chapel at Westminister Abbey in the presence of His Royal Highness, the Prince of Wales, Grand Master of the Order. With the assistance of the Herald of the College of Arms, I had undertaken the task of creating a new personal coat of arms, as is illustrated. The helmet and shield were surmounted by a Royal Naval King's Crown, over which stood a boar rampant in blue and white quarters. The shield was of red and gold cheque, taken from a known Moravian shield of the middle ages and crossed by a white Bar Dexter on which were emblazoned four blue roses representing 'endeavour' (since no one has yet succeeded in creating a blue rose). My choice of a Moravian shield represented the very important part, as my story has revealed (Book 1), that the Moravian Church played the lives of many of our ancestors. The two 'supporters' for my shield were heraldic Sea Dogs in blue and gold. The motto beneath, which I chose as representing what I sought to achive through my lifetime, was "Harmony with Honour". The 'badge' for the use of my family, is of the Boar, blue and white quartered, surrounded by a blue circlet.

Sir Admiral James Eberle

The Author

Sir James (Jim) Eberle was born in Bristol on the 31st of May 1927. He entered the Royal Naval College, Dartmouth in 1941, and went to sea on operational service in mid 1944. He first served in motor gunboats in the English Channel, and subsequently in the Indian Ocean and the British Pacific Fleet. At the end of World War II, he was serving in HMS Belfast that was part of the first US-British Task Force to enter Shanghai. He served in HMS Cossack in the Far East from 1947 to 1949; and again in HMS Belfast as the Second Gunnery Officer during the later stages of the Korean War. He specialised in naval gunnery and was deeply involved in the development of the early naval surface-to-air guided weapons.

After early advancement to Commander and Captain, and a period of study as a Defence Fellow at University College, Oxford, he was selected for promotion to Rear Admiral in 1971, one of the three youngest British admirals of the twentieth century.

His Flag Rank appointments included the Flag Officer Sea Training, Flag Officer Carriers and Amphibious Ships, NATO Commander of the UK Atlantic Strike Group; and a member of Naval Board of the Defence Council as Chief of Fleet Support. In 1979, he took over command of the British Fleet, and as NATO Commander in Chief of the Eastern Atlantic and Allied Commander-in-Chief Channel. Following his Fleet Command, he served as Commander-in-Chief of the Naval Home Command during the Falkland war, prior to his retirement from active service in 1983.

In 1984, he was appointed Director of the Royal Institute of International Affairs, a post he held until 1991. In this position he established high-level contacts with many other countries within Western Europe, and also with Russia, Argentina and Japan.

Sir James was awarded the Knight Grand Cross of the Order of the Bath in 1978. His banner, based on a Moravian shield of the seventeenth century, is hung in St George's Chapel of

Westminster Abbey. He has served as Vice Admiral of the United Kingdom and as ADC to Her Majesty the Queen. He was granted the Honorary position of Admiral in the Texan and Georgian Navies.

He is a Freeman of the City of London (1991) and of the City of Bristol (1947) He holds an Honorary Doctorate of Laws at Bristol University (1989) and an Honorary Degree of Doctor of Letters at Sussex University (1992). He was a member of the Vice Chancellor of Exeter University's Advisory Board for Development (1993). He was Chairman of the Council of Clifton College (1984-1994). He was for many years Chairman of the naval professional journal, the Naval Review. He has strong countryside interests having farmed on Dartmoor. He is a Board member of the Countryside Alliance. He has been a Master of the Britannia Beagles at the RN College Dartmouth for fifty years. He played tennis for the Royal Navy for many years and is a member of the All England Lawn Tennis Club at Wimbledon.

He has published three other books – "British Space Policy and International Collaboration" (1987), in conjunction with Dr Helen Wallace (Chatham House Paper no 42) – "Jim. First of the Pack" (1982) a centenary history of the Royal Navy's Britannia Beagles. – and "Management in the Armed Forces" in conjunction with Air Vice Marshal John Downey.

"For'd on"